Endorsements

It's time to work on how we work. If you've gotten hooked on being perfect instead of being of service, this book will be a balm. Share it with someone who needs your help.

Seth Godin
Author,
The Song of Significance

I so wanted to write that *Flawed* is perfect! It covers very important material in a highly engaging style, drawing from extensive clinical research. But I avoid the obvious and ironic error to say instead that *Flawed* offers a comprehensive look at the dangers of perfectionism in teams and organizations – and offers a way out. Author Greg Chasson adds a crucial new perspective to existing resources on perfectionism in individuals by bringing his considerable clinical expertise to the workplace.

Amy C. Edmondson
Novartis Professor of Leadership,
Harvard Business School
Author,
Right Kind of Wrong: The Science of Failing Well (Atria 2023)

Flawed is one of those precious books that comes along just at the right moment. It's well-researched, chock-full of illuminating case studies, and offers a treasure trove of clinically-informed strategies to manage both our own perfectionism and the perfectionism of other people. Like spending time with a close friend, by the end of it I was sad to put it down. It's the only book on perfectionism that business leaders will ever need.

Thomas Curran
Associate Professor of Psychology, London School of Economics
Author, *The Perfection Trap: Embracing the Power of Good Enough*

In *Flawed*, Greg Chasson tackles toxic achievement culture head-on. He exposes the widespread harm of perfectionism in the workplace and provides practical frameworks and solutions for leaders and managers. Flawed is a must-read for anyone with an interest in workplace health and looking for a healthy way forward.

Jennifer Breheny Wallace
New York Times Best-Selling Author,
Never Enough: When Achievement Culture Becomes Toxic-and What We Can Do About It

Perfectionism is a secret saboteur of organizational efficiency, but Greg's engrossing and timeless book delivers an innovative framework and practical solutions for addressing perfectionism in your teams. *Flawed* needs to be required reading for every manager and any business leader with a stake in a thriving workplace culture.

Nick Sonnenberg
Wall Street Journal Best-Selling Author,
Come Up for Air: How Teams Can Leverage Systems and Tools to Stop Drowning in Work

Time for companies to stop hailing perfection as the only destination and recognize flexible thinking as a viable direction. Fixating on unreasonable expectations is a surefire way to act inauthentically and unnaturally, while also undermining your personal and professional potential. Chasson's entertaining and informative book masterfully changes the way we think about perfection. This book will help leaders and perfectionists alike.

Colin Coggins
Wall Street Journal Best-Selling Co-Author,
The Unsold Mindset: Redefining What It Means to Sell

Perfectionists on your team can become crippled by their own strategies, albeit with the best of intentions. Their behavior seems self-defeating and paradoxical. And they can bog down your entire team. Greg Chasson gives expert guidance about how managers can root out the cause of inefficiency and obstacles to success by helping you spot perfectionistic employees. And more importantly, he provides you with a multitude of strategies that you can use to help these employees truly tap into their potential.

Jeff Szymanski
CEO, Getting to the Next Level Consulting
Clinical Instructor (part-time), Harvard Medical School
Clinical Associate, McLean Hospital,
Author, *The Perfectionist's Handbook*

Overcoming "analysis-paralysis" by embracing uncertainty and imperfection is essential for operators to realize their full potential. Dr. Chasson has tremendously utilized his expertise as an OCD specialist and his adept teaching ability to assist leaders in mastering this important skill.

Stephen Smith
Founder and CEO,
NOCD

Chasson earns points for tackling a serious, largely underreported condition in plain, direct language, at times with a biting wit and much practical, hard-won guidance and illuminating tools, including his own "Emphasis Framework" crafted for "understanding behavior in a context of effort-value pressures." Chasson's prose is as clear as his thinking and approaches are rigorous. His examination of the inner conflict that arises in the ongoing struggle over whether he should or should not fold the household towels employs a simple, everyday example to drive home key points of being true to one's values vs. the overall good of an organization—in this case his marriage. Many readers will immediately turn to revelatory the chapter about dealing with a perfectionist boss.

[*Flawed* is an] eye-opening guide to the problems of workplace perfectionism and how to face them.

BookLife (by Publisher's Weekly) Editorial Review

Author Greg Chasson has crafted a skilled and inspiring book where his expertise is evident on every page, providing a solid foundation for understanding the detrimental impact of perfectionism on organizational productivity. What I found particularly valuable was the practical nature of the book, which offers actionable strategies and tactics for managers and business leaders to address perfectionism within their teams. Chasson's authoritative voice instilled confidence in the efficacy of the solutions proposed, yet there's a gentility and a smoothness to the tone that makes it feel as though you're getting advice from a wise mentor-friend rather than a hierarchical superior. The result is a work that sheds light on the complexities of perfectionism in the workplace in a positive, motivating way that makes you want to put the book down and take action. Overall, *Flawed* serves as a transformative guide for leaders seeking to build cohesive teams and drive success in the face of perfectionism-related challenges, and I would not hesitate to recommend it.

Readers' Favorite

5-Star Editorial Review

FLAWED

FLAWED

Why Perfectionism
Is a Challenge for
Management

GREG CHASSON
PhD, ABPP

Foreword by JASON NAZAR

Illustrated by JOSEPH TUMILTY

TRANSLATIONAL MENTAL HEALTH
FROM THE CLINIC TO THE COMMUNITY

Printed in the United States of America.
First edition 2024

Illustrations by Joseph Tumilty
Copy edited by David Woods-Hale
Cover and layout design by G Sharp Design, LLC

Visit the author's website: www.gregchasson.com or scan:

ISBN 979-8-9900688-0-3 (paperback)
ISBN 979-8-9900688-2-7 (ebook)
ISBN 979-8-9900688-1-0 (audiobook)

Library of Congress Control Number: 2024903714

To my supportive and loving wife, Tasha. I don't believe anyone is perfect, except for my wife, because suggesting otherwise would be idiotic.

ABOUT THE AUTHOR

Gregory S. Chasson, PhD, ABPP, is an esteemed psychologist, board-certified cognitive-behavioral therapist, researcher, educator, and international invited speaker helping organizations, communities, and individuals address mental health challenges, such as perfectionism, using practical and feasible strategies. He sees the inner workings of perfectionism and its pitfalls, as well as how best to dismantle it with tips and insights grounded in science and honed through real world practice.

He has served on the Board of Directors for a variety of professional non-profit organizations (e.g., Maryland Psychological Association) and owned and operated two mental health practices, giving him an intimate familiarity with how organizations and teams function.

Dr. Chasson is an Associate Professor at the University of Chicago in the Department of Psychiatry and Behavioral Neuroscience, where he's also the Director of Behavioral Interventions of the Obsessive-Compulsive & Related Disorders Clinic. He specializes in the nature and treatment of obsessive-compulsive disorder (OCD) and related conditions (including perfectionism), high-functioning autism spectrum conditions, and anxiety disorders. He has provided cognitive-behavioral therapy for clinically severe perfectionism for nearly 20 years.

As an active scholar, Dr. Chasson has authored or co-authored more than 70 scientific publications and one academic book (Hoarding Disorder: Advances in Psychotherapy –Evidence-Based Practice). He serves as the Editor of the scientific journal, the *Behavior Therapist*.

Learn more about Dr. Chasson, his work, his speaking, his national and international workshops, and his training courses by visiting his website: www.gregchasson.com or by scanning the QR code below:

TABLE OF CONTENTS

Perfectionism, How to Spot It, and Why It Wrecks the Workplace

How Perfectionism Sabotages the Workplace and Solutions for Managers

TABLE OF FIGURES

FOREWORD

I OFTEN FIND myself telling my teams: Don't let perfection be the enemy of progress. It can sound like a strange sentiment to share; shouldn't we all want to strive for perfection? We're trained in our youth and academia to find the "right" answer. High achievers are often rewarded and stand out among their peers because they know the correct answers. The more they get right, the more they're rewarded. However, many business environments don't operate on the same principles. There can be a variety of ways to get to an outcome; speed can sometimes matter more than accuracy; risk-taking and experimentation lead to outsized outcomes; and sometimes we just get too caught up in how things have always been done.

Perfection can take on many forms, but it's often most insidious when it's no longer in service of an outcome and instead about the ego of contributors and managers. Just like in our youth, we often care too much about how we are perceived by others. We should be focused on how to achieve meaningful goals with ethics and urgency. I saw this many times over the course of two decades while starting and selling various technology companies like Docstoc, Comparably, and Clovers.ai. Particularly in these startup environments, I often found employees who were so worried about making mistakes that they didn't get things done. Sometimes they were too sure something had to be done a certain way; they weren't willing to break the mold and find new and better avenues for success. And other times, "it's always been done this way," was actually used as an excuse not to go the extra mile.

Show me any hyper-growth company that's the envy of the market, competitors, and investors... and I'll show you the inner workings of an organization barely keeping the trains on the track, complex systems held together with duct tape, and high performing teams who break every norm and standard. So why then do we hold ourselves to these standards of perfection in the workplace so often?

Dr. Chasson's examination of perfectionism illuminates its multifaceted nature, addressing not only the classic high-achiever, but also those entrenched in traditional approaches and those quick to pass judgment on deviations from the norm. Offering rich examples, this book delves into the psychological underpinnings of perfectionism, offering a comprehensive framework that resonates with real-world scenarios.

Flawed offers practical strategies that are grounded in psychological theory and evidence. They are designed for leaders to dismantle the perfectionist culture and foster one that celebrates continuous improvement and prioritizes outcomes over rigid adherence to perfection. To this end, Dr. Chasson's insights provide leaders with a valuable playbook to navigate the complexities of managing teams and addressing perfectionism at its roots.

Dr. Chasson's perspective and solutions are timeless. The book is a formative intersection of mental health and team dynamics within the context of organizational culture. Navigating this intersection is a tricky enterprise, but Dr. Chasson is the ideal expert for the task. As an expert in mental health, including perfectionism, he uniquely offers a rich psychological perspective to enhance our understanding of employee well-being and organizational efficiency. *Flawed* serves as a compelling resource, shedding light on a challenge that transcends industries and resonates with professionals at all levels.

I've built products that over a billion people have used, started and sold numerous software companies, have raised over $100M in capital for various technology ventures, and have served as an advisor, investor, and board member for multiple billion-dollar exits and IPOs. Never have I found a 'perfect' way to success. In fact, the distinguishing characteristic of so many extraordinarily successful founders and leaders is their ability to embrace the unconventional path, the less tried-and-tested formula in favor of the more perfect outcome.

Dr. Chasson's expertise and thoughtful exploration of perfectionism provides an invaluable contribution to the literature on leadership and organizational dynamics and serves as a practical roadmap for managers, leaders, and anyone navigating the intricacies of organizational dynamics to better equip their teams with frameworks and strategies that lead to more winning and less angst.

Flawed is the perfect read for anyone who has experienced the trappings of perfection.

Jason Nazar
CEO and Serial Entrepreneur

INTRODUCTION

WHAT IS YOUR GREATEST WEAKNESS?

"I'm a perfectionist," replied Gary, the job interviewee. He looked confident and safe in his response.

Troubling answer.

This was my first thought when Gary answered the age-old interview question, "What is your greatest weakness?"

It's as if he had confessed a crime. The poor interviewee didn't know that *perfectionism* is a loaded answer in my line of work.

How could he? People think perfectionism is, at worst, a quirk. Many consider it admirable, which is probably why this interview response has become so predictable and tired. The response is strategic: by claiming perfectionism as a weakness, Gary flips the question to avoid an answer that reflects a true liability and instead offers a response that highlights another potential strength. The spin is not subtle.

It's clear that perfectionism is double-edged. Otherwise, this classic interview response wouldn't have developed in the first place.

Perfectionism is mysterious, but the full landscape is underappreciated, misunderstood, and minimized.

Perfectionism is not the same as *pursuing perfection* or *pursuing excellence*, as we will discover later in this book. Pursuing perfection isn't necessarily a problem, but for some individuals, this pursuit can become rigid and get out of control, causing major complications. This is perfectionism.

For some individuals, perfectionistic tendencies are minimal or yield positive outcomes, such as better grades, promotions at work, or compliments on your outfit. For others, perfectionistic tendencies can be so disabling that they obstruct basic activities, such as getting dressed, cooking, working, and socializing. Most presentations of perfectionism are associated with effects that fall somewhere between these two extremes.

This book focuses mainly on employees with elevated but **nonextreme** levels of perfectionism that disrupt the workplace and teams as a result. These negative effects, if left unchecked, can create a culture of perfectionism that will spread insidiously and destroy businesses.

By managing the negative effects, you provide an opportunity to leverage the many strengths that coincide with perfectionism. Indeed, perfectionists often present with a range of positive features that enhance the workplace. For example, they can be especially conscientious, detail-oriented, loyal, and honest.

But what does perfectionism in the workplace resemble? It could manifest in employees who:

→ Exhibit anxiety before, during, and after a job task—particularly novel or complex ones;

→ Procrastinate and avoid tasks because of anxiety;

→ Miss deadlines to fix products and get them *just right*;

→ Submit pristine products, albeit late;

→ Freeze with dread when faced with being responsible for completing a task;

→ Become fixated on planning, list-making, and completing tasks in an effective and efficient manner;

→ Find it difficult to prioritize tasks because they all seem equally important;

→ Become rigid about enforcing rules even when doing so undermines important principles;[1]

→ Get stuck on details instead of seeing the big picture;

→ Find it problematic to be flexible in their expectations and beliefs about success;

→ Become petrified when asked to make even minor decisions;

→ Seek reassurance from others excessively;

→ Compulsively check performance indicators;

→ Show an inability to accept or appreciate well-earned praise and positive feedback, such as being sad despite winning a first-place ribbon;

→ Seem unsurprised by negative feedback—as if it were expected—but also act crushed emotionally by it anyway;

→ Exhibit oversensitivity to actual and perceived criticism;

→ Are preoccupied with doing what they think is *right* or *should* be done;

→ Moralize and sometimes come across as snooty;

---

1 A classic example of this is Swiss Psychologist Lawrence Kohlberg's Heinz dilemma. Is it morally permissible for a husband to steal unaffordable medicine to save the life of his wife? Is the *rule* of not stealing more important than the *principle* of preserving human life?

→ Seem underemployed or have a confusing work history despite having substantial ambition and skill;

→ Push unrealistic and rigid standards on others;

→ Show a hesitancy and difficulty with delegating tasks to others.

If these signs seem familiar, this book is for you. If your workplace culture is saddled with perfectionism, there are solutions. So, if you're looking for ways to loosen the vice that perfectionism has on your workplace and employees, please keep reading.

When unmanaged, perfectionism is bad for business—it slows productivity,[2] directly and indirectly. But what do these negative effects look like? Perfectionism may contribute to:

→ Reduced profit;

→ Inordinate employee turnover;

→ Elevated employee absenteeism;

→ Poor workplace reputation;

→ Difficulty recruiting new talent;

→ Increased unnecessary spending;

→ Angry and dissatisfied clients;

→ Missed deadlines;

→ Slowed productivity;

→ Declining creativity;

→ Toxic workplace culture and mood;

→ Employee and manager resentment.

2 Sherry et al., "Perfectionism Dimensions and Research Productivity in Psychology Professors."

In short, the potential effects of perfectionism are profoundly disruptive to an organization's health and employee well-being. These consequences will be revisited throughout the book. They underscore why *perfectionism* is a loaded answer when an interviewee self-assuredly declares this as their greatest weakness.

The Purpose of *Flawed*

While self-help tools are available for individuals who suffer from perfectionism, no tools exist for those who lead a workforce and manage in an organizational setting. This book fills that void and offers practical solutions for businesses.

Written for decision makers, business leaders, and HR managers who struggle to deal with employee burnout, procrastination, anxiety, and turnover risk—perhaps even quiet quitting—the book is designed as an approachable guide for understanding, detecting, and alleviating the ways that perfectionism undermines the workplace.

How to Use *Flawed*

Flawed is divided into two parts. Part I provides a definition and broad overview of perfectionism (chapter 1). This is followed by a summary of perfectionism features (chapter 2). I then provide tips for how you can detect perfectionism at work (chapter 3). Part I concludes with a discussion of why perfectionism is bad for your workplace and the bottom line of the business (chapter 4).

Filled with clear examples, Part II characterizes specific ways that perfectionism hinders the workplace (chapters 5–9). I focus on five predominant problems, which include (1) a dysfunctional emphasis framework; (2) process paralysis; (3) confounding rules and principles; (4) cognitive rigidity; and (5) other-oriented moralism. Each of these is covered in detail in their respective chapters.

Part II offers practical solutions for these specific problems. These comprise a range of practical antiperfectionism strategies and tactics. They are separated into group-level and employee-level strategies. The former represents top-down approaches for leaders that can influence the workplace culture. The latter provides tools for leaders who need to work with employees at the individual level.

As a bonus, a final chapter reverses the dynamic emphasized in the rest of the book. It offers strategies for recognizing and coping with a perfectionistic boss (chapter 10). It's also applicable for handling perfectionistic individuals who are higher than your boss on the organizational chart (e.g., CEO, Board of Directors).

Flawed contains many resources, all of which you can adopt at your discretion for enhancing your workplace. This includes all figures, blank versions of select figures to tailor to your team circumstances, and recommended non-*Flawed* resources for perfectionists and their families. All these items can be downloaded for free from my website, which you can visit at www.gregchasson.com/flawedresources or by scanning the following QR Code:

About Me

I'm a clinical psychologist and board certified cognitive-behavioral therapist who specializes in the nature and treatment of OCD and related conditions, including perfectionism.

I'm an Associate Professor and the Director of Behavioral Interventions for the OCD and Related Disorders Clinic at the University of Chicago. My career has included tens of thousands of hours of conducting research on OCD and related conditions, treating clients with perfectionism and anxiety, and teaching dozens of psychologists in training how to provide such services.

In my work as a psychologist, it sometimes feels like perfectionism is everywhere.[3] I'm inundated each week with client stories about the tremendous toll perfectionism exacts on emotional well-being and quality of life. I see the way it hampers work performance and job satisfaction. I witness it in C-suite executives, physicians, professional athletes, politicians, attorneys, engineers, teachers, graphic designers, artists, psychologists—the list is extensive.

I've supervised countless staff and students who struggle with perfectionism but, even as an expert, I find it challenging to help somebody with these difficulties. Leaders may find it daunting to deal with this problem in their workforce, especially if they have limited exposure to mental health knowledge and techniques—and that's if they can even detect perfectionism successfully in the first place. My guess is that many managers don't recognize how it is playing a role in their team's daily operations.

This is why I've written *Flawed*. I'm not a Fortune 500 business influencer, but I've owned and operated businesses in the mental health sector. I've managed and led people for nearly 15 years. My hope is that the book can bridge the gap between my expertise in mental health and the workplace culture in which it's embedded,

---

3 Granted, I see a subset of the community who seek me out specifically for help with these conditions, so my perspective is skewed. This is an example of what's called the *availability heuristic*.

specifically when it comes to the underappreciated challenge of perfectionism.

Perfectionism doesn't need to wreck your workplace. Organizations can address this overlooked challenge. It's okay to promote a work environment that not only accepts flaws—and uses flaws to its advantage—but also promotes making mistakes **on purpose**, among other strategies.

Making mistakes on purpose? I know—it sounds absurd. I promise it'll make sense by the end of this book. By the end, like me, you'll never react the same way again to the interviewee response, "*I'm a perfectionist.*"

No, Gary—being *flawed* is not a weakness… but claiming to be a perfectionist might be.

Perfectionism, How to Spot It, and Why It Wrecks the Workplace

CHAPTER 1

NUKING THE FLY: AN IMPERFECT INTRODUCTION TO PERFECTIONISM

"I am careful not to confuse excellence
with perfection. Excellence, I can reach
for; perfection is God's business."[4]

MICHAEL J. FOX
Actor, Parkinson's Disease Advocate

MICHAEL J. FOX gets it. His quote sums up the common confusion with the term *perfection* and how it's confounded with *excellence* and *high standards*. Fox's quote carries a subtext: perfection is valued by society.

But I would add the prefix *over* to his comment: much of society *over*values perfection. At the same time, however, they seem not to understand that this represents an unreasonable and harmful standard.

4 Fox, *Lucky Man: A Memoir.*

Inflating the value of perfection in this way creates a culture of tremendous pressure and dissatisfaction across many areas of living. For example, in one sphere in which there is some growing recognition that perfection standards are toxic, research points to the damaging effects from airbrushed photographs of models to hone body shape, color, and size.[5] Growing social media use compounds the effects of this type of body image standard. Processes of perfectionism and their impact extend into many aspects of life, and workplace culture is no exception.

What's particularly alarming is that perfectionism is on the rise around the globe.[6] Based on fascinating research by Dr. Thomas Curran and colleagues, perfectionism has increased over time in young adults from 1990 to 2015. The cause of this increase is unclear, but Curran offers some compelling hypotheses related to individualism and achievement (and their parenting influences) as growing society values. These emphases are magnified in a world with instant social media feedback. Curran's fascinating book, *The Perfection Trap*, delves into these topics in more detail.

I also believe perfectionism has qualities that make it inherently self-perpetuating at the individual and societal level, as we will discover throughout this book.

But what is meant by *perfectionism*?

Perfection versus Perfectionism

The word *perfect* floods everyday jargon. In many ways, its meaning has been diluted to the point of no longer making sense. People often mistake it with *satisfactory* or *sufficient*.

---

5 Derenne and Beresin, "Body Image, Media, and Eating Disorders—A 10-Year Update."

6 Curran and Hill, "Perfectionism Is Increasing over Time."; Curran, The Perfection Trap: Embracing the Power of Good Enough.

"That's perfect," says the patron watching the waiter shred parmesan cheese on their spaghetti.

I couldn't stop chuckling when it came time to decide how I wanted this book printed. For those holding a physical copy of the book instead of the e-book, take a moment to admire its binding. This form of binding is called *perfect bound*. Apparently, we've reached the pinnacle of book binding innovations.

As a word, perfect has a complicated meaning that depends on its application. Sometimes its use can get conflated. *Perfectionism* is not the same as perfection; the two are not interchangeable. Although both are nouns, the former is similar to a personality type or disposition whereas the latter is a generic noun to describe a flawless state of being. For example, when I tell my neighbor that her soufflé is a work of *perfection*, she often refuses the praise because of her *perfectionism*.

Definition of Perfectionism

Ask different experts to define perfectionism and you'll get different answers. There isn't a consensus on the full definition of perfectionism and its various elements, but there are some common threads.

According to seminal theory and research,[7] perfectionism is a worldview described by extreme and rigid expectations of oneself or others. Often, it's characterized as an approach to the world driven by a belief that mistakes are unacceptable. The perfectionist's thinking is highly inflexible and can be narrow. They also doubt their actions. For example, they might spend significant amounts of time preoccupied with worry that they or others have completed tasks in a non-optimal way.

7 Hewitt and Flett, "Perfectionism in the Self and Social Contexts"; Frost et al., "The Dimensions of Perfectionism."

The lens through which the perfectionist sees the world has a broad view, and it expands to multiple situations and settings. For instance, somebody exhibiting perfectionism at work also tends to have these tendencies when dating, exercising at the gym, etc. For many—but not all—people with perfectionism, the extreme expectations are consistent with their personal values and sense of self. To them, this is the way the world *should be,* and it's an entrenched worldview.

The perfectionist has a contradictory relationship with control. On one hand, they overestimate the amount of control they have when completing tasks. It's impossible for anybody to perform flawlessly on a constant basis, but this doesn't stop the perfectionist from believing they can do so. This is true even if the outcomes are influenced by random chance, which is usually the case. For example, a wedding planner with perfectionism might express demoralization and self-blame about rain on the wedding day[8] (e.g., "I should have convinced them to have the wedding inside.")

On the other hand, even though a perfectionist overestimates their control in situations, they also describe their anxiety as a universal feeling of being out of control. This is probably due to the compulsive and seemingly pressured nature of perfectionistic behavior (which I'll discuss further in the next chapter). The anxiety may also result from attempting to control too much but inevitably failing much of the time, because their expectations are unreasonable.

Perfectionism is a dimension in the same way as measures of height or income.[9] In other words, we all fall somewhere on the "perfectionism scale," with most people landing in the middle range. For

8 Which is *not* ironic, Alanis Morissette. It just sucks. I wonder how many times Alanis has dealt with these criticisms.

9 Broman-Fulks, Hill, and Green, "Is Perfectionism Categorical or Dimensional?"

example, I probably drafted this sentence a dozen times because it didn't sound *just right*. Some people present with extreme perfectionism, which is debilitating across multiple life domains (e.g., work, home, social life). In these instances, they are incapacitated by anxiety and fear[10] and often cannot work. Somebody with extreme perfectionism might draft this sentence hundreds of times over several hours because it doesn't seem *just right*. They might become so paralyzed that they give up on the task altogether.

As a clinical psychologist, I would diagnose and treat extreme perfectionism as a mental health condition, often obsessive-compulsive disorder (OCD) or a related syndrome.[11] This book does not focus on the extreme groups or delve into details about OCD and related disorders. Though, if you would like resources for finding professional help for perfectionism, please follow the instructions at the end of the book for accessing a list or go to www.gregchasson.com/flawedresources.

Perfectionism is widespread and not synonymous with a mental health disorder in general, nor OCD specifically. Millions of people exhibit perfectionistic tendencies but are not diagnosable with a disorder.

Healthy and High Standards versus Perfectionism

Perfectionism compels you to launch a nuclear attack in order to kill a fly, when all you need is a swatter or a newspaper.[12] The nuke will succeed in killing the fly, but is it worth it? The strategy is prohibitive

10 Fear and anxiety are related emotions. In this book, I use *fear* to refer to immediate threat reactions—fight, flight, and freeze reactions. I use *anxiety* to refer to anticipated threats in the future.

11 Frost and DiBartolo, "Perfectionism, Anxiety, and Obsessive-Compulsive Disorder."

12 This is an adaptation of a Korean proverb: "Do not draw your sword to kill a fly." Other iterations of this phrase exist, although the supposed meaning seems to vary. Sometimes it serves as a caution about aggressive responses, and at other times it means acting in an extreme way that goes well beyond what's required to meet a goal. I've discovered adaptations that use different insects (e.g., mosquitos) and less destructive weapons, like a sledgehammer instead of a nuke. Though, the latter seems more apropos of the collateral damage that perfectionism causes.

in myriad ways. Was setting off a nuclear weapon worth the hassle? Why not use the swatter to save time, money, and energy? Also, what about the collateral damage from the nuclear blast? Yes, the poor fly is atomized—and maybe a few other flies in the process—but in doing so, the blast demolished city blocks.

A nuke can kill a fly, so some perfectionism scholars and experts suggest that perfectionism has a healthy version.[13] They see some presentations of perfectionism as positive, but I don't conceptualize it this way.

Perfectionism is defined primarily by one holding unreasonable and rigid expectations about outcomes and processes to achieve those outcomes. I'm not convinced rigidity and unreasonable expectations are healthy, no matter the degree. Even if modest, these characteristics are problematic, regardless of whether perfectionistic tendencies can be adaptive and lead to positive effects sometimes (e.g., A+ on a test).

Healthy expectations are not unreasonable or rigid.

I often use the extreme example of snorting cocaine to illustrate this point. If a healthy individual inhales cocaine before taking a test—even if a small amount—their performance will probably improve. This is not necessarily evidence that cocaine use is healthy or positive. It's evidence that an approach to test-taking had some positive effects, but the net healthiness of the approach is dubious.[14] Repeated and long-term use of cocaine as a test-taking strategy comes with tremendous health, financial, social, and other costs.

13 Szymanski, *The Perfectionist's Handbook: Take Risks, Invite Criticism, and Make the Most of Your Mistakes*; Ong and Twohig, *The Anxious Perfectionist: How to Manage Perfectionism-Driven Anxiety Using Acceptance & Commitment Therapy*.

14 It's worth acknowledging that cocaine is a stimulant. Several prescription medications prescribed for attention-deficit/hyperactivity disorder (ADHD) are also classed stimulants. One could argue that cocaine use in this example is like stimulant use for ADHD. I am in no way implying that stimulant use for ADHD, as prescribed, is unhealthy, wrong, or problematic.

Ultimately, the "healthy" version to which others refer probably isn't perfectionism at all, but rather, *high standards* and *pursuing perfection*. Maintaining high standards and pursuing perfection can be carried out in a nonperfectionistic manner—flexible and without causing distress and impairment. You know when you're dealing with perfectionism when those two negative features present themselves.

Work Example of Perfectionism versus High Expectations

Imagine a sales team. A perfectionistic manager might expect their team to meet sales figures that are unreasonable by industry standards or to achieve sales goals across an unreasonable number of territories (i.e., excessive expectation). Even if the team was to approach the lofty sales goals but falls shy of the target—with good reason—a manager with perfectionism might react in an inflexible manner, perhaps giving off an impression of disappointment, focusing on the missed goals, and muting praise and celebration (i.e., rigid adherence to expectation).

High standards, conversely, are flexible. A nonperfectionist updates expectations in real-time to calibrate them to the situation and adjust based on circumstances. They may adopt a high standard, but it's not rigid or excessive. Levels of expectations vary across context and are informed by unique circumstances. For example, perfectionists might have high standards when dating, but lower expectations at the gym.

Imagine that same sales team with a nonperfectionistic manager. Original expectations for sales figures might be high, but they aren't unreasonable (i.e., practical expectations). If the team was to approach the sales goals but falls shy of the target, a nonperfectionistic manager might flexibly reforecast the expectations as needed to account for unique circumstances (e.g., an employee was sick and missed sales in a territory[15]). Doing so would foster a feeling of success, place a focus on achievements, and provide a reason for celebration (i.e., flexible calibration of expectations).

Enabling Perfectionism

Perfectionism doesn't happen in isolation. Coworkers—including peers, supervisors, and subordinates—are drawn easily into the perfectionistic behaviors of other employees. Colleagues act as enablers for perfectionistic behavior by granting deadline extensions, providing excessive reassurance, or excusing tardiness or absences, for example.

Sometimes the enabling is inadvertent, but occasionally it's purposeful, perhaps to protect the employee with perfectionism. The enabling, however, erodes team dynamics. Over time, the workplace becomes a powder keg of resentment between coworkers because it suggests special treatment and inequity.

It's usually the case that enabling behavior is well-intentioned by the enabler. For example, a boss who grants a deadline extension for their perfectionistic employee often does so because they want to be helpful or flexible. Few people like to watch others suffer from anxiety, self-doubt, and perfectionistic behavior.[16] It's uncomfortable.

Why am I referring to this type of "helpful" behavior as *enabling*? It's a harsh characterization, but it's warranted. This "helpful" behavior is not really helping at all. Instead, it's making the situation worse. When I work with extreme cases of clinically severe perfectionism,

---

15 This is another example of overestimating control. The perfectionistic manager in the same scenario would believe they have total control over meeting sales goals, but it's an illusion. It's not totally within their control. For example, they cannot control if their sales associate becomes ill and can't sell for a day (assuming there are no reasonable coverage options).

16 Insert cliché joke about your sadistic mother-in-law being the exception. For the record, my mother-in-law doesn't fit this profile one bit. She's a masochist. ☺

these types of enabling behaviors within a family are a high priority treatment target.

Chances are that you've enabled one of your perfectionistic team members in the past. We all have. I literally get paid not to succumb to this type of behavior, yet I still give in on occasion. It's really difficult. Try not to beat yourself up.

Perpetuation of Perfectionism

Perfectionism can slip under the radar early in life. As kids, we have far fewer demands compared to when we're adults. When we're young, we can nuke a fly and get away with it. If we want to overkill a task, doing so may not carry much opportunity cost. A child can use a strategy of applying all their effort to every task and still have time left over.

Adults can't do this. The façade of relying on this strategy shifts around middle school. Based on my observations, this is about the age in which perfectionistic children start to suffer and become debilitated from these tendencies. Early adolescence seems to be the life stage in which the complexity and number of demands reach a tipping point. At this age you lose the ability to devote 100% effort to each demand. It's just not feasible to do so. Kids who adhere to a perfectionistic approach don't adapt to this tipping point because of their rigid thinking.

You may wonder why some kids shift and accommodate the difference in demands while others do not. The answer isn't clear, but it involves a mixture of biological (e.g., genetics) and environmental (e.g., learning, family modeling) factors.[17] One likely contributor is that perfectionistic children are rewarded for their performance and

---

17 Egan et al., *Cognitive-Behavioral Treatment of Perfectionism.*

encouraged to keep up the good work. This is one reason why perfectionism is self-sustaining.

Early in life—when perfectionists are overkilling tasks—the products are beautiful. Much like the example above with body image perfectionism in adolescent girls, kids who create pristine product using perfectionistic tendencies are praised, which rewards the overkill strategy. The statement, "Your project was perfect—you're so smart and talented," works in the same manner for a perfectionistic child as, "You look great—I can tell you've lost weight," for adolescents with unrealistic body image expectations. Both serve to increase the perfectionistic mindset and behavior.

Three Forces of Perfectionism

Perfectionistic approaches to the world stem from three primary driving forces.[18] First, perfectionism is often *self-oriented*, which refers to rigid and excessive expectations that are derived from and imposed on oneself as a driving force. For example, a perfectionist labors over a project proposal because they believe anything less than perfect is unacceptable for success. The excessive and unreasonable standards are self-derived. They are personal and not implied necessarily by the organizational culture or actions.

Second, self-oriented perfectionism is sometimes—but not always—accompanied by *other-oriented* perfectionism, which is a driving force in which one insists on excessive and rigid performance from others. The other-oriented perfectionist pushes these standards on others, sometimes unknowingly. In other words, one's self-oriented

18 Hewitt and Flett, "Perfectionism in the Self and Social Contexts."

perfectionistic standards are projected outward to affect others in the environment. This often occurs in a workplace.

Third, a common driving force concerns *socially prescribed* perfectionism, which refers to rigid and excessive expectations that are self-imposed but are perceived to come from the world. This can be macro, such as a perceived industry pressure for an academic to publish research in premier scientific journals. It's often more local, however, such as when an employee perceives implicit messages from their workplace culture to pursue excessive and unreasonable goals.

These perfectionism driving forces are not mutually exclusive and often feed into each other to amplify effects. A realtor may have their own need to be the top seller at their company (i.e., self-oriented perfectionism). This drive may be strengthened by the real estate industry, which places considerable emphasis on sales figures as a metric of success (i.e., socially prescribed perfectionism). These two forces may then interact to create an attitude in which the realtor expects the same drive among colleagues that sell houses (i.e., other-oriented perfectionism).

It's not clear where and how a cycle of perfectionism begins. In fact, the starting point might depend on the circumstance. Ultimately, however, you can see how different forces of perfectionism can become entwined over time.

This connected relationship between the three forces may also account for the increase in perfectionism over the generations. As a first generation exhibits perfectionism, it takes hold and becomes an important value. As the perfectionists of the first generation carry on their lives, the perfectionism solidifies and grows because of its self-sustaining qualities. This value is then transmitted to the second generation, but the starting point of collective perfectionistic tenden-

cies has a higher baseline than where it started with the first generation. You can imagine how this pattern continues on to the third and
fourth generations, and so on.

Don't Slam the Perfectionist

Let me be clear. This book is not meant to slam the perfectionist.
I don't believe they should be identified and removed in a workplace
witch hunt. Perfectionists are some of the most industrious, brilliant,
honest, and thoughtful employees in your organization.

My intention is for you to leverage the strengths of these employees
and provide opportunities for them to reduce any negative impact
from perfectionism—much of which can be done through changes to
the workplace culture. The hope is that many of them, with support,
can shift from being perfectionistic to having a mentality of high and
flexible expectations. The rest of this book will go into detail about
some of these solutions. Spoiler alert: none of the solutions require
or recommend the elimination of perfectionists from the workplace.

What Are Some of the Positive Features of Perfectionism?

Team members with perfectionism can be highly loyal, which is
a blessing for a workplace. If they leave a company, it's not usually
because they don't believe in the organization's mission. It's more likely
they don't believe in themselves and their ability to contribute to
that mission.

Perfectionists can be the most honest workers on your team.
When I've needed the details of a workplace incident, I often rely on
perfectionistic colleagues to give me the unfiltered truth. This type of
honesty is critical for enhancing a workplace culture of trust.

Individuals with perfectionism often have a knack for focusing on the details of a project. This proclivity can be useful for certain professions. Several years ago, for instance, I was introduced to a clever software company that specifically hires individuals on the autism spectrum to beta test all its computer programs for finding bugs and user-interface errors. Autism has been linked with higher rates of perfectionism[19] and tendencies to zoom in on details.[20] The company leverages the strengths of individuals with autism, such as attention to details and perfectionistic tendencies, to improve its product. It's a win-win for the company and the employees with perfectionism.

Workers with perfectionism are often the most industrious on your team. This is likely the result of years of learning to accommodate their perfectionistic tendencies by doubling down on their task effort. If you use a blitzkrieg approach when finishing tasks, nobody will deny your hard work, although you won't be praised for your efficiency.

Perfectionism is positively correlated with conscientiousness,[21] which is associated with a range of positive tendencies that benefit a team. This includes characteristics such as being responsible, persistent, goal-oriented, and organized.[22] If you could create an ideal employee from scratch,[23] it would probably start with a liberal pinch of conscientiousness.

---

19 Greenaway and Howlin, "Dysfunctional Attitudes and Perfectionism and Their Relationship to Anxious and Depressive Symptoms in Boys with Autism Spectrum Disorders."

20 Happé and Frith, "The Weak Coherence Account."

21 Stoeber, Otto, and Dalbert, "Perfectionism and the Big Five."

22 Huo and Jiang, "Trait Conscientiousness, Thriving at Work, Career Satisfaction and Job Satisfaction."

23 Perhaps using *science* with electrodes and a doll, such as in John Hughes's 1985 classic film, *Weird Science*. Thankfully, creating the ideal employee was not the premise of a cringey sequel.

➤ Chapter Conclusion and Takeaways

This chapter provided a broad overview of perfection, including its definition and some of the forces that shape and perpetuate it. Here are some key takeaways:

→ Perfectionism, which is on the rise over the generations, reflects society's overvaluation of achieving perfection.

→ *Perfectionism* is not the same as *perfection*. Perfectionism is a worldview and set of behaviors characterized by unreasonable and rigid expectations, inflexible thinking, high levels of doubt, and preoccupations with making mistakes.

→ *High expectations* are distinct from perfectionism, as they are flexible and healthy. Perfectionism is not healthy.

→ Perfectionism has the added drawback of drawing in others in the environment, which leads to enabling. This, in turn, creates toxic team dynamics.

→ The presentation of perfectionism is complicated, but it's influenced by three connected forces: self-oriented, other-oriented, and socially prescribed perfectionism.

→ This chapter is not a call to ban perfectionists from the workplace. When taught to manage their tendencies, perfectionists represent some of the most dedicated and hard-working employees on your team. This is because perfectionism is associated with a host of correlated strengths, such as conscientiousness, loyalty, and attention to detail.

Getting on the same page with terminology is important for launching into the rest of the book, including strategies for addressing perfectionism in the workplace. Now you can be like Michael J. Fox and be "careful not to confuse excellence with perfection."

CHAPTER 2

GOOD HAS PERFECT: OVERVIEW OF PERFECTIONISM CHARACTERISTICS

"The better is the mortal enemy of the good."[24]

**CHARLES LOUIS DE SECONDAT BARON
DE LA BRÈDE ET DE MONTESQUIEU**
18th Century French Philosopher

YOU MAY HAVE heard the aphorism, "Don't let the perfect be the enemy of the good," which has been attributed to enlightenment philosopher Voltaire. Though, the Montesquieu quote provided above preceded Voltaire and may represent the earliest known version of the saying.

It's a simple, yet powerful statement that leverages our human tendency to pit hero versus enemy. Batman has the Joker. Dantes has Mondego. Harry has Voldemort.[25] Skywalker has Vader. Barcelona has Real Madrid.[26] Good has Perfect.

---

24 Montesquieu, *Essays on Montesquieu and on the Enlightenment.*

25 Not only did I state the name of "He Who Must Not Be Named," I printed it. Take *that* superstition! While I'm at it: Candyman, Candyman, Candyman and Beettlejuice, Beettlejuice, Beettlejuice. I might have a very **lively** evening.

26 Or maybe Real Madrid has Barcelona, depending on your allegiance.

The meaning behind this aphorism is that seeking perfection often causes you to engage in behavior that obstructs completion of the task and undermines the creation of a *good* product, much less a perfect one. In saying that, I would contend that *seeking perfection* isn't the problem, but rather, the unwillingness to flex that goal when circumstances necessitate doing so.

But this elicits the question: what are the features of perfectionism that separate it from simply seeking perfection? As a complement to the broad concepts outlined in chapter 1, this chapter highlights the characteristics of perfectionism.

Cognitive Rigidity

Although neuropsychological data is lacking,[27] perfectionism is defined by a rigid thinking style.[28] Cognitive flexibility (sometimes known as *set shifting*) is the opposite of rigid thinking and refers to an ability to switch between mental states, mindsets, and contexts.[29] It causes problems with appraising the importance of tasks—all seem equally important. This, in turn, results in substantial difficulty when prioritizing activities. Preliminary evidence also suggests that perfectionism is associated with reduced creativity,[30] which may be related to rigid thinking (i.e., the inability to think outside the box).

When a perfectionist exhibits difficulties with cognitive rigidity, they find it challenging to shift to new mentalities when contradictory evidence is presented. They also can't shift strategies and tactics in the moment, and as needed, when completing a task. For example,

27 Robinson and Abramovitch, "A Neuropsychological Investigation of Perfectionism."

28 Egan et al., *Cognitive-Behavioral Treatment of Perfectionism.*

29 Diamond, "Executive Functions."

30 Goulet-Pelletier, Gaudreau, and Cousineau, "Is Perfectionism a Killer of Creative Thinking?"

somebody with cognitive rigidity might struggle to switch tactics when playing chess, even when the original gameplan is not working.

Cognitive flexibility is part of executive functioning, which refers to a suite of higher-order cognitive skills and processes that are analogous to a C-suite for your mind. They include processes such as planning, deciding, categorizing, and inhibiting unwanted responses[31] (e.g., stopping yourself from blurting out what you really think about your coworker's ghastly new haircut). I like to imagine executive functioning as little imps of the mind[32] sitting in their executive chairs, wearing tiny three-piece suits, and pulling cortical levers. In the case of perfectionism, the levers get stuck.

Safety Behaviors

For a perfectionist, escaping, avoiding, and ritualizing represent hallmark behavioral responses when navigating life.[33] Many in my field lump these concepts into a family of related compulsive behaviors, for which we use the umbrella term *safety behaviors*.

Examples of safety behaviors in those with perfectionist tendencies include being absent from activities because they cause anxiety, reviewing and fixing projects for too long because of concerns about making a mistake, apologizing excessively for minor mistakes (or non-mistakes), and procrastinating on dreaded tasks.

Safety behaviors all share a common purpose: they are carried out with the intention of reducing or preventing fear and anxiety.[34]

31 Diamond, "Executive Functions."

32 In honor of Lee Baer; Baer, *The Imp of the Mind: Exploring the Silent Epidemic of Obsessive Bad Thoughts.*

33 Egan et al., *Cognitive-Behavioral Treatment of Perfectionism.*

34 Why do we call them safety behaviors? It's because escape, avoidance, and ritualizing behaviors maximize feelings of *safety*.

They provide immediate relief, or at least they did at some point in the individual's past. In anticipation, perfectionists might chase this relief even if they no longer experience it, because of their learning history.

Figure 1 outlines an example of how safety behaviors cause problems over time. This effect is called the *sawtooth effect* because it looks like the teeth of a saw when plotted on a graph. Over time, as anxiety creeps up from encountering an anxiety-provoking object or situation (e.g., making a mistake on a work assignment), the perfectionist will engage in a safety behavior to reduce that anxiety—it's a coping strategy that makes complete sense in the moment.

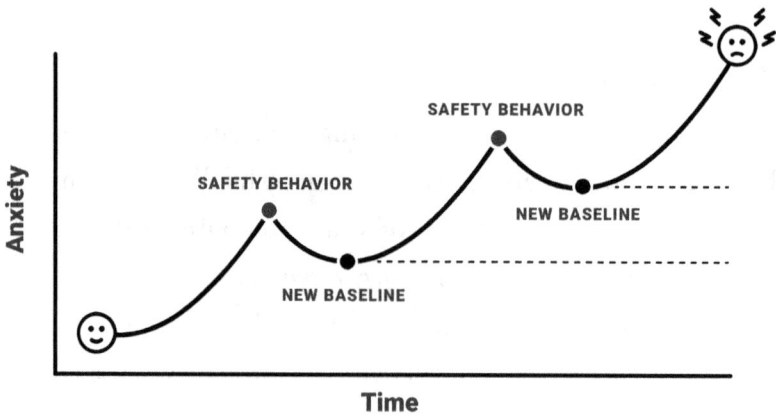

Figure 1: Anxiety and Safety Behavior Sawtooth Effect

As you can see in the figure, the anxiety starts to dissipate, but the relief is short lived. The anxiety starts to increase again, but from a new and higher baseline compared to before. This then cues the need for another safety behavior to elicit relief. As the pattern shows, much like a tumor, the safety behaviors grow and become more complex and debilitating over time.

Negative Reinforcement. In my field, the mechanism for the sawtooth effect is called *negative reinforcement.*[35] Decreasing negative feelings, such as anxiety, is relieving and therefore rewarding. You are removing an unwanted stimulus (i.e., the *negative* part of the term, negative reinforcement[36]) and, as a result, you are strengthening the behavior and increasing the likelihood that the behavior occurs again in the future (i.e., the *reinforcement* part of the term, negative reinforcement).

Negative reinforcement is a behavioral learning law that you experience all the time. For example, a screaming baby (i.e., unpleasant stimulus) cues a parent to grab the bottle and feed them to reduce the horrible screaming and experience relief. The parent has been negatively reinforced to feed the baby when they hear or anticipate hearing the screaming. The relief from the screaming has increased the likelihood of grabbing the bottle more quickly and strongly when the baby screams again in the future.[37]

Incidentally, from the perspective of the baby, screaming also is negatively reinforced. Why? It's because hunger is an unpleasant stimulus that's relieved by screaming and getting fed. The baby will scream more loudly and more strongly each time they get hungry, as parents negatively reinforce this behavior when they give food in response. This is a natural and completely healthy pattern among newborns and parents. It's an illustration of how this behavioral law integrates into our everyday behavior without much awareness.

35 Mowrer, "On the Dual Nature of Learning—a Re-Interpretation of 'Conditioning' and 'Problem-Solving.'"

36 Many people confuse this concept. It's *negative* in the sense of *removal*, not "bad" or "unpleasant." Negative punishment, for example, means *removing* something desired (e.g., losing computer privileges).

37 Or, for some parents, grabbing their own "adult" bottle, but not of milk.

Escape and Avoidance Behaviors. These behaviors are similar to each other but have subtle differences. *Escape* refers to discontinuing a task prematurely once initiated, such as a coworker who starts working on a data entry assignment but gives up during the process because of feeling overwhelmed. *Avoidance* means not initiating tasks in the first place. For example, the previous coworker might find an excuse to dodge the assignment altogether out of fear or anxiety.

Procrastination. Avoidance and escape behavior often take the form of procrastination. Procrastination is a near-universal feature of perfectionism. It's negatively reinforcing to delay working on a dreaded task. By doing so, you don't have to experience the uncomfortable feelings that come with working on the unwanted activity. With procrastination, the undesirable task is a problem for future *you*, not current *you*.

The story for procrastination doesn't end there, though. If you end up ditching a dreaded activity in favor of a preferred one, which is rewarding (e.g., binge watching your favorite show), you're positively reinforcing the preferred activity. As a result, because you're adding a wanted stimulus (i.e., the *positive* part of the term, *positive reinforcement*), you are strengthening the behavior and increasing the likelihood that the behavior occurs again in the future (i.e., the *reinforcement* part of the term, positive reinforcement).

As such, procrastination is a double whammy of reinforcement. You're rewarded for not doing the unwanted activity (i.e., negative reinforcement), and you're also rewarded for doing the wanted activity (i.e., positive reinforcement). No wonder procrastination cycles are so difficult to break.[38]

Ritualizing. When it serves as a safety behavior, ritualizing involves carrying out repetitive behavior with the purpose of decreasing anxiety or fear arising because of a task. As an example, a coworker might recheck a data entry point 20-30 times to make sure they didn't make a mistake. Another common example is reassurance-seeking—the coworker might ask their boss repeatedly if there's been a data entry mistake or if everything is alright. It helps to think about ritualizing as the addition of a behavior (e.g., adding extra checking to a task), whereas avoidance and escape represent subtractions of behavior (e.g., subtracting necessary work on a task).

Please note that ritualizing is not inherently problematic. We all seek reassurance from others, or check our work, as part of completing daily tasks. It's the quantity and quality of the ritualizing that cause problems. With perfectionism the ritualizing is excessive, rigid, and pressured. The perfectionist asks for reassurance so many times that their supervisor becomes frustrated, or they check for mistakes so many times that it causes them to miss deadlines. The ritualizing is compulsive and inflexible. It's as if the perfectionist is compelled to complete these behaviors and has no choice.

Avoidance of New Activities and Learning New Skills

Perfectionism also seems to limit a willingness to try new activities and learn new skills.[39] It may represent a form of safety behavior,

---

38 I'll explain the procrastination cycle in more detail in a future book, maybe after I finish one more episode of *Downton Abbey*.

39 Goulet-Pelletier, Gaudreau, and Cousineau, "Is Perfectionism a Killer of Creative Thinking?"

specifically avoidance. The perfectionist becomes distressed easily—experiencing frustration, shame, or embarrassment—when they try a new activity and believe they stink at it.

Very few people are naturals when picking up a new activity. For the mere mortals of the world, we practice, fail often, look stupid trying, and try again. And again. Perfectionists can't handle that process. Instead, it's easier just to avoid trying new activities and learning new skills.

The Irony of Perfectionism

The degree of situational irony of perfectionism[40]—specifically of the self-fulfilling prophecy variety—cannot be understated. When a perfectionist attempts to control so many factors for optimizing performance, they ultimately undermine their own success. It's ironic when a college student who obsesses for days over the perfect essay ends up procrastinating and not submitting it at all. The preoccupation and ritualizing were carried out to facilitate an A+ grade, but the safety behaviors ultimately contributed to an F grade.

Take another example of a perfectionistic employee who gets stuck rechecking and fixing their draft email to their boss. The employee reviews the message repeatedly to make sure there are no grammar and spelling mistakes, the subject heading isn't misleading, the salutation is respectful, and the tone is deferential. The individual is preoccupied with sending the correct message and being a good employee.

In the process, however, the email requires hours of effort and is delayed substantially. In turn, this delay results in the boss missing

---

40 Real irony, Alanis.

a key piece of information that disrupts productivity. In the end, the compulsive checking and fixing behavior resulted in the opposite effect for the employee—instead of helpful, they come across as obstructive. The optics look awful for the employee.

Cognitive-Behavioral Components of Perfectionism

Psychologists and allied disciplines have been researching perfectionism for decades. Most advances in understanding and treating it have come from the tradition of cognitive-behavioral therapy (CBT). CBT is a treatment orientation that emphasizes the interconnectedness of a person's thoughts, feelings, and behaviors in various situations.

CBT targets unhealthy patterns within that interconnectedness. The triangle is a universal symbol for CBT, with each of the three corners representing one of the three components of a person's reaction: thoughts, feelings, and behaviors. The sides of the triangle represent the interconnectedness of each of these components. Let me illustrate:

Trey has called in sick from work for three days straight, which has been problematic because he is expected to present to the company's board of directors next week.

His division chief wants to review the presentation and requested a copy of the slideshow last week, but it hasn't been provided. As a result, the chief has emailed terse messages to Trey pointing out the tardiness. Trey feels very depressed and hopeless because he isn't even close to finishing the presentation. This state makes him even less motivated to work on the presentation. He is thinking about resigning because of his high anxiety and low mood.

Trey's situation might have a variety of explanations, but a CBT conceptualization is a strong starting point. Figure 2 provides a CBT breakdown of the various components of Trey's problematic situation. It shows the interplay between—and within—the three CBT components: thoughts, feelings, and behaviors.

Figure 2: Trey's Patterns of Thoughts, Feelings, and Behaviors

Imagine the context in which Trey has been tweaking different versions of the slideshow compulsively—trapped by attempts to improve different slides—for more than a week. This is a classic safety behavior for a perfectionist. Trey experiences a range of beliefs (i.e., *thoughts*). He becomes preoccupied with his lack of progress from getting stuck on the assignment. He doesn't think the product is good enough because of the importance of the presentation. As a result of being stuck and perceiving pressure to complete the assignment, Trey starts to believe he's incompetent and unworthy of his place on the team. He anticipates that his division chief is furious and wants to fire him.

Based on all these thoughts and his lack of progress on the slides, Trey starts experiencing strong emotions (i.e., *feelings*). He is terrified that he won't complete the slideshow, will let down the team, and will be fired. This even results in panic sensations, such as racing heart, sweating, shaking, and feeling nauseated. He experiences guilt and shame due to being stuck and not meeting his job expectations. His anxiety often converts to hopelessness and lack of motivation.

Trey's thoughts and feelings in this situation influence his response, most notably a range of safety actions (i.e., *behaviors*). The email causes Trey to freeze because of his anxiety and desperation—he can't resume the work. He avoids responding to all emails, including those from his division chief, due to shame, guilt, and anxiety. Trey checks the social media posts of his colleagues constantly to see if there are any clues about how they might be feeling or what they might be thinking.

One colleague posted: "Brutal day at work—there's just not enough time!"

For Trey, this post is consonant with his mood and beliefs and strengthens the cognitive-behavioral pattern. He blames himself for his coworker's brutal workday.

As a result of his anticipation of failure and angering his division chief, Trey starts drafting a resignation letter he can't finish. He pauses, becomes demoralized, and retreats to his bedroom to isolate, although he musters enough energy to call in sick. He is so paralyzed by perfectionism that he can't even quit his job.

The thoughts, feelings, and behaviors outlined in this situation also provoke a nasty feedback loop of more thoughts, feelings, and behaviors. Trey's absenteeism elicits frustration from his coworkers, who must pick up the slack. Their resentment prompts them to call and email Trey with pleas for assistance, all met with silence. It's not long before the coworkers reach out to the division chief and complain about workload and Trey's lack of participation. As a result of the complaints, the division chief sends off a quick and perhaps curt email to Trey: "Please prioritize the end-year reports, as they seem to be accumulating and causing delays."

Trey interprets the email—accurate or otherwise—as evidence that his division chief is furious. This conclusion worsens his overall cycle of self-loathing, shame, and guilt. Trey spirals into further hopelessness and withdrawal. After a while, Trey's isolation and procrastination do, in fact, color his chief's opinion of him in a negative light. It's a self-defeating and self-fulfilling prophecy.[41]

The Cognitive-Behavioral Model of Perfectionism

This previous section highlights a broad application of a CBT perspective to Trey's circumstances. Over the years, researchers, clinicians, and theorists have refined generic CBT perspectives to map against the patterns of perfectionism more specifically. In one excellent example, Shafran, Egan, and Wade (2010)[42] published a CBT model

---

41 ♪ Isn't it ironic, don't you think? ♪
42 Shafran, Egan, and Wade, *Overcoming Perfectionism*.

of perfectionism that depicts a looped cause-and-effect flow of CBT components (i.e., thoughts, feelings, and behaviors). I find the model intuitive and useful for considering the elements at play across different presentations of perfectionism.

The CBT model of perfectionism starts with the individual overrelying on and overvaluing achievements for defining their self-worth. Achievements become the core of their self-esteem. This is true at the exclusion of other features that many of us use to define ourselves, such as our values, interests, and circumstances.

When cognitive rigidity is added to the mix, this leads to rigid standards around performance. The individual attempts to achieve goals within the context of these rigid standards. At this point, three outcomes are possible: they (a) meet the standard, (b) do not meet the standard, or (c) avoid or escape trying to meet the standard.

Regardless, the individual does not interpret the results objectively. They view their performance with myriad biases, such as beliefs about society's rules and hyperfocusing on minor mistakes.

According to the model, when the individual fails to meet the rigid standards or they avoid trying to achieve goals (i.e., outcomes *b* and *c* above), they engage in self-criticism and self-destructive behavior—for example, resigning from a job. Then, the self-criticism and self-destructive behavior feed back into the beginning of the model to undermine the individual's sense of self-worth. This reinstigates the cascade.

Even if the individual meets the initial rigid standards (i.e., outcome *a*), the sense of achievement only lasts for the short-term. This is because the perfectionist drifts in how they appraise their performance and starts doubting whether it was enough, much like gaslighting oneself. At this point, the gaslighting starts to work, and the individual interprets their performance in a negative light.

In addition, I would add to the model that ritualizing undermines the perfectionist's ownership of positive results and feelings of satisfaction. For example, they might downplay positive results because they needed reassurance from others or spent an unreasonable amount of time trying to achieve it: "Sure, I finished, but it took me forever."

Ultimately, self-gaslighting and ritualizing feed back into the beginning of the model to weaken self-worth. This pattern also reinstigates the cascade.

Common Perfectionism Biases

We're wired to take shortcuts when perceiving and thinking. For example, we often miss mistakes when process written material. Did you notice in the previous sentence that I omitted the suffix -ing on the word *processing*? If you missed it, you could thank your mind's ability to fix these types of errors automatically on your behalf without spending too much precious mental energy. This is why book editing is such a difficult task. [43] When reviewing this book, the editor must override strong automatic processing of words to discover subtle errors. Our minds reflexively fill in the blanks for us constantly. It's very useful; imagine having to process every detail—exhausting!

The mind works similarly when you encounter missing or ambiguous information in the environment. For example, imagine if your coworker were to show up to work late, seeming agitated, clutching a wad of napkins, with an unsightly coffee stain on their shirt. You'd probably take it for granted, but your brain would help you draw an inference based

---

43 Yes, this is a shameless attempt at soliciting a discount from my editor.

on the circumstantial evidence. Even now, you've probably jumped to the conclusion that they were late because they spilled coffee on their clothes and needed to clean it. Attorneys often rely on this automatic processing when making a case to the jury or judge.

When your assumptions lean in a certain direction consistently across situations—even in the face of contrary evidence—they might be biased. For example, you might always assume the driver of a car speeding past you on the highway is a reckless jerk on a joy ride.[44] That's an assumption, and it could reflect a bias shaped by a variety of factors, such as your current mood and past experiences.

Sometimes the mind fills in the blanks with assumptions that are wrong. The driver of the car speeding past you might be rushing their spouse to the hospital. When you're feeling depressed or anxious, the mind tends to fill in the blanks with assumptions that match your negative state.

For instance, let's say you send a text message to your boss notifying them that you're running a few minutes behind. If your boss sends a cryptic reply that says, "Okay," your mind may start racing with assumptions. Those assumptions might take on characteristics of your emotional state. If depressed, you might have a bias in which you assume your boss is being curt because they think you're worthless. If anxious, you might have a bias in which you assume your boss is angry and will fire you.

Perfectionism has its own set of common biases.[45] Figure 3 offers a nonexhaustive list and examples of common biases exhibited by

44 If you can stomach some profanity, I encourage you to search for George Carlin's take on fast and slow cars in traffic. The late comedian's take on this was genius and the inspiration for this example.

45 Antony and Swinson, *When Perfect Isn't Good Enough: Strategies for Coping with Perfectionism*; Egan et al., *Cognitive-Behavioral Treatment of Perfectionism*.

individuals with perfectionism. Per the CBT model of perfectionism, these biases are pivotal for understanding how individuals with perfectionism develop rigid expectations, overvalue their achievements when determining self-worth, and consider their outcomes as failures. These biases also represent key targets for change efforts in the workplace.

Definition	Workplace Example
All-or-None Thinking	
Seeing the world as binary—black or white—and not seeing degrees in between categories	You're either loyal to the company's mission or not.
Catastrophizing	
Predicting the worst possible outcomes or negative effects	I'm late on this project, so the client will drop our firm and I'll be fired.
Emotional Reasoning	
Believing that your emotional reaction—instead of objective data—makes something fact or true	This report doesn't feel complete, so it must not be done.
Filtering	
Discounting positive evidence and focusing on the negative evidence	My efforts weren't successful because only one grant proposal was funded and not the other five.
Fortune-Telling	
Making predictions about the future that are unsupported by objective data	I probably won't reach my annual sales target in the next 12 months.
Labeling	
Applying extreme and rigid category labels—often with negative connotation—to describe	I'm a moron. I accidentally provided the wrong information to the client.
Mind-Reading	
Thinking that you know somebody's beliefs or intentions without objective data	After I made my comment at the meeting, my boss looked unimpressed; they must think I'm incompetent.
Over-Generalization	
Using one instance to draw conclusions about all instances	I sent a suggestion for a new strategy but it wasn't selected. My suggestions are never taken seriously.
Should Statement	
Placing extreme and rigid demands on oneself or others and perceiving those demands as universal by everyone	I should catch all errors while data cleaning.

Figure 3: Table of Common Cognitive Distortions Associated with Perfectionism

Cognitive biases in perfectionism are worsened by cognitive rigidity. When a perfectionist exhibits a biased perspective, the effects are amplified because they tend to get fixated on those biased beliefs. They get stuck shifting to new ways of thinking when presented with contrary evidence.

The All-or-None Bias

For the moment, let's focus on one pervasive bias that may underlie all others, at least when considering perfectionism. This is the *all-or-none bias*, which refers to a worldview that forces a binary system on everything it touches. You're good or bad, smart or stupid, competent or incompetent. You've failed or succeeded, finished or not finished, won or lost. Middle grounds don't exist in this mindset; dimensions are replaced with dichotomies. You're not smarter or less smart, just placed in bins of *smart* or *stupid*.

Should Statements

Should statements[46] are the most toxic form of the all-or-none bias. Should statements reflect a worldview characterized by global and rigid life expectations. Perfectionists believe that these expectations are universal to life. I *should* be a good manager. I *must* be an attentive parent. I *ought* to be on time. I *have to* exercise. These should statements take on a life of their own and start to dictate one's behavior, even if harmful.

Process Paralysis

Often, perfectionists become preoccupied with achieving perfect efficiency by optimizing task processes. This tendency results in them

---

46 Crafty synonyms can't help you, as the bias includes cousins of *should*, such as *ought to, must, supposed to, have to.*

getting stuck trying to identify and execute a plan—*process paralysis*. An example of this includes researching and comparing options to identify the ideal strategy to carry out a task. This can take the form of countless hours of Internet research and seeking reassurance from others.

Another example involves the perfectionist engaging in compulsive overanalysis to determine the optimal order of steps for completing a task. They might identify and compare all the different combinations of steps. This also tends to include considerable reassurance-seeking from others.

The perfectionistic tendency for process paralysis also coincides with excessive list-making behavior. We all leverage lists in our lives. Without lists, I'd be returning to the grocery store a dozen times while making dinner. A modest degree of list-making is adaptive, but it's problematic when making lists gets in the way of completing the tasks for which they were created. For example, imagine I spend two hours creating a perfect grocery list but, as a result, I can't get to the store before it closes. This is process paralysis.

Moralism

Perfectionistic tendencies often associate with rigid and extreme moral reasoning.[47] The way in which moral reasoning and behavior show up differs by self-oriented versus other-oriented perfectionism. A perfectionist can present with both self- and other-oriented moral reasoning, though.

For individuals with perfectionism, the rigid and extreme moral reasoning involves preoccupation with being good or holy (i.e., not offending a deity). It often presents with a tendency for

---

47 Nelson et al., "Scrupulosity in Patients with Obsessive-Compulsive Disorder"; Ojserkis and McKay, "Scrupulosity and Slowness in OCD."

self-flagellation. You can imagine a coworker who feels compelled to confess mistakes and self-impose punishments, even if the rest of the team and their supervisor believe it's being blown out of proportion. When this self-oriented moral reasoning and behavior are extreme and cause life impairment and distress, it's sometimes called *scrupulosity*, a form of OCD.

It's common in these situations for the perfectionist to apologize profusely and to do so even if it's inappropriate or unwarranted. It's driven typically by fears of burdening others and therefore not being a good or perfect person. In this case, apologizing is a safety behavior. The perfectionist's intention—within their awareness or otherwise—is to decrease anxiety in the event they're imposing on others. This goes beyond the societal tendency to overapologize; it comes across as pressured and compulsive.

With other-oriented perfectionism, the reasoning involves holding others to rigid and extreme religious or moral standards. It often presents as self-righteous indignation and preaching behavior. Individuals exhibiting other-oriented perfectionism tend to teach others moral lessons, even passive-aggressively. This type of behavior destroys relationships with others. This extends to organizational culture. Most people can point to working with a moralizing colleague at some point in their career. It can be toxic.

Please note that extreme and rigid moral reasoning and behavior do not require high levels of religiosity or a fear of offending a deity. A perfectionist can present with this type of reasoning and behavior and identify as atheist, [48] agnostic, or nonreligious. If you investi-

48 Phillips and Fisak, "An Examination of the Factor Structure of the Penn Inventory of Scrupulosity-Revised (PIOS-R) in Atheist and Christian Samples."

gate scrupulosity on the Internet, please don't be misled by an over-emphasis on religion.

Other Related Features of Perfectionism

Perfectionism can perform as a solo artist or sing on stage as part of an ensemble. In other words, perfectionism sometimes—but not always—presents alongside other common characteristics. These associated features complicate the picture and can alter the landscape of a workplace.

Inflated Sense of Responsibility. The perfectionist often holds unreasonable beliefs about their responsibility for outcomes.[49] They often overestimate their amount of control in a situation (i.e., *over-control*) and believe they must prevent bad things from happening. This tendency often presents with should statements, for example, "I should have known that my colleague was unhappy and wanted to quit—I could have done something to stop it."

Just In Case (JIC).[50] Related to the inflated sense of responsibility, JIC is a perfectionist's bias to always attempt to pre-empt and avoid bad outcomes, even if the probability of the bad outcome is low and the cost of the behavior is prohibitive. For example, a perfectionist might rationalize reviewing their proposal draft one more time, *just in case* they missed an error. They might follow all assignment directions, even if unnecessary or optional, *just in case* they're accused of not

---

49 Woods, Tolin, and Abramowitz, "Dimensionality of the Obsessive Beliefs Questionnaire (OBQ)."

50 In this case, I'm not referring to the JIC term adopted in inventory strategy, but the underlying principle of both JIC concepts are the same. For inventory, JIC is a strategy in which companies warehouse extra product inventory *just in case* there is an unexpected run on the product—think toilet paper fever during the early stages of the Covid pandemic.

working hard enough. They might add that extra section to the report, *just in case* their boss wants it and would be upset if it were missing.

Cognitive rigidity interacts with the JIC mentality. The perfectionist has difficulty differentiating which JIC behaviors are necessary and when they're best employed. They cannot prioritize the JIC opportunities flexibly and therefore overcommit to completing too many.

The draw of JIC is that it usually only requires a rapid and inexpensive response—one quick review; one extra step; one additional sentence. They're often small acts, all justified by the thought that doing the JIC behaviors can avert large problems later. After all, an ounce of prevention is worth a pound of cure, so they say. The cost of doing a single JIC behavior seems minor compared to the possible consequences of skipping it.

What's not considered enough, however, are the costs that accumulate from giving in excessively to the JIC behaviors. The costs can include social, financial, emotional, and physical impacts, among many others. The JIC behaviors add up and become impairing. It's death by a thousand tiny cuts.

Indecisiveness. Related to process paralysis, indecisiveness is a common feature of perfectionism. Often the perfectionist waffles between two or more options and cannot decide. This can slow down work processes or bring them to a halt. Perfectionists often worry about making the wrong or imperfect choice and being the one to blame. For this reason, indecisiveness also connects to an inflated sense of responsibility.

Not Just Right Experiences (NJREs). Sometimes referred to as *not just right feelings,* NJREs represent an oft-overlooked correlate of perfectionism.[51] This concept refers to feelings and thoughts that something doesn't feel right. It doesn't feel complete. It's a gut feeling and, in perfectionism, this intuition seems to go awry.

Exhibiting a form of cognitive rigidity, the perfectionist becomes stuck revising a product until it feels right. Conversely, a nonperfectionist might get that same feeling but stop working on the task and accept that it feels complete or right "enough." For example, you might wash a countertop until it feels clean. If that feeling never comes or is unclear, you might get stuck wiping down the counter for a long time. The nonperfectionist can ignore this, decide the countertop is clean enough, and stop.

NJREs are a form of emotional reasoning: when one draws conclusions based on emotion rather than reason. Specifically, the perfectionist feels that something isn't complete, even if reason and evidence suggest that the task is, in fact, done. They draw the conclusion that the task isn't complete because it doesn't "feel" as though it is. Emotional reasoning is another example of a cognitive bias.

Difficulty Delegating. Individuals with perfectionism often have difficulty delegating tasks for which they are responsible. This hesitancy may be due to a variety of factors, but it's often triggered by anxiety about the performance of others. In some instances, they may trust the work performance of others, but the anxiety is too overwhelming to take a chance. This reluctance can be conceptualized as a safety behavior—specifically avoidance.

In other instances, perfectionists may not trust the work of their colleagues. Either way, delegating is a key part of the workplace and

---

51 Coles et al., "Not Just Right Experiences and Obsessive–Compulsive Features."1 (1995

for most job roles. For this reason, this perfectionism tendency can obstruct workplace efficiency and effectiveness.

Local Processing Tendency. As noted in the previous chapter, it's a common perfectionistic tendency to zoom in on the details at the expense of appreciating the big picture. It's comparable to the saying, *can't see the forest for the trees.*[52] The problem with overactive local processing is that it causes perfectionists to become engrossed in the minutiae of a task. They become consumed by project details and fail to keep the overarching purpose in mind when working.

Stinginess. Individuals with perfectionism tend to spend resources in a thrifty manner. It's sometimes driven by moralistic beliefs about spending wastefully and limiting extravagance. In other instances, it might be caused by rigid adherence to spending rules.

For the budget-minded organizational leader, this characteristic of perfectionism might be welcomed. Please note, however, that stingy tendencies have a downside. Under-resourced work environments can be frustrating and demoralizing for a workplace culture. This sends a message to employees about being undervalued.

Clutter. Hoarding is one of my professional areas of expertise. It's part of the family of OCD conditions. When giving presentations, I love to *wow* the audience by revealing that hoarding is positively correlated with perfectionism.[53] This means that higher perfectionism is connected to more

52 For British English speakers, the saying is *can't see the wood for the trees.*

53 Frost and Gross, "The Hoarding of Possessions"; Martinelli et al., "Perfectionism Dimensions as Predictors of Symptom Dimensions of Obsessive-Compulsive Disorder"; Wetterneck et al., "Obsessive–Compulsive Personality Traits."

hoarding behavior.[54] In fact, many of those severe cases of hoarding you see on reality television shows have pronounced levels of perfectionism.

How can that be?

Clutter is associated with a range of beliefs and behaviors, but some are relevant to perfectionism. Often, individuals have a vision for how to set up their space, create an optimal system, or build an inspired project. If that vision is extreme and rigid—and therefore infeasible to implement—individuals with perfectionism will procrastinate or give up altogether. As such, they will give up organizing the space, developing the optimal system, or working on the inspired project. Over time, this tendency recurs and develops into mountains of clutter that consists of ingredients for partially designed systems and well-intentioned projects.

It's important to note that these *other related features* of perfectionism are not mutually exclusive nor are they a necessary part of the presentation. In other words, any combination of them may present in a perfectionistic employee. And, as a reminder, they are not inherently problematic in and of themselves.

In fact, some of the features may be helpful, such as a strong sense of responsibility, which is often a positive quality in a worker. Stinginess can be conceptualized as wise budgeting. Similarly, many leaders swear by instinctual decision-making, and you could argue that NJREs are an example of this approach (i.e., "the project isn't done until my gut says so").

---

54 On the flip side, lower perfectionism is connected to lower hoarding behavior.

➤ Chapter Conclusion and Takeaways

This chapter highlights core features of perfectionism. Here are some key takeaways:

- → Perfectionism is defined in large part by cognitive rigidity.
- → Safety behaviors are a common perfectionistic response to navigating the world, and this includes escape, avoidance, and ritualizing behaviors. These behaviors function to reduce immediate anxiety and fear in the short-term but come with substantial cost to functioning.
- → The current conceptualization of perfectionism is expressed within a CBT framework. A specific CBT for perfectionism model provides insights for understanding common patterns of thoughts, feelings, and behaviors that arise when a perfectionist approaches a task.
- → As part of the CBT framework, common cognitive biases— such as all-or-none thinking and its derivative, the should statement—complicate the perfectionism picture.
- → Perfectionism is associated with a range of other characteristics that worsen impairment and distress. Some examples include indecisiveness, NJREs, moralism, difficulty delegating, and the local processing bias.

Striving for perfection is not necessarily a problem. The difficulty arises when striving for perfection coincides with a range of problematic features that capture the very nature of perfectionism. Although some aspects of perfectionism can be conceptualized as strengths, in most instances, those aspects promote an unhealthy pursuit of perfection that serves as a "mortal enemy of the good."

CHAPTER 3

HIGH ON THE KOOKOMETER: DETECTING PERFECTIONISM IN THE WORKPLACE

"The other day I noticed my 12-year-old daughter was getting stressed about a grade she was due on a science test. The grade came back, and it was absolutely fine, but she felt it wasn't good enough. That was my red alert for this issue of perfectionism."[55]

KATTY KAY
Journalist, Author, Broadcaster

NOW THAT YOU'RE more familiar with the concept of perfectionism, we can turn our attention to strategies for spotting it in the wild (i.e., your workplace). It's not always easy to notice perfectionistic traits in others, but as Katty Kay quotes above, sometimes it hits like a left hook from Mike Tyson. At other times, it's subtle and easy to miss.

---

55 King, "How To Ditch The 'Good Girl' Routine."

Spotting a perfectionist will involve confirmation from many different types of data sources. A single piece of evidence will rarely result in a confident conclusion. In fact, I'd encourage you to be skeptical until multiple pieces of evidence for perfectionism emerge.

In many ways, this chapter reads like a logical extension of chapter 2. For example, in the previous chapter, I introduced the concept of cognitive rigidity. Chapter 3 will carry that idea forward and outline methods for noticing cognitive rigidity in your employees. In this chapter, all methods for identifying perfectionism will be informal,[56] and many of these strategies also work for screening for perfectionism in job candidates.

As a reminder, this book was not published to target perfectionists and rid them from the workplace. Employees with perfectionism tend to exhibit the type of aptitude, effort, and skills necessary for success. Instead, my aim is for you to find ways of mitigating any negative impact of perfectionism—for example by adjusting the organizational climate, supervisory styles, methods of communication, and other possible changes. Individuals with perfectionism often represent a strong, positive force in your workplace. With the right approach, these employees can become rockstars for your mission and bottom line.

Common Denominator of a Slowed Workflow

Perfectionism assaults workplace efficiency. A good first step would consist of checking productivity metrics to find patterns that point to aspects of the workflow that have slowed or held up other components of the process.

---

56 I will skip discussing formal methods—those employed by a trained professional, such as a psychometrician or psychologist. If more formal and structured methods are needed in your workplace, I would recommend a consultation from an expert.

Perfectionism is much like the slow group ahead of you on the miniature golf course. You must wait until they finish if you're unwilling to play through and skip holes. In this analogy, holes represent critical tasks that support the workflow and overall productivity. With one slow golf group, the entire system can grind to a halt, creating a bottleneck for productivity.

You may find an area of your team's work processes that places a stranglehold on efficient workflow. If this is the case, dig deeper to examine individual contributions and performance. You might find that the deceleration is due to one or two members of the team who take longer to complete their tasks, even if their products are stellar.

The slowing at the individual level might not seem awful, but it adds up across tasks and team members. Individual perfectionistic performances might reduce the entire workflow by fractions of percentages, but for overall productivity, they become noticeable at the cumulative level. If Joe in accounting, Tonya in client relations, and Jianping in project management each contribute 0.5% to a slowing of workflow pace, this adds up to 1.5% to the overall bottleneck effect, assuming each team member's performances are independent of each other.

By the way, the assumption of independence is probably a stretch. It would be unsurprising if there were an interactive effect between the individual contributions to slowing, thereby intensifying the workflow bottleneck. For example, Tonya's perfectionism-driven procrastination with returning calls from irate clients might be worsened by Jianping's perfectionism-driven slow pace with finalizing the addition of a new product feature. This is especially true if the client is irate because of missed product launch deadlines. In short, the combined contributions to a throttled workflow from Tonya and Jianping are not as simple as adding each percentage, but rather, are multiplied based on their effect on each other.

A strong approach would consist of examining individual contributions to workflow across different tasks and processes over time. Perfectionists exhibit broad applications of these tendencies across different tasks, and the pattern is consistent over time. If a perfectionistic employee is the common denominator linked with multiple slowed processes, your hypothesis seems even more valid.

Beautiful but Late

Keep an eye out for employees who produce beautiful work, but it's chronically late. I was once able to identify a perfectionistic doctoral student who produced the most sophisticated, well-written manuscripts. The first draft required very few revisions and was ready to submit for publication.

Sounds lovely, right? Not entirely. The problem is that the manuscript was months overdue. It required me to provide considerable check-ins for accountability and caused me substantial confusion around the reason for the delays. It was clear the student had the aptitude and skill—in fact, they were superior to their peers. Perfectionism sabotaged their progress.

The Handwriting Hack

There is one possible way to spot a perfectionist that doesn't usually get discussed: handwriting. In this age, handwriting is a dying art, but if you have an opportunity to observe an employee or job candidate's handwriting—printed or cursive—you might be able to identify a perfectionist. Be sure to look at the form of the writing and the amount of time it takes them to write.

This is not a universal observation, but individuals with perfectionism tend to exhibit some of the neatest and most symmetrical handwriting you'll ever see. It often looks artificial. If the handwriting requires an unreasonable amount of time to complete, this could be another sign of perfectionism. This is all to say that asking an employee or job candidate to write out an answer to a question by hand, while you observe, might be a clever hack for spotting a perfectionist.

Signals of Safety Behaviors

Escape and Avoidance. One of the easiest ways to tell if somebody is a perfectionist is by noticing their overt behavior. In this case, that means observing their safety behaviors. Avoidance and escape are often straightforward to identify.

This is especially the case if they are exhibiting procrastination. This also includes employees who cram just before the assignment is due, even if they meet the deadline. This tendency also presents as repeated requests for deadline extensions. It's important to note that procrastination can result from a variety of factors, but if you observe it in the workplace, it's reasonable to bet that perfectionism is one cause.

Radio silence is another key indicator of perfectionism. If you request a task or follow up on task progress, a perfectionist often delays responding and finally does so well beyond a reasonable timeframe. This unresponsiveness is a common version of avoidance behavior and driven, in a large part, by shame and guilt. The perfectionist knows they've let their perfectionism obstruct their performance, which elicits strong feelings of shame and guilt.

Shame is an underrated paralyzing agent. It's awful to experience, hard to self-identify, and slow to disappear. I find that it's second only to anxiety—or fear—in terms of negative emotions that perfectionists work tirelessly to avoid.

A perfectionist's safety behaviors also tend to include the avoidance of career-advancing opportunities. For example, you may be stunned to learn that your employee declined a promotion or the opportunity to deliver a key presentation. This baffles employers because they leverage career advancement as a critical reward mechanism to motivate employees. It therefore seems unusual for employees to turn down such opportunities.

There are several reasons that may explain these curious decisions, but a common factor is perfectionism. The perfectionist hesitates to accept new responsibilities out of fear of failure and—because of all-or-none thinking—is reluctant to accept rewards because they often feel undeserving.

Another area of perfectionistic avoidance concerns difficulty delegating tasks to others. It might strike you as odd or problematic that an employee opts to fly solo on a project and hesitates to involve others in the process. Many reasons could explain this tendency, but it might be perfectionism. Maybe the perfectionist doesn't trust others to complete the project, or they are unwilling to give up control. If this occurs occasionally, it's probably not a concern, but if this is a recurring pattern across projects from an employee, it may signal perfectionism.

Ritualizing. Many forms of ritualizing are noticeable to others. Some perfectionistic rituals can be private and out of sight—such as compulsively checking and reviewing products for mistakes—but others cannot be hidden. Pressured reassurance-seeking, confessing, and apologizing fit into this category. These types of rituals extend into the perfectionist's social world and draw in people around them.

The excessive and rigid nature of these behaviors cause them to stand out, but they also have other signals of being socially bizarre. These behaviors can present as quite off-putting to others because they tend to violate social scripts, contracts, and other norms. I use a fabricated 1-10 scale as a measure of weirdness or kookiness, and I call it the *Kookometer*™.[57]

If an employee is constantly confessing minor mistakes and apologizing ad nauseum, this sticks out as odd. It's not just about rigidity and excessiveness; the behavior is just socially inappropriate. It's probably high on the Kookometer, and it's likely there's some form of perfectionism at play.

Figure 4 illustrates an example of the Kookometer with hypothetical ratings of perfectionistic behaviors. I've also included a blank copy as part of the book's online resources for you to tailor to your own workplace. To access the blank copy, please follow the instructions at the end of the book for accessing the figures or go to www.gregchasson.com/flawedresources.

---

57 If you're not appreciating the label of *bizarre, weird,* and *kooky*, I get it. Change up the name to whatever makes sense to you. (I couldn't call it an *Odd*ometer.)

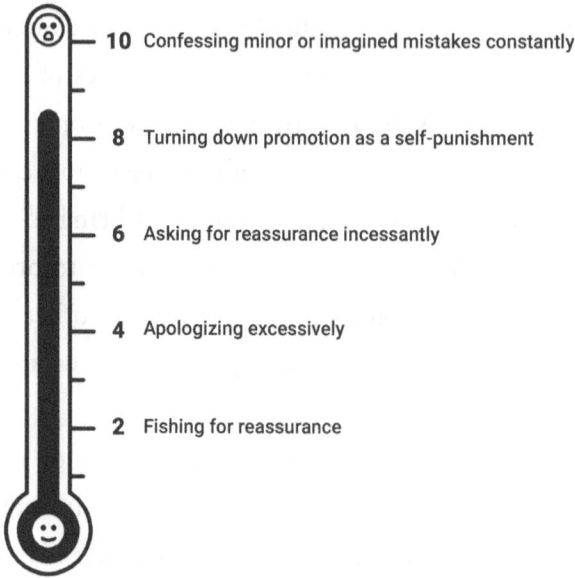

Figure 4: An example of the Kookometer

Individuals with perfectionism often have some self-awareness of the Kookometer and therefore attempt to camouflage any ritualistic behavior. In this way, the behaviors can become more discreet over time. For example, if a perfectionist is worried about their performance on a task, they might engage in subtle communication attempts to see their manager's microreactions. I call this *fishing for reassurance*.

To illustrate this fishing, consider a perfectionist who's been told by management to cease requesting reassurance from others because it's become excessive and exhausting. Now imagine this perfectionist the morning after submitting a critical proposal draft and feeling nervous about their performance. The employee can't ask for reassurance from their boss outright, as this has been flagged as a problem behavior, so the perfectionist needs to camouflage the intentions of any reassurance-seeking. It's more indirect and might look something like this:

Perfectionist: *Good morning! How was your evening?* [Scans boss for facial expressions and overall mood to identify evidence that boss had a difficult evening, which could signal being upset about the proposal quality.]

Boss: *Good morning. My evening was okay.* [Looks gloomy and exhausted.]

Perfectionist: [Anxiety increases because the boss doesn't look thrilled, and *okay* is an ambiguous descriptor and might mean *bad.*] *Just the usual then?* [Repeats subtle attempt at clarifying the emotional state of the boss's evening. More scanning of facial expressions and mood.]

Boss: *No, not really. I didn't sleep very well.* [Still looks gloomy and exhausted.]

Perfectionist: [Starts to worry that a poor proposal draft caused the boss to become sleepless. Anxiety increases. Pressure to seek reassurance skyrockets.] *Sorry to hear that.* [Decides next—within their awareness or otherwise—to use light, self-deprecating humor as a fishing strategy.] *I didn't think our proposal needed THAT much work!* [Laughs ever so slightly and artificially. More scanning of facial expressions and mood.]

Boss: [Provides awkward compulsory laugh.] No, my dog was up all night vomiting. I couldn't even get to the proposal.

Perfectionist: [Takes comfort in the reassurance that everything is alright for now.] *That's awful. Hope your pup is okay.* [Mission accomplished.]

You may suspect that your perfectionistic employee has learned to choreograph their reassurance-seeking, confessing, and apologizing behavior in subtle ways to prevent elevations on the Kookometer. It's always a good strategy to ask yourself about the function of their behavior. I always tell my trainees it's all about the function, function, function.

In the example above, the function of the perfectionist's questioning of the boss had nothing to do with a genuine interest in the boss's sleep quality, concern with the dog, nor desire to strengthen their relationship. The sole function was to seek evidence that their relationship with their boss is undamaged. This, in turn, serves the function of reducing the perfectionist's momentary anxiety that their work performance was insufficient.

Oversensitivity

Oversensitivity is a common and observable aspect of perfectionism.[58] It's important to acknowledge that, although some people handle criticism well, few enjoy it. They might appreciate it as a way to learn and grow, but enjoying critical feedback seems like a stretch. I saw a meme floating around that stated, "Unsolicited advice is always received as criticism." This is a powerful reminder that criticism is a matter of perspective. Even in the absence of an intention to criticize, it may be interpreted this way.

---

58 Dunkley, Zuroff, and Blankstein, "Specific Perfectionism Components versus Self-Criticism in Predicting Maladjustment."

That being said, individuals with perfectionism tend to handle criticism—even if delivered diplomatically and without intention—more poorly than most, and this causes considerable distress.[59] This oversensitivity to feedback can manifest in multiple ways. For example, the perfectionist might interpret neutral feedback as criticism. They often amplify the comments they receive such that they're perceived as stronger or more negative than intended.

You might feel like you're walking on eggshells around oversensitive employees because of concerns about being perceived as critical. That gut feeling—being worried about somebody's oversensitivity—might be a signal that you're dealing with an employee with perfectionism.

Rigid and Biased Cognition

Cognitive Rigidity. Rigid thinking often becomes noticeable to others and represents a key signal that you're dealing with a perfectionist. This can be witnessed in an employee who struggles to shift work strategies when needed, to abandon a project temporarily to deal with a different and urgent priority, or to accept and participate in organizational change efforts that don't match their view of right or wrong. They get stuck. Their momentum carries them forward with outdated perspectives while others have shifted to new perspectives in a more fluid manner.

Unreasonable or inflexible goals might stem from naiveté. One way to tell the difference between naiveté and perfectionism is by asking a role-reversal question. If you ask an employee if their coworker should be held to the same standard as them, a naïve employee will

59 Dunkley, Zuroff, and Blankstein.

agree. For them, the goal would be consistent across workers because they're ignorant about the unreasonableness of the expectation. For a perfectionist, the employee would disagree and hold themselves to the unreasonable standard but not expect the same from their colleagues. Why? They tend to have some self-insight and don't want to impose unreasonable and inflexible standards on others.

This strategy only works if the employee exhibits self-oriented rather than other-oriented perfectionism. With other-oriented perfectionism, or if the employee demonstrates both forces of perfectionism, they will show little to no insight that the expectation is unreasonable or inflexible. This therefore precludes a differentiation between naiveté and perfectionism.

Cognitive Biases. You might get whiffs of cognitive bias as you interact with the perfectionistic employee. They might have a hard time stopping a task at the opportune moment. This is a result of the employee appraising their work quality negatively and placing it in the *bad* category because it's not good enough (i.e., all-or-none thinking). Perfectionists rarely show satisfaction—indirectly or directly—based on their performance outcomes or praise from others. In fact, they might minimize or dismiss praise altogether.

Declining praise and not gleaning satisfaction from performance are behaviors often driven by should statements, as perfectionists establish unrealistic, universal, and rigid expectations. Perfectionists hold themselves accountable whenever a behavior doesn't align with a should statement. This type of cognitive rigidity can be identified by listening for key words or subtext in the employee's dialogue—*should,* *ought to, have to, must.*[60]

Local Processing. The propensity to process local details and miss the big picture is a possible signal of perfectionism. You might notice that your perfectionistic employee just doesn't appreciate the big picture purpose of a task or work process. They may become preoccupied with the details and technical aspects of the work. Focusing on those details might be their strength, but they would be unreliable and unhelpful for contributing at the holistic level.

Other Related Features of Perfectionism

As noted in chapter 2, there is a collection of related features that could be used for identifying perfectionism in your workplace. For example, an employee with a cluttered office might struggle with perfectionism. Other factors may explain the clutter, such as depression and attention-deficit/hyperactivity disorder, but perfectionism is a strong contending hypothesis.

Confirming the link between clutter and perfectionism can be tricky without asking directly, and this can get awkward. With employees who struggle with clutter, keep an ear out for rationalizations. With reference to their office clutter—of which they are usually ashamed—the employee might declare a half-baked intention to create an ideal organizational system or to finalize a neat project. Though, those intentions never or rarely come to fruition.

Look out for employees who seem stuck on trying to control outcomes that are outside their ability to control. They may exhibit

---

60 But I wouldn't go so far as to say these types of words *should* never be used.

indecisiveness and an inflated sense of responsibility, take ownership of bad outcomes that they couldn't prevent, and present as ashamed and guilty in a situation when others might not feel this way.

Why don't others feel this way? It's because the nonperfectionist understands that their responsibility for the bad outcome was minimal to zero, or—at the very least—their beliefs about responsibility are flexible and can be challenged quickly by others.

Another correlate of perfectionism is moralism,[61] as noted in chapter 2. If an employee seems overly rigid about, and preoccupied with, their own scruples, it might be worth investigating self-oriented perfectionism. If the moralism is projected outward in such a way that individuals are rigid about, and preoccupied with, coworkers' scruples, this pattern could reflect other-oriented perfectionism. In the latter instance, the behavior might come across as self-righteous—a possible signal of moralism.

If you investigate the function of safety behaviors, you may get some hints that suggest perfectionism is the cause. For example, a perfectionist may get stuck on reviewing and fixing a project, but when asked, they may have difficulty articulating the moment that they will know their work is done. It might seem like they're waiting for it to feel *just right* (i.e., NJREs). Similarly, a perfectionist might express the conservative stance that it's best to take that extra step *just in case* it ends up being needed (i.e., JIC). These types of rationales are signals of perfectionism.

61 Nelson et al., "Scrupulosity in Patients with Obsessive-Compulsive Disorder."

Job Candidates and Reading Between the Lines

With the exception of offering a quick hack for testing a job candidate's handwriting for clues, this chapter has focused exclusively on detecting perfectionism in your current workplace instead of considering it as part of the job hiring process. There are methods for sniffing out perfectionism as part of the recruitment process, but please do so with considerable caution.

The process of sensing perfectionism in job candidates is a minefield. Although candidates may self-disclose having perfectionism, it's usually downplayed in the moment, spun as a strength, or used as a strategic attempt to answer the interviewer's inquiries about their "weaknesses." When it comes to the level of perfectionism discussed in this book, however, self-disclosure is rare. For example, job candidates are not inclined to confess a history of becoming paralyzed when working on tasks.

Even if there are hints of perfectionism in a candidate's presentation and materials, it typically seems shaky to draw conclusions about perfectionism from indirect data. With that caveat, below I provide some tips for finding evidence of perfectionism, but none are definitive. In fact, most evidence can be dismissed easily by considering alternative explanations, many of which are reasonable.

Some of the time, however, perfectionism is the clear cause.

Please also remember that weeding out perfectionists from a pool of candidates would be disadvantageous. Perfectionists can be star employees if their proclivities are managed effectively. If you identify a job candidate's perfectionistic tendencies in advance, and if they're hired, you can help them mitigate negative effects from the perfectionism and leverage its positive correlates to enhance your team and productivity.

Résumé Evidence. The résumé is, fundamentally, a sales instrument influenced by a heavy dose of impression management. It's therefore contrived and carefully curated for that purpose, often by selecting which information is revealed and which is omitted strategically. Any explicit confession of perfectionism on a résumé is rare.

Résumés can provide some clues of perfectionism, nonetheless. It's a red flag if a job candidate's résumé shows certain patterns in their work and education history. For instance, it raises questions if a job candidate started their undergraduate education in 2008 but didn't graduate until 2015. This doesn't mean perfectionism explains the seven-year undergraduate career, nor does it mean that taking that time to complete a bachelor's degree is inherently bad. It simply raises the question: *Why did it take that long?* Perfectionism can be the culprit.

Delayed graduation always piques my interest. I've seen full-time doctoral students take 15 years to complete a degree designed to be completed in five. Perfectionism is usually the primary explanation for this delay. In fact, this pattern is so common in doctoral education that we have a label to describe it—*All But Dissertation (ABD)*—as in, *Jane Smith, ABD.* I've always considered this label unfortunate; it makes light of this pattern, which often is silently devastating for the person experiencing it.

Perfectionism can be deduced from other patterns on a résumé. For example, does the job candidate seem underemployed given their education level and time since graduation? As an extreme illustration, it raises questions if a job candidate earned a PhD in economics from the University of Chicago in 2004 but is employed currently as a bank teller. The time since graduation and current job title do not match expectations for that type and year of degree. It would be more common for that degree and graduation date to be associated with a university professor, private sector consultant, etc. Again, there is nothing wrong or inherently bad about being a bank teller.[62] The concern is that the job candidate is overqualified for their current job. They might even be overqualified for the job for which they're interviewing.

Consistent and extended unemployment also raise red flags. Individuals might have employment gaps on a résumé for a variety of reasons, which are often valid (e.g., career change, medical leave), but they still raise questions as to *why*. It might be a result of perfectionism.

A final note about résumés. I would not use the visual presentation or the degree of detail orientation of a résumé as evidence of perfectionism. Given the impression management function of a résumé, this is one area in which all job candidates will have invested considerable energy. It's a common message by others that the résumé should be free from errors. In fact, this is one example where I'd consider sloppy mistakes a bigger red flag than a clean and beautiful résumé.

References. A job candidate's selection of references is problematic for similar reasons to the résumé. While the perfectionist can't control the specifics of a reference's recommendation, the candidate does get to decide which references to list in the first place. It's rare for references to reveal explicit evidence that the candidate exhibits a level of perfectionism characterized in this book. It must be inferred from indirect data. If a reference mentions perfectionism without being prompted to discuss candidate liabilities, you would be wise to interpret this information as a red flag. I'd also advise caution when a reference or letter

62 I chose this job title on purpose because of my tremendous respect for it. My late mother, Robin, was a bank teller for decades. It's an honorable, challenging, and satisfying career.

of recommendation omits comments about a candidate's personality or interpersonal characteristics. This could be a subtle way for the reference to indicate that a candidate is challenging as a coworker.

Dig Deeper. During a job interview or when speaking to a reference, one way to glean more information about perfectionism is to ask about it directly. Listen carefully for evidence of downplaying perfectionistic tendencies. Press for more information if perfectionism or related concepts are disclosed without explicit mitigating information, or if perfectionism is used as a cavalier response to the interviewer's question about the candidate's weaknesses. Below is a nonexhaustive set of example questions.[63]

- → Has perfectionism reduced your pace of completing projects? Do you seek deadline extensions or miss deadlines? How often does this occur?
- → Have coworkers or bosses ever talked with you about being too slow to complete projects, procrastinating, or seeking extension of deadlines or missing deadlines?
- → Do you become preoccupied with the quality of your work and get stuck finishing it? Do you get stuck because your work doesn't seem good enough or doesn't feel just right or complete enough? If so, has this tendency caused issues for you at work, such as missing deadlines or seeking deadline extensions?
- → Have you ever been reprimanded at work or let go from a job for being too slow to complete your work or for missing deadlines?

---

63 These need to be reworded slightly if they are asked of references instead of the candidate themselves.

→ Have you ever been reprimanded at work or let go from a job for being too slow to respond, or altogether nonresponsive, to communications from others, such as emails or voicemails?

→ How important to you is turning in perfect work? Do you think other people need to turn in perfect work? Do you have a hard time trusting the work of others?

→ Do you have a hard time delegating work to others because you worry about the work quality they produce?

→ Do you have the mentality that it's easier just to do the job yourself? For example, do you agree strongly with the saying, *If you want something done right, do it yourself?*

→ Do you tend to be persistent in your beliefs? Do people have a hard time changing your mind if you believe something? Have you been described as stubborn or rigid?

→ Do you love having control over all details of a task? Is control over all task elements important to you? Do you find it distressing not having control over task elements?

There's no guarantee you'll get honest answers, but direct questioning is a helpful tactic for maximizing the chance you get evidence of perfectionism. The questions above are close-ended for the most part. This helps with soliciting unambiguous answers. However, these questions can be followed up with more open-ended questions to solicit details about specific candidate responses.

➡ Chapter Conclusion and Takeaways

Spotting a perfectionist in your workplace can be a challenge. It's not always obvious, but there are clues, which were highlighted in this chapter. Here are some key takeaways:

- → If you notice a bottleneck in the overall efficiency of work processes, a fine-grained analysis of the individual contributions to that slowing is warranted. You might find that an individual on your team is struggling with perfectionistic tendencies.

- → Perfectionism can show up as a bright employee who submits pristine products, but they're chronically late. Part of the process may include multiple requests for extension and periods of radio silence, as the employee avoids responding to your correspondence.

- → Ritualistic behaviors may be a sign of perfectionism. Common examples include reassurance-seeking, confessing, and apologizing.

- → I use an informal measure of weirdness called the Kookometer. It can be useful for quantifying socially inappropriate behavior resulting from perfectionism, such as excessive and unwarranted apologizing in a social context.

- → Cognitive rigidity is a hallmark of perfectionism and therefore useful to monitor in the workplace.

- → There are signs of a perfectionistic candidate when conducting a job search. Be cautious, however, as drawing inferences about perfectionism during a job hire is loaded with risk of forming incorrect conclusions.

→ Weeding out perfectionists is not ideal. They can be star workers, but they may need a different management and leadership strategy to thrive and not be damaging within the business.

There is no foolproof way of spotting a perfectionist in the workplace, but the strategies noted in this chapter are a helpful starting point. My guess is that once you've identified perfectionism in your workplace, you'll start to see it everywhere. It's like when you notice a car model that you think looks sleek and then start seeing it everywhere on the roads. The car probably isn't more common. It's just that you've become tuned in to the car in the environment and notice it more.

Seeing perfectionism in the world works similarly. The first instance of spotting perfectionism might feel like an "aha moment"—perhaps even a "red alert," as Katty Kay noted—but soon it can become commonplace in your approach to evaluating your work environment.

CHAPTER 4

DEEPLY INFILTRATED SABOTEUR: PERFECTIONISM IS BAD FOR BUSINESS

"Some people will always be driven
by ambition, enjoyment, perfectionism
or insecurity to do more than is asked
of them, but if you expect everyone
to do that, by definition it isn't 'above
and beyond' anymore."[64]

SARAH O'CONNOR
Employment Columnist, The Financial Times

THE PRIMARY MESSAGE of this book—you know, the one
with which I've been torturing you since page one—is that perfectionism sabotages the workplace. For many, this message seems
counterintuitive. Indeed, the first three chapters acknowledge that
perfectionism can yield positive outcomes. The nuked fly disintegrates
without question.[65]

64 O'Connor, "The Term 'Quiet Quitting' Is Worse than Nonsense."
65 No flies were harmed in the making of this book. Entomologists, please stand down.

How does perfectionism damage a workplace? Case illustrations are a useful vehicle for providing explanations. Let's break it down.

Case Illustration: Mika

Mika manages a team of junior executives at a marketing firm but feels daily pressure from her supervisor to improve performance. Her supervisor often provides feedback that the team's work quality is excellent but slow to develop, which undercuts the department's productivity. This, in turn, endangers relationships with trusted clients and jeopardizes revenue streams.

Her supervisor also expresses concern frequently about the high employee turnover rate and its negative effects on the operating budget. In addition, there are fewer staff to handle client relations, which causes delays in customer service. The clients have expressed dissatisfaction, which further jeopardizes revenue streams.

Mika's team members procrastinate on tasks, seek considerable reassurance about their work quality, submit partially completed products, and miss internal deadlines. As a result, Mika assumes the responsibility of completing the team's incomplete projects regularly, adding to her own overstuffed to-do list.

Compounding Mika's distress, a recently hired team member has resigned after receiving feedback for failing to meet productivity benchmarks.

Constantly on the brink of emotional exhaustion after burning the candle at both ends, Mika notices her own work quality is suffering. She also finds herself resentful and becoming irritable with her team, especially when they fail to deliver and meet deadlines. Her prickly reactions worsen the negative workplace vibe. Job dissatisfaction among the team members soars to new heights. Work motivation plummets.

Her team is not improving no matter what she tries. This lack of progress, in turn, contributes to Mika's emotional exhaustion, feeding back negatively into the workplace mood.

She needs a fresh perspective to diagnose the problem and implement solutions.

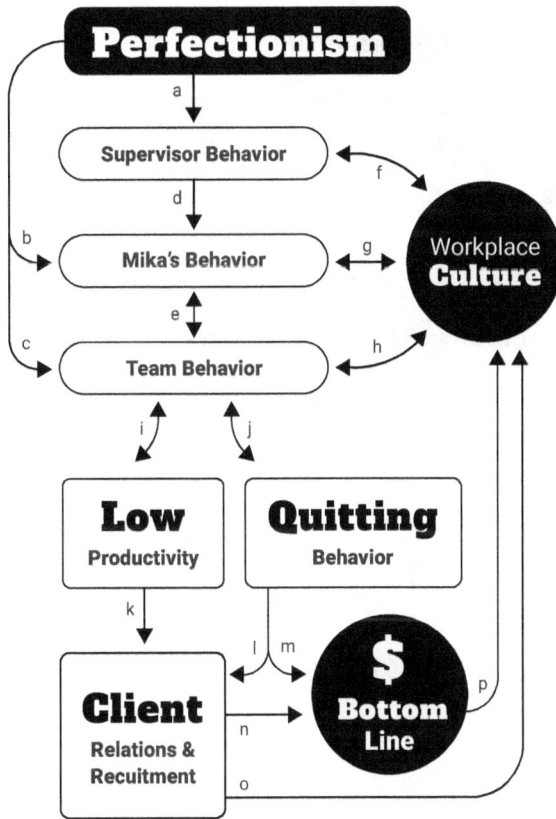

Figure 5: A Model of Mika's Perfectionism in the Workplace

Mika's plight might stem from a range of variables. Perfectionism is not a universal explanation for workplace ills. Nevertheless, it could be a common denominator. By the law of Occam's razor—which favors simple over complex explanations—perfectionism might be a powerful variable explaining much of the dysfunction and distress in Mika's workplace. Let's break down where and how.

Figure 5 provides a big picture illustration of how the perfectionism factors converge in this case. Figures 5.1-5.4 break down figure 5 into local sections for easier discussion. For the sake of discussion, it helps to consider the case in reverse. So, let's start with the bottom line.

Perfectionism Plunders Profit

If you inspect figure 5.1, you'll see one direct consequence of perfectionism on the bottom line. The high turnover rates in Mika's workplace are placing a heavy burden on operating budgets and eating into profits (*Path m* in figure 5.1). It's costly to hire and train new staff, whether from direct expenditures (e.g., advertising a vacancy, instructing search consultants) to indirect ones (e.g., opportunity cost of diverted personnel effort).

The bottom line is also harmed by two indirect impacts. First, the high turnover rate is hurting client retention and recruitment (*Path l* in figure 5.1), as there aren't enough people to manage the client-facing needs. This threatens revenue streams critical to the bottom line (*Path n*).

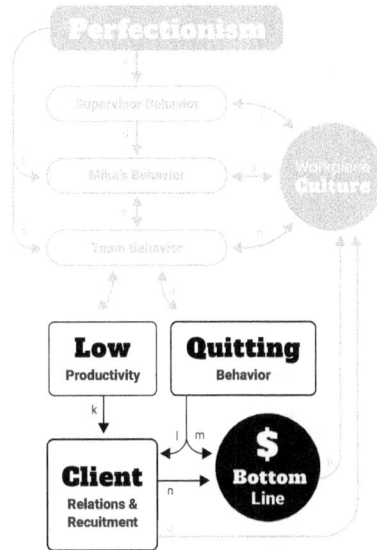

Figure 5.1: A Model of Mika's Perfectionism in the Workplace: Perfectionism Plunders Profit

In this sense, employee turnover inflicts a double whammy. High attrition negatively impacts the bottom line directly through added costs associated with hiring and training (i.e., first whammy), as well as indirectly through poor client relations (i.e., second whammy). This is a clue that strategies to mitigate team member turnover are essential for protecting the bottom line, especially in markets with thin margins.

Second, the bottom line is jeopardized indirectly by reduced team member productivity. The reduction in work output is due to the slowing of employee task pace because of perfectionism. Clients become dissatisfied with the lack of timely products and services (*Path k* to *Path n* in Figure 5.1).

It would be easy to lump lower productivity (*Path k*) with employee turnover (*Path l*) when considering client dissatisfaction, but doing so would result in a loss of information by confounding two paths. In this case, client dissatisfaction is driven by two different forces, albeit connected by reduced work output overall (i.e., addressing client-facing needs as one work output and producing timely products as the second work output).

Regardless of the specifics, the take-home message is that multiple issues are angering clients, and this is not a good strategy for a healthy bottom line.

As you continue exploring the model, you'll see that all these negative outcomes for the bottom line represent a cascade of consequences originating from perfectionism: high rates of turnover from quitting and sluggish team member productivity don't occur in a vacuum. They were driven by other factors in the case model, which we will discuss next.

The Team Loses Steam

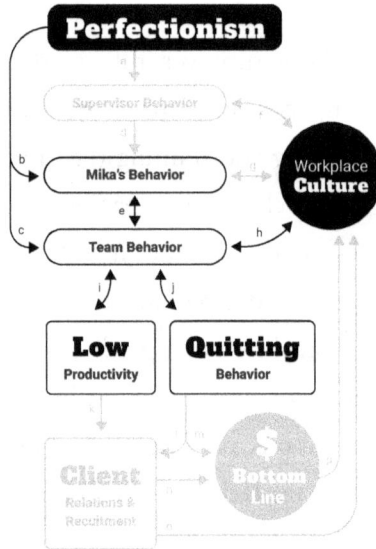

Figure 5.2: A Model of Mika's Perfectionism in the Workplace: The Team Loses Steam

For the case model in figure 5.2, the overall effects of employee behavior result in hampered productivity and increased rates of turnover

(*Path i* and *Path j*). By definition, perfectionism has a direct influence on team behavior (*Path c*). For specific details about how and why, see chapters 1 and 2. To identify it in your workplace, see chapter 3.

Aside from the direct effects of perfectionism (*Path b*), Mika's behavior (*Path e*) and the workplace culture (*Path h*) both impact the team directly. Mika's influence on the team is characterized by exhaustion, irritability, and resentment. These mix to produce prickly behavior. Also, her own work quality is suffering, which worsens difficulties with the team's low work productivity (*Path i*).

Workplace culture takes on a life of its own in this model. A toxic workplace culture, as described in the case, devastates team cohesion and behavior (*Path h*). This also worsens workplace culture reciprocally. Job dissatisfaction is soaring and work motivation is plummeting. Both contribute powerfully to problematic team behavior, such as slower work pace, stifled productivity, and more instances of job quitting.

Mika Needs a Moment

With this case example, Mika may be the character for whom you have the most empathy. This makes sense, given just how much she is impacted by the four negative forces coming from different directions.[66]

First, it's important to remember that Mika's behavior may be influenced directly by perfectionistic tendencies of her own (*Path b*). This isn't mentioned explicitly in the case narrative, but it might not be surprising to learn that Mika's decisions to assume extra

---

66 Perhaps this explains the unfortunate reputation of "squeezed" middle management roles.

responsibilities and burn the candle at both ends reflect her own perfectionistic expectations.

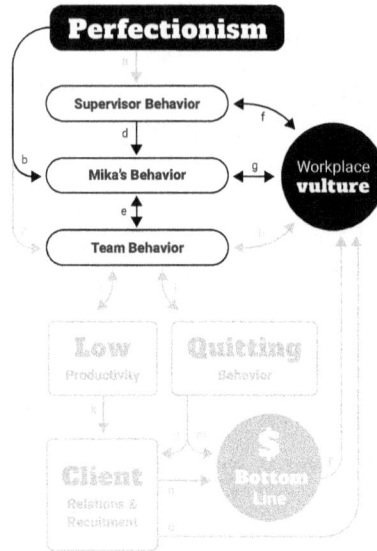

Figure 5.3: A Model of Mika's Perfectionism in the Workplace: Mika Needs a Moment

Second, Mika is directly and deeply impacted by her team's perfectionistic behavior. Her prickly behavior—elicited by exhaustion, irritability, and resentment—works in both directions. It both causes and is affected by (*Path e*) the team's perfectionistic behavior. This includes team behaviors described in the case, such as procrastination, reassurance-seeking, and turning in partially completed assignments. These behaviors, in turn, cause Mika to assume the team's responsibilities and work overtime, thereby resulting in exhaustion, irritability, and resentment.

Third, there is a bidirectional impact between Mika's behavior and workplace culture (*Path g*). Her mood spoils the workplace culture, but the workplace culture—itself damaged by the team members' dissatisfaction and low motivation—is partially responsible for Mika's spoiled mood in the first place.

Fourth, Mika's current experience is shaped by her supervisor's behavior, which presents directly (*Path d*) and indirectly (*Path f* and *Path g*). The direct impact is that the supervisor pressures Mika daily to improve her performance and expresses concern about turnover frequently. It's not unreasonable for a supervisor to voice a concern about employee performance and turnover (I'd be worried if a supervisor failed to communicate about such vital issues), but it's all about the details in how the communication is carried out and how often. In this case, these details are unclear.

The indirect path is the one by which the supervisor influences the workplace culture (*Path f*), which then influences Mika's behavior indirectly (*Path g*), not to mention all other components downstream. The power of the supervisor's behavior at this level to affect the entire system has no equal in the model. This is the pathway by which the supervisor establishes a workplace culture, tone, policies, and expectations. In fact, much of part II of this book offers antiperfection solutions that center on this pathway, plus those related to Mika's behavior.

Stay tuned.

The Merciless Merry-Go-Round

The supervisor's behavior doesn't occur in a vacuum. When you work backwards from the end of the model, the supervisor's behavior seems like a natural starting point. As the proverb goes, *the fish rots from the head down*. If the workplace is falling apart, eyes tend to look to the person in charge.

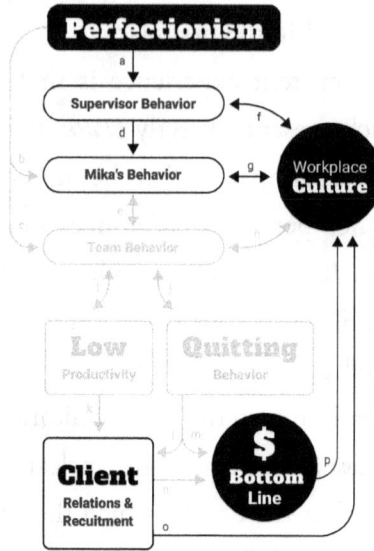

Figure 5.4: A Model of Mika's Perfectionism in the Workplace: The Merciless Merry-Go-Round

This case model is no different. The supervisor's behavior is being influenced by perfectionism (*Path a*). The supervisor approaches their duties within this cancerous framework that spreads to everything that follows. For example, perfectionism influences the supervisor's behavior (*Path a*). This, in turn, impacts the workplace culture (*Path f*) and Mika's behavior (directly via *Path d* and indirectly via *Path f* and *Path g*). Directly and indirectly through the workplace culture and Mika's behavior, the supervisor's behavior—influenced by perfectionism[67]—disrupts the team's behavior.

We all know how that ends for the bottom line...

---

[67] For tips on how to manage a perfectionistic boss, please see chapter 10.

As if that weren't enough workplace drama, there's more to the story. This case model depicts a self-perpetuating cycle. After all this, when the bottom line starts to suffer, there's a feedback loop. As the bottom line crumbles, the workplace culture is harmed (*Path p*). This is also the case for the negative feedback from the clients (*Path o*). The supervisor will inevitably be alarmed by any drops in revenue (*Path f*) and therefore respond accordingly. For a perfectionist such as the supervisor, this would probably resemble a fear-based response, worsening any perfectionistic influences on Mika's behavior (*Path d*) and the workplace culture (*Path f*). This reinstigates the entire cycle in the model, like a merciless merry-go-round.

The Road to Bankruptcy is Paved with Good Intentions

The case example and discussion in this chapter illustrate specific ways in which perfectionism can wreck a workplace and ultimately undermine business success. This case example and my discussion are by no means an exhaustive description. Perfectionism is a far-reaching and deeply infiltrated saboteur.

Much of the time, the intentions of perfectionism are positive. For example, the head honcho might believe that it's motivating for employees to be immersed in a culture that reinforces expectations of perfection. They may believe that requiring anything less of their workers will result in loafing and excuses. They adopt this framework with the utmost confidence and optimism in its efficacy. They probably don't consider it much, and they don't seem to doubt it.

Here's the problem: perfectionism doesn't work well in most social dynamics, no matter how large or small the group. Most research on perfectionism is carried out at the individual level, but research that extends outward and looks at relationships begins to tell a clear story about how the toxicity of these tendencies affect social dynamics.[68] For example, perfectionistic behavior by a partner in a marriage is suffocating, anxiety-provoking, and may be abusive.[69,70]

Similarly, much has been written about the damage caused by expectations placed upon children by perfectionistic parents.[71] In fact, several formal measures of perfectionism include a set of questionnaire items that capture the nature and consequences of this parent-child dynamic specifically.[72] The mental health industry could probably be sustained by the therapy fees collected from patients needing help with this circumstance.

As you move to consider larger and more complex social groups, the negative influence of perfectionism doesn't waiver. I've seen perfectionism disrupt healthy dynamics within sports teams. It's invaded the health and well-being of congregants of religious organizations. It even sneaks its way into law and regulation via political pressure and lobbying. In that sense, it affects entire populations. There really are very few limits to its potential reach.

This is all to say that leaders within the workplace might think they're doing good deeds by promoting a perfectionistic framework and supporting it through policies and messaging, but it's doing the opposite. It's harming their entire climate. Unbeknownst to them, they have promulgated their organization's values, such that it hampers their

---

68 Stoeber, "Dyadic Perfectionism in Romantic Relationships"; Mackinnon et al., "Caught in a Bad Romance"; Habke and Flynn, "Interpersonal Aspects of Trait Perfectionism."

69 Lafontaine et al., "Romantic Perfectionism and Perceived Conflict Mediate the Link between Insecure Romantic Attachment and Intimate Partner Violence in Undergraduate Students."

70 For a classic and intense cinematic depiction of this marital dynamic, see *Sleeping with the Enemy*. Patrick Bergin's character is the epitome of somebody exuding self- and other-oriented perfectionism, among other issues. It's a haunting portrayal.

71 Flett et al., "Perfectionism in Children and Their Parents."

72 Frost et al., "The Dimensions of Perfectionism."

organization's very mission. This, I suppose, is an organizational-level, rather than individual-level, perfectionism irony (i.e., self-fulfilling prophecy). As the aphorism states, "The road to hell is paved with good intentions." In the business world, I imagine that *hell* equates to bankruptcy and liquidation.

Perfectionistic Propaganda and Pressures

I'd like to paint a picture of what it might be like to work in an environment characterized by high levels of perfectionism. It can provide more understanding of what the employee experiences. This might then provide a window through which you can understand why it's bad for business in the long-term.

An employee who enters a workplace as a new hire is overwhelmed immediately with company data about expectations, policy, and culture. This barrage of information starts the moment they see the job advertisement, examine the company's website with all its public-facing messaging, lurk around social media profiles of current employees, and investigate online reviews.

The immersion increases tremendously once the onboarding orientation begins. The induction process for new recruits is the most effective vehicle for downloading perfectionistic propaganda directly into the employee's brain. The employee handbook—perhaps the second-best vehicle for perfectionism brainwashing—is a written record of this propaganda.

The new employee begins their job in earnest. After drinking the Kool-Aid, they undoubtedly become believers and champion the same ideals, at least at the outset. As the first few days and then weeks unfold, the employee starts receiving feedback about their performance. This can be direct and even gentle, such as a project manager saying something such as, "You're really picking this up, but I'm going to have Aiden take it from here. We need this to be perfect."

Feedback can also be indirect—learning through observing others—such as watching a coworker get chastised by the boss for forgetting to carbon copy[73] them on an email. These types of observations start to provide concrete examples of perfectionism to complement the more abstract messaging downloaded into their brain at the outset.

Given the nature of perfectionism, the new hire starts to struggle with keeping up with the quantity and quality of work expected of everyone in this type of environment. This is true for the new hire despite their profound sacrifices to work-life balance as a result of tripling down on their effort. Initially, the new hire might be committed in full to this sacrifice. The downloaded propaganda worked to a large degree, but the foundations start to crumble over time.

At some point, the situation is worsened by additional—typically well-intentioned—messaging in the workplace. For example, the workplace might use a whiteboard for showcasing the high achievers (e.g., employee rankings of the highest sales last week). Now imagine these high achievers are praised and rewarded with a token of appreciation as part of a weekly public ceremony in the workplace. This tactic might be motivating for some, but for others—such as our new hire who has devoted every speck of life energy to their job—not being ranked and being embarrassed by the silence around their performance may add to the distress. It sends the new hire a silent message that they're not doing enough.

---

73 That's the same as "CCing" for those who can't remember or weren't born yet when paper was the hottest commodity.

In these moments, the individual reaction by the new hire depends considerably on what my field calls their *locus of control*.[74] Although an overly simplistic definition, this concept refers to an individual's typical beliefs about what causes events to occur—their causal attributions.[75] People have different styles when it comes to beliefs about what causes events to occur—an external or internal locus of control.

Let's differentiate external and internal locus of control. For a new hire that has a susceptibility to an external style—that is, blaming people or circumstances that are external to themselves—they may start to harbor resentment about these expectations and the lack of work recognition. They blame all their suffering and their behaviors on the world and people around them (e.g., "I stole the car because the system is rigged against people like me"). They take little to no responsibility for any of it. In this case, we'd see the new hire become bitter and angry towards others and the organization. They might even become aggressive or passive-aggressive.

If the new hire is more susceptible to an internal locus of control—that is, blaming variables that are internal to themselves—they may start to feel demoralized and ashamed. Employees with an internal locus of control tend to own all the mess as their own ("I stole the car because I'm a bad and broken human being"). They feel accountable for any distress and behavior, even in situations in which external variables are an obvious cause. They see the situation as consequences of their choices. A negative self-image often sets in at this point, strengthening any latent imposter syndrome that may

74 The first time I heard this as an undergraduate student, I thought they said *locust* of control. Now, that insect scenario might justify a nuke.

75 Rotter, "Generalized Expectancies for Internal versus External Control of Reinforcement."

have existed. An internal locus of control also tends to coincide with beliefs that they don't belong and that they're a burden to others at the company and unworthy of their job.

We all fall somewhere on internal and external locus of control. Falling in the middle is adaptive in the workplace much of the time, whereas extremes are not in the best interests of a workplace. You can imagine how extreme internal and external locus of control might produce different sets of behaviors and pollute the workplace climate in unique ways. Employees with either extreme type of locus of control are not destined for longevity at the company.

Psychological Safety

In this chapter, I've provided some concrete examples of how perfectionism undermines a healthy company culture, but you might be left craving more theory.

What exactly is happening in workplace dynamics when perfectionism takes a toll?

For this question, I turn to a construct called *psychological safety*, which is distinct from perfectionistic safety behaviors introduced in chapter 2. Both concepts involve perceptions of safety, but that's where the similarities end.

First solidified as a concept in the 1990s by Dr. Amy Edmondson, psychological safety refers to a sense of feeling secure in taking interpersonal risks in a business environment, such as voicing honest feedback to others, asking questions, expressing candid opinions to a manager, and offering ideas freely. This concept can be assessed at multiple levels: individuals can feel psychologically safe, and organizations can foster an unthreatening culture and facilitate a sense of collective psychological safety.

What are the possible benefits of high psychological safety?
Plenty.

A comprehensive review of the research literature links the concept to a host of positive outcomes such as increasing innovation, facilitating performance on tasks, improving employee learning, enhancing job satisfaction, boosting job engagement, reducing burnout, and buttressing diversity, equity, and inclusion efforts.[76]

I won't belabor the benefits associated with psychological safety. This topic has been researched for decades. Edmondson has written several books that draw from her experience and work.[77] Indeed, her most recent book on leveraging failure is pertinent to the topic of perfectionism.

And that's where my interests lie—the intersection of psychological safety and perfectionism. It's theorized, with some empirical support,[78] that benefits of psychological safety may be due to reductions in *fear of failure*. For example, an organizational culture that fosters psychological safety improves an employee's job satisfaction because it likely reduces or protects against their fear of failure.

Enter perfectionism—the "king of fear of failure."

If perfectionists become paralyzed with the prospect of failing, does this tendency worsen or improve based on their perceived psychological safety? Alternatively, maybe the reverse question is more interesting: How does perfectionism shape perceptions of psychological safety at the individual and group level?[79]

76 Edmondson and Bransby, "Psychological Safety Comes of Age."

77 Edmondson, *The Fearless Organization: Creating Psychological Safety in the Workplace for Learning, Innovation, and Growth*; Edmondson, *Right Kind of Wrong: The Science of Failing Well*.

78 Deng et al., "Slacking off in Comfort."

79 Who am I kidding? I'm a nerd—both questions are interesting.

There are no clear answers to these questions at the moment. Unfortunately, there's a lack of published research on the relation between perfectionism and psychological safety, specifically. If I were a betting man, however, I'd predict a bidirectional relation: perfectionism reduces perceived psychological safety, which exacerbates perfectionistic tendencies reciprocally.

Regardless, if you're interested in building theory to explain why perfectionism has a negative impact on the workplace, I'd start with psychological safety.

The Quiet Quitting Quandary

I'd be remiss not to mention quiet quitting. I hope you can see, based on how I've described the new hire scenario above, how easy it would be for a quiet quitting mentality to develop. For those who are unfamiliar, quiet quitting is a slang term for a workplace behavioral pattern. It refers to the situation in which an employee engages purposefully in the bare minimum work necessary to meet their obligations.[80]

The definition starts to get muddy once you consider the supposed function of the behavior. Why is the employee quiet quitting? My guess is that it varies by person and that no universal definition is appropriate. I'll go with the definition that implies some underlying evil genius who's playing three-dimensional occupational chess and is cackling at their cubicle. With that image in mind, quiet quitting is enacted to skirt the system, stay under the radar, collect a paycheck,

---

80 Sarah O'Connor, quoted at the beginning of this chapter ("The Term 'Quiet Quitting' Is Worse than Nonsense."), suggests in the same blog post, that the "bare minimum of work to meet their obligations" is just a euphemism for work duties.

and siphon resources. Their tagline is probably, *stick it to the man discreetly and do it with a paycheck and a smile.*

If you think about the new hire example for a moment, you can see how quiet quitting emerges. I'd go so far as to say that I appreciate why the new hire might do this, regardless of external or internal locus of control tendencies. For external locus of control, the growing resentment fuels a passive-aggressive quiet quitting approach. It's a way to stick it to the organization but with a sense of financial and professional security. For internal locus of control, the quiet quitting might be an attempt to reduce their perceived burden on the organization or serve as an avoidance strategy to cope with fear, anxiety, shame, and other dreadful emotions.

The concept of quiet quitting isn't necessarily new, but it's picked up steam recently in the public discourse as an identifiable pattern. One could argue that it's received some support from workers as a reasonable and conventional strategy to deal with a difficult work context. I would bet that a non-negligible proportion of quiet quitting is driven by work-related distress tied to perfectionism in some capacity. We may find that this hypothesis is tested and refuted in the coming years but, if confirmed, it would provide yet another compelling reason to address perfectionism in the workplace.

➡ Chapter Conclusion and Takeaways

This chapter opened with a promise to illustrate how perfectionism is bad for business. To do so, I presented a case and its cyclical model as a mechanism for making this argument. Here are key takeaways:

- → Perfectionism may explain much of the dysfunction and distress in a workplace.
- → A company's bottom line is affected negatively by high turnover and reduced productivity, both of which are worsened by employee perfectionism.
- → There is a vicious cycle in which the team's perfectionistic tendencies result from, but also cause, a perfectionistic workplace culture.
- → Middle management is often sandwiched between perfectionistic employees and perfectionistic bosses, causing distress.
- → Perfectionistic bosses serve as a top-down and primary influence on a workplace culture, causing a cascade effect of perfectionism.
- → The negative effects of this cascade feed back into the workplace culture, amplifying the entire cascade and its consequences.
- → When a worker joins an organization, perfectionism brainwashing often begins early in the onboarding process.
- → Psychological safety may be the most fruitful theoretical framework for understanding how perfectionism disrupts a workplace culture.
- → Quiet quitting may, in part, be caused by socially prescribed perfectionism (i.e., excessive and unreasonable workplace expectations).

This brings us back to the start of the chapter, where I provided a sage quote about quiet quitting by journalist Sarah O'Connor. Apropos of my primary argument, her quote invokes the construct of perfectionism. I agree with her sentiments. Expectations of folks in the workforce have become contradictory. Some workers excel and attempt to go above and beyond, maybe even pursue perfection, "but if you expect everyone to do that, by definition it isn't 'above and beyond' anymore."

How Perfectionism Sabotages the Workplace and Solutions for Managers

CHAPTER 5

GUNSHOT WOUNDS VS. RAGING HEMORRHOIDS: DYSFUNCTIONAL EMPHASIS FRAMEWORK

"Pursuit of perfection is futile. Instead,
I prioritize and often realize goals or tasks I've
been aiming for just aren't that important."[81]

AISHA TYLER
Actor and Talk Show Host

CHEERS TO AISHA Tyler for discovering a key principle in the fight against perfectionism.

It's impressive that she boiled it down in such a simple and direct way. Fighting perfectionism is about prioritizing tasks based on your values. This chapter will provide more details about Tyler's nugget of wisdom and how to apply this principle to the workplace.

---

81 Platon, "Last Laugh: Aisha Tyler On Being A Woman In Comedy."

Szymanski Plans

When thinking about perfectionism, I like to use a framework—which I call the Emphasis Framework—that I've developed from a seed planted by Dr. Jeff Szymanski in his excellent self-help guide on perfectionism: *The Perfectionist's Handbook*.[82] This book is full of sage tips and commentary on the topic. In fact, my own formula for understanding perfectionism was inspired by an enriching two-page section of his book.

Szymanski introduces his model of effort allocation according to personal values, which to emphasize Tyler's quote, supports the notion that not all priorities of tasks are meant to be uniform.

Szymanski conveys a simple categorization system—based on conventional A through F letter grades in the US but without the D grade (or, for that matter, the letter E[83])—to describe effort allocation for completing tasks. For example, he calls tasks to which you devote 100% effort because they align with your values, Plan A. Plan B is one step down—80% effort—as it aligns with values that are important and warrants effort that would yield a B grade. Plan C is for tasks that require average effort and performance, such as striving for a grade of C on an assignment. Last, he describes F tasks, to which you devote attention but do so begrudgingly because they seem inconsistent with your needs and values.

Although this brief section of Szymanski's book is important to his overall messaging, it hardly represents the linchpin of his conceptualization of perfectionism. Though, when I read it, I saw an

---

82 Szymanski, *The Perfectionist's Handbook: Take Risks, Invite Criticism, and Make the Most of Your Mistakes.*

83 For readers outside the US, the letter E has been skipped as the lowest grade option since the early 20th century, when it was changed to the letter F to signify "Fail." Apparently, until that time, heroic and clever children were telling their parents that a grade of E meant "Excellent."

opportunity for its expansion into something bigger and more crucial. It could provide a rich framework for understanding the nature of perfectionism—a framework that provides a shared language to promote change at the individual and social level, including in the workplace.

Before introducing my own Emphasis Framework, it's important to describe another model that contextualizes my framework: the Effort-Value Model.

Overview of the Effort-Value Model

First described by Stephen R. Covey,[84] the Effort-Value Model is a well-known bidimensional concept for conceptualizing prioritization, which has implications for perfectionism. Bidimensional refers to the model's two dimensions: *effort* and *value*. The two dimensions bisect each other at right angles and form a plus-sign graph with four quadrants. See figure 6 for a visual depiction of the Effort-Value Model.

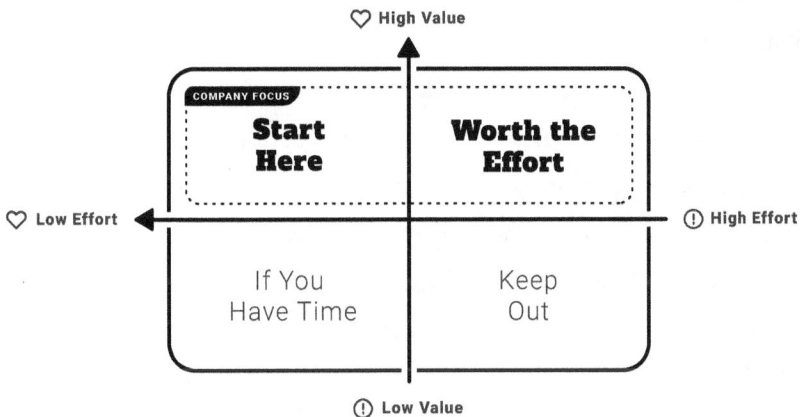

Figure 6: Effort-Value Model

---

84 Covey, *The 7 Habits of Highly Effective People: Powerful Lessons in Personal Change.*

You can think of the effort-value graph quadrants as representing different task types. Tasks with high-effort and high-value tend to require the most resources, but the expenditure is worth it. Tasks with low-effort and high-value are your "low hanging fruit"—the tasks that don't require much expenditure but yield valuable outcomes. Tasks with high-effort and low-value are a waste of resources because they require considerable expenditures for outcomes of questionable value. Then there are the tasks characterized by low-effort and low-value outcomes, which require little resource but yield little reward. These are unnecessary tasks.

Emphasis Framework

Building on both the Effort-Value Model and Szymanski's work, I suggest a framework that's helpful for understanding behavior in a context of effort-value pressures in a workplace. I see a tug of war between three strategies for completing a task: Emphasis A, Emphasis B, and Emphasis C.

According to the framework, Emphasis A is a strategy designed for maximal effort. This means these tasks are critical and best met with tremendous energy and resource allocation. These might be reserved for high-effort and high-value tasks.

Emphasis B, on the other hand, is a strategy designed for exerting the least amount of effort necessary for completing the task. I call this the "git 'er done" strategy. The final product doesn't need to be amazing, but it doesn't need to be awful. Emphasis B revolves around completing the task in a way that's sufficient for its purpose. These tasks aren't throw-away tasks that you resent having to complete. Instead, these are more like Szymanski's Plan B and C. This strategy probably makes the most sense for low-effort and high-value tasks, as well as any low-value tasks that are mandatory.

Emphasis C involves not completing the task at all—zero effort. In a healthy implementation of this model, Emphasis C is purposeful and strategic, particularly for low-effort and low-value tasks, as well as high-effort and low-value tasks that are not mandatory. In the context of perfectionism, however, Emphasis C can become a safety behavior—more on this later in the chapter.

There are no inherent judgments associated with any Emphasis approach. For example, Emphasis A isn't inherently better than Emphasis B or C. It all depends on the circumstance, which includes the unique scenario in which an individual finds themselves, plus their personal life values. For example, some scenarios call for an Emphasis A approach, whereas others might call for an Emphasis B strategy. Ignoring the task altogether—Emphasis C—is often on the table as a legitimate option.

This framework includes six key changes to Szymanski's approach:

1. The Emphasis Framework is not intended to merely describe different types of tasks and efforts. Instead, it offers a larger framework for understanding and communicating about perfectionism.

2. I've pared down the number of levels. My scheme includes three levels instead of the four levels in Szymanski's model. A three-level model provides a streamlined framework for articulating big picture perfectionism processes, dissecting specific moments of perfectionism, and communicating change efforts for improving perfectionism in the workplace.

3. I've added a level to the framework to represent a strategy of ignoring the task altogether (i.e., Emphasis C).

4. I've eliminated specific effort percentages (e.g., 100%, 80%) and instead applied effort and value descriptions. I emphasize task value when defining effort levels. This last tweak isn't different in spirit from Szymanski's approach, but my framework amplifies the influence of values.

5. My framework eliminates the letter grade scheme. My levels are agnostic to judgment and appraisal of performance (i.e., letter grades imply judgment). Using the strategies for a given level is not better or worse, good or bad, etc. Their use depends entirely on context.

6. I ditch the term *Plan* for *Emphasis* because it started to become awkward when I told people to "use Plan B," especially teenagers sitting next to their parents.[85]

Prioritizing Based on Values and Available Resources

What determines if a task requires Emphasis A, B, or C? Personal life values and the availability of resources. First, tasks must be evaluated in the context of your values. For example, publishing this book has been an important goal of mine, and it's embedded within my personal values of spreading knowledge to others, facilitating the health of organizations, and becoming wealthy from billions of dollars in royalties.[86] As such, I have opted to use Emphasis A to write my book.

Second, you only have finite resources to devote to life's tasks. Life requires you to choose where to allocate your efforts. It's like triaging emergency room patients. If a patient is wheeled in with a critical

85 *Plan B* is a contraceptive.
86 The last one is sarcasm in case you thought it was serious.

gunshot wound to the chest, they'll be brought back for treatment immediately. They'll get prioritized over all other patients, such as the one with the raging hemorrhoids who has been waiting for 12 hours to be seen. The system would fall apart if the patient with the gunshot wound had to wait based on a policy of first-come, first-served. Determining which tasks require Emphasis A, B, or C is like determining which cases get to skip the line for emergency room services.

Predictable Emphasis Patterns

Although each life circumstance is different, Emphasis A, B, and C have general patterns of when they make the most sense to adopt. With finite resources, Emphasis A makes the most sense for a small subset of life tasks that you've deemed valuable.

An undergraduate student seeking admission into law school might opt to use Emphasis A when studying for the entrance exam because they value a law career. An engaged couple might decide to adopt Emphasis A for their wedding plans because they value celebrating this milestone with family. An author might decide to use Emphasis A when writing their memoir because they value leaving a legacy. A CEO who values a positive and inspiring work culture might employ Emphasis A strategies to revamp their organization's employee policies.

Emphasis B makes sense for most of life's tasks. This is because most tasks in life don't need to be completed with maximal effort. They just aren't that important (to you). They don't carry critical consequences for unexceptional performance. Emphasis B tasks don't warrant extra effort, especially if that added effort would jeopardize your effort on tasks that you've determined are worth Emphasis A.

I often encourage my clients to "Emphasis B the daylights out of most things." It might make sense to adopt Emphasis B to mow the lawn in the backyard and deal with the possibility that you miss a tiny section. Perhaps corresponding with your cousin isn't that important to you, so you decide to communicate with an Emphasis B approach (e.g., short but pleasant messages every few months). Maybe your job requires completing recurring professional education, trainings you've completed a dozen times. You could probably get away with an Emphasis B technique of paying partial attention to the presentation and then completing the quiz at the end and earning a grade just above the 70% pass threshold. In that circumstance, does it really make sense to use Emphasis A for training and pass at 100% if it doesn't yield anything positive for you?

Emphasis C is the option that usually makes people most uncomfortable when I introduce it. The idea that we can opt not to complete a task—as a strategy—seems foreign to many. There are many real-world examples of Emphasis C in action. Whenever my mobile carrier asks for me to complete a customer satisfaction survey at the end of my call, I opt to "Emphasis C the daylights out of it." It's not much of a conscious decision at this point. It's intuitive. I've determined, outside of awareness for the most part, that I don't want to spend my resources on a satisfaction survey. It's not important to me.

As another example, as a university professor, I often have conversations with students who feel compelled to take the final exam in my course. Taking a final exam might seem mandatory, so let me explain. Imagine, in this scenario, that the university only offers grades of A through F, with no plus or minus distinctions. Let's say the test is worth only 5% of the grade, and the student already has a cumulative course grade of 100%. The student could score a 0% on the final and see no change in their overall course grade (i.e., 90-100% yields a grade of A).

The student might choose to study and take the final anyway, perhaps because they value learning, or maybe they value my opinion of them. I can appreciate those reasons. It becomes problematic, however, when a student opts to study and take the final exam in my course if doing so means they don't study for a final exam in another course. If not studying for the exam in the other course results in a lower grade in that course, then it was a dubious allocation of resources.

In that scenario, choosing to use Emphasis C for the final exam in my course, in which they have a grade of 100%, is the strategic decision.

Clash of Values

Sometimes we opt for an Emphasis strategy that seems unaligned with our values. My favorite example of this probably resonates with couples everywhere. I hate folding towels and can probably write an entire book about why. Let me be extra clear: I don't disagree with the idea of folding towels in some capacity; what I mean is that I hate folding towels so that they're symmetrical and beautiful (i.e., Emphasis A), which my wife values. From my values-laden perspective, it seems like a waste of time. They are shoved in a linen closet, remain unseen by the public, and are unfolded immediately when needed. Why on Earth do we need symmetrically folded towels? Whom are they benefitting?

Given what I've just confessed, you might be surprised to learn that I fold the towels in my household, simply because I'm tasked with doing the laundry in our grand marital puzzle called *division of labor*. Although I'm sure my wife would passionately disagree,[87] I try to fold the towels to meet this need for symmetry and beauty. Why do I attempt to fold the towels neatly if doing so doesn't align with my values? It's because I value my wife.[88]

My relationship with my wife and her well-being are both critical personal values in my world. By engaging in Emphasis A of tasks that are aligned with her personal values, I'm leaning indirectly into my own values. My own values, in this case, have nothing to do with towel aesthetics. My dislike of folding towels isn't so strong that it gets in the way of my pursuit of personal values unrelated to towels (i.e., my marriage). It's just an annoyance. It's worth it to attempt a quality fold on my wife's behalf.

If folding towels somehow violates a fundamental value in my life, the situation becomes more complicated. My value of marriage would be pitted against my value of freeing the towels. In this case, choosing whether to fold the towels would require some mental calculus that weighs the net gains and losses of each choice. Net gains or losses of what? Fidelity—it requires an abstract appraisal of my fidelity (i.e., faithfulness) to my values and sense of self. A mismatch between my behaviors and my values is emotionally disturbing and causes all sorts of problems.

It might help to swap out *folding towels* with a different example that depicts a personal values clash. Let's say my wife asks me to vote *Yes* to the development of a new apartment complex to replace the park in my neighborhood. Let's say I'm strongly opposed to this new development because it contradicts my personal values of protecting the environment and reducing suburban congestion.

---

87 My folding is abysmal, but not because I'm not trying. It's because I'm inept at it. My wife refolds the towels that I've butchered.

88 See, honey, it ends on a sweet note.

My wife's request therefore creates a dilemma. On one hand, if I vote *Yes*, I score marriage points and lean into my value of a harmonious marriage. On the other hand, if I vote *Yes*, I lean away from my values of protecting the environment and limiting suburban congestion.

My decision—that is, my vote—will require some mental calculus to figure out the net dissonance from each option. It might feel worse overall to vote *Yes* and compromise my environment and congestion values, even if I leaned into my marriage value. Alternatively, maybe it feels worse overall to vote *No* and compromise my marriage value, even if I leaned into my environment and congestion values. You can see how it gets complicated. Imagine adding even more values to the mix.

Perfectionism within the Emphasis Framework

How does the Emphasis Framework integrate with the concept of perfectionism? Perfectionists try to use Emphasis A for way too many tasks. This poses a major problem because there just isn't enough time and energy for a person to meet the demands of approaching every task this way. The perfectionist tries to do so anyway—often it feels compulsive. They inevitably fail to meet this Emphasis A standard for all tasks. They spread themselves thin and diffuse effort across tasks and ultimately accomplish very little (or nothing). Overzealous attempts at Emphasis A lead to a forced version of Emphasis C.

For the nonperfectionist, Emphasis C is strategic. It's used purposefully for tasks that warrant low effort and have low-value outcomes, or for nonmandatory tasks that require high effort and yield low-value outcomes. For perfectionists, however, an Emphasis C strategy is forced on them because they cannot meet the widespread demands of attempting to use Emphasis A for everything. When perfectionists try to adopt Emphasis A for everything, safety behaviors such as procrastination, rechecking, and fixing start to dictate the outcome.

Ultimately, excessive safety behaviors result in avoidance of the task—Emphasis C—but not as a conscious strategy. In the end, perfectionism has dictated your priorities, instead of your values doing so.

This perfectionistic formula—overcommitting to Emphasis A, which leads to Emphasis C—can be fixed with promoting more use of Emphasis B instead of Emphasis A. A perfectionist with a dysfunctional Emphasis Framework exhibits a highly skewed ratio of Emphasis A to Emphasis B. In other words, for a perfectionist, Emphasis A is adopted most of the time and under most circumstances. Conversely, for the nonperfectionist, the ratio skews in favor of Emphasis B.

Most of the time and under most circumstances, Emphasis B is the best strategy for a task, but it comes with some risk. It's possible that you opt to approach a task with Emphasis B when Emphasis A is more appropriate. Similarly, you might use Emphasis C when Emphasis B makes more sense.

In other words, the outcomes from your Emphasis choices can backfire. It's best to sit with the risk and possibility of a backfire. The benefits of freeing yourself from perfectionism far outweigh the inevitable but relatively infrequent costs of misjudging which Emphasis level a task requires (e.g., Emphasis B selected when Emphasis A was necessary).

Disguised Exposure Therapy

Exposure Therapy with Patients. The Emphasis Framework is a means for implementing exposure therapy. Exposure therapy is a type of cognitive-behavioral therapy (CBT) technique in which individuals with anxiety and fear systematically encounter the very objects or situations that scare them. During these exercises, these individuals abstain voluntarily from carrying out safety behaviors that serve to decrease their anxiety and protect them in the moment of the exposure exercise. These exercises are carried out in a formal and systematic way with the support of a trained therapist; it's never coerced, and it's always done collaboratively.

For perfectionists working with a CBT-trained clinician, it's customary for the patient and therapist to design and carry out exposure therapy exercises[89] that encourage the individual to face their fears of being imperfect.[90] The exercises are unique to everyone, but a common example might include doing work and making mistakes purposefully without engaging in safety behaviors. An individual might be asked to write an email to their coworker within a short time frame to limit ritualizing behavior, urged to misspell the sign off phrase on purpose (e.g., "cordally yours"), hit *Send,* and sit with the anxiety that this mistake is a disaster or that the patient can't handle the negative emotional state it causes.

---

89 Sometimes you might hear these referred to as *behavioral experiments* instead of *exposure therapy* exercises. In my field, some professionals believe these are the same techniques, but not everyone agrees. The distinction between the two has become even less clear over the last decade with the emergence of the inhibitory learning model of exposure therapy. I tend to think the mechanisms of the two techniques are virtually indistinguishable. I use *exposure* in this book because I'm partial.

90 Egan et al., *Cognitive-Behavioral Treatment of Perfectionism*; Antony and Swinson, *When Perfect Isn't Good Enough: Strategies for Coping with Perfectionism.*

These types of exercises are carried out repeatedly with an increasing degree of difficulty each time. For example, the individual could sign off with a misspelling in an email to their boss (instead of to their coworker, which is easier) or submit a work report with a misspelling (instead of in an email). In doing so, the perfectionist learns to tolerate the anxiety and that these types of mistakes are not so devastating. Their cognition starts to become more flexible. The learning generalizes over time—their thoughts about mistakes and the need for perfection start to loosen in other domains of life (e.g., chores at home, communicating with clients).

Translating Exposure Principles to the Workplace. By helping perfectionistic employees use Emphasis B for tasks they otherwise feel compelled to carry out using Emphasis A, they're inherently doing an exposure exercise. The anxiety stems from bona fide risk. Applying an Emphasis B strategy to a task is an inherent gamble, especially from the perspective of the perfectionist.

If a perfectionistic employee believes a task should be approached with Emphasis A, but they force themselves to use Emphasis B, there is a risk that their strategy was insufficient. In this case, when the task outcome is poor, it's easy to develop the belief that the task should have been approached with Emphasis A from the outset. It's this *possibility* that makes decisions to use Emphasis B in lieu of Emphasis A[91] an exposure exercise. This is a direct challenge to their inflated sense of responsibility and overcontrol tendencies.

Do we need to disguise exposure therapy principles? We don't really. Exposure therapy is the gold-standard and by far most

---

91 The same is true for the decision to use Emphasis C in lieu of Emphasis B.

effective behavioral treatment for anxiety and fear.[92] Though, it can help to disguise it sometimes. Psychologists and allied mental health disciplines are infamously terrible with marketing and public relations.

Case in point: the term *exposure therapy*. What a terrible name for the public. It elicits images of medieval torture or middle-aged white men in trench coats flashing their genitals.

Poor name notwithstanding, exposure exercises are the most effective approaches for reducing anxiety in the long-term. This includes perfectionistic anxiety. Whether you call it exposure exercises is up to you, but by advocating for Emphasis B at times when your team believes in using Emphasis A, you are using exposure principles.

Case Illustration: Kabir

The following case example of perfectionism in the workplace illustrates how the Emphasis Framework can help with thinking about the case. Using the case as a vehicle, I will discuss specific individual and group-based strategies based on this framework for mitigating perfectionism.

> Kabir is a new hire in your department and has been part of the team you lead. He comes highly recommended from academic experts and senior leaders in your organization. He recently graduated from a prestigious graduate program and has been touted by industry figures as a "true visionary" set to have a tremendous impact on the field. Your organization has undoubtedly paid a fortune to recruit Kabir

92 Abramowitz, Deacon, and Whiteside, *Exposure Therapy for Anxiety*.

and considers it a victory to have landed him, given all the wooing from top employers.

Kabir started his gig relatively smoothly about 12 weeks ago. He's been well-liked by others in the department and has been surprisingly humble. It strikes you as impressive—albeit odd—that such a rising star isn't more overconfident. He's eased into the daily operations. When he speaks up in meetings and offers his unique perspective, his genius is apparent. He's a critical thinker, offers innovative ideas, and provides a fresh approach to an otherwise tired formula. Early on, you've been very pleased with his contributions.

Over the next several weeks, however, subtle moments with Kabir start to give you pause—nothing horrible, just curious. You've been waiting for two weeks for him to clarify one of his reports, but he hasn't complied, despite your friendly follow-up email request. When you see him in person and ask for an update, he responds, "Sorry, I'm on it." After several more days go by with no response, you send him another message, this time firmer in tone. The clarification finally hits your inbox several days later with no apology. You decide not to pursue any corrective actions to address Kabir's tardiness, as his clarification was thoughtful, comprehensive, and elegant.

But problems continue to compound with Kabir's performance. You start getting reports from multiple sources within and across teams that Kabir has not been meeting his deadlines and has been unresponsive to requests for updates and final products. His coworkers tiptoe around the issue, because they like Kabir, but the resentment and concerns grow.

You decide to investigate. After collecting data from multiple collateral sources throughout the organization, you start to develop a clear picture. Kabir is working across multiple projects but has delivered on very few of them. When he does deliver, the work is stellar, but the amount of time and human capital spent nudging Kabir and securing his completed work are enormous.

Armed with an extensive list of incomplete projects to which Kabir has committed but failed to deliver, you approach him with your concerns. Kabir breaks down in your office and acknowledges that he's been overwhelmed by the amount of work and ashamed of his inability to carry through. He notes profound procrastination and getting stuck with checking and rechecking his work.

You are shocked by this circumstance for two reasons. First, the workload is comparable to those of his peers. It's not negligible, but it's a standard workload in the industry. Second, you don't understand how somebody of this pedigree and reputation could be struggling so much with this work.

You want to help and decide to work with him to dissect the needs of the various projects and teams. You intend to help him prioritize tasks and develop a plan for completing everything. As you approach this process with him, the primary problem becomes obvious. He can't prioritize tasks because he believes all of them are equally and highly important. He believes everything is critical, so he invests all his energy into each task and making sure all are perfect.

He can't keep up with the approach to all his tasks.

Kabir's Dysfunctional Emphasis Framework

Kabir's case is familiar to anyone who works with perfectionism. It's a composite example of how a rising star gets derailed early in their career because of these tendencies. His perfectionism and its consequences were probably overlooked or enabled when he was a student, especially given his tremendous promise as a future visionary.

In this case, Kabir can't keep up with the workload, not because it's an unrealistic amount or too complicated for his aptitude level. Rather, it's because he's doing too much for every assignment on his to-do list, without prioritizing them by importance.

Kabir is exhibiting a classic dysfunction of the Emphasis Framework. He's approaching his job duties in a way that fails to discriminate the importance of each task and how it's connected to his values. He finds each task equally important and therefore struggles to determine which tasks require more immediate effort, as well as the amount and quality of that effort. In other words, Kabir is attempting to use Emphasis A for way too many tasks, but ultimately this is causing Emphasis C unintentionally. The tasks aren't getting done because of safety behaviors (e.g., procrastination, ritualistic behavior), but not because it was a strategic move based on values and prioritization. Perfectionism forced a haphazard prioritization scheme on him.

You're likely to encounter a worker such as Kabir in your organization who gets stuck with the dysfunctional approach of trying to employ Emphasis A for too many tasks. The next section presents some strategies for mitigating the negative impact of this dysfunctional tendency in your workplace. The solutions are presented as group-level approaches (i.e., top-down culture changes) and employee-level approaches (i.e., bottom-up assistance for a specific employee).

Group-Level Solutions for a Dysfunctional Emphasis Framework in the Workplace

Leaders at every level of an organization are positioned to set the tone and have an opportunity to build antiperfectionism messaging into that tone. You can do this subtly or not-so-subtly. I prefer the latter approach because it leans heavily into a public display of antiperfectionism and its value in the workplace culture. Subtle messaging can be missed and doesn't communicate the value of antiperfectionism clearly.

What does a top-down, group-level approach look like? You can start like how I initiated this chapter, by talking about Covey's Effort-Value Model. You can present and describe this as shown in figure 6.

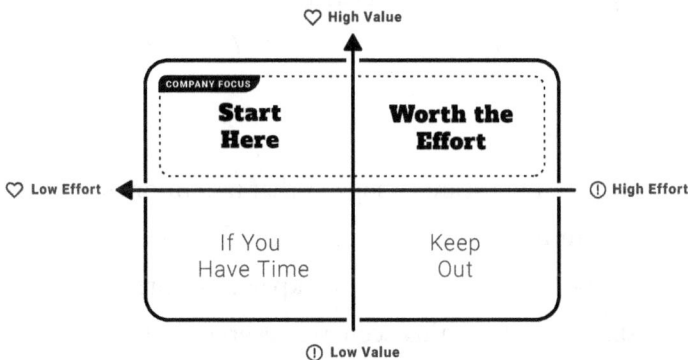

A top-down approach also looks like a work environment that integrates the Emphasis Framework into everyday planning and language. Do employees within your division know about this framework? Can they use its language to describe their priorities and to-do list? For example, if the Emphasis Framework has become embedded successfully into the culture of your workplace, conversations in a meeting might sounds something like this:

> Manager: *Okay, so the Smith Co project is next on the docket. Per the email this morning, we designated it as an Emphasis A task that warrants top resources. Bill, can you give us an update on this project?*

> Bill: *I've shifted my attention to the project now that it's Emphasis A. The Jones Co project has been pushed to Emphasis B and reassigned to Brenda's group, which has more availability until December. The Jones Co project is still in good hands, but now we can have "all hands on deck" for Smith Co.*

> Brenda: *Yep, we've accommodated the Jones Co project, but this required us to use Emphasis C for the annual retreat planning until December. It won't get abandoned completely, but it can wait.*

This illustration is not meant to suggest that task prioritization is innovative. It's meant to show that the Emphasis Framework concept and language can be integrated into a workplace culture so that it's used fluidly in discussions. In this scenario, everyone in that meeting is knowledgeable of the Emphasis A, B, and C distinctions. Although not obvious in the dialogue, they probably understand the pitfalls of the perfectionism pattern—Emphasis A forced to Emphasis C.

Introducing and supporting this messaging provides shared language and antiperfectionistic expectations. It will have a minimal negative impact on work quality but will enhance work efficiency. The tasks that are critical for the organization will receive the most effort. Those that receive less effort will do so because that's sufficient, by the definition of Emphasis B. Most importantly, however, the expectations and communication contribute to a healthy workplace culture, which then facilitates growth and satisfaction at the individual level of the employee. Expectations are super clear. The ripple effects of this can be robust, such as word-of-mouth via the Internet about your highly supportive and inviting workplace.

Integrating this type of framework into the workplace can take a variety of forms. Here are some examples, not all of which will apply to your workplace or are within your power to implement.

- → The employee handbook can discuss the framework explicitly.
- → New hire trainings can emphasize this framework to set the stage from the outset of employment.
- → The framework can be integrated into the organization's critical identity messaging, such as the organization's vision, mission, and values statements.
- → Emphasis A, B, and C language can be used as part of communication within the organization, such as via email, as part of newsletters, etc.
- → The Emphasis Framework can be used for strategizing during meetings and assigning action items. Doing so means that all parties are aware of the importance of each task.

→ Model—as a leader, you can show your employees how to follow this framework by doing so yourself. Minimize hypocrisy by managing your own perfectionism.

→ Promote an environmental cueing system. Create a public display of tasks and categorize them by Emphasis level. For example, there can be a whiteboard in the office or on a channel in your workplace application that lists each project in different sections, one for each Emphasis level.

→ Reward healthy framework use during yearly employee evaluations or on a more frequent and smaller scale (e.g., weekly praise). Provide direct feedback on Emphasis level balance during employee reviews. It can be its own review item, which also sends a message about the importance of this framework to your employees.

→ Using an Emphasis B approach assumes some risk. If the risky outcome does occur, absorb the negative impact, blunt the outrage, roll with the punch, and remind the team that this was always a possibility. Model acceptance. Don't abandon the framework.

→ Discuss the framework as exposure to perfectionistic anxiety. Some workers might feel empowered by the strong evidence supporting exposure techniques. Perhaps ditch the word *exposure* and instead discuss it as embracing anxiety, fear, and uncertainty of making a mistake or using Emphasis B or C at an inopportune time.

Every workplace would benefit from an antiperfectionistic worldview, which comes from the top down. You are in a unique position—whether local to your team or more global to the whole organization—to influence workplace culture and foster an environment that embraces flaws, creates shared expectations and language, and enhances the health and satisfaction of your employees. It also provides fertile conditions for helping the perfectionist on your team at the individual level, discussed next.

Employee-Level Solutions for a Dysfunctional Emphasis Framework in the Workplace

Gather Details about Self-Awareness and Skills. If you've deduced that an employee under your supervision is succumbing to problematic perfectionistic tendencies, you may have some options for providing a supportive environment to help them overcome these challenges. Doing so is a win-win; it's good for the employee and good for you. It's also good for the organization.

My first instinct with any employee involves being direct and putting the issue out into the ether, but respectfully and in private. Outline your concerns to the perfectionistic employee individually and observe their reaction. By being direct, you can gauge whether they have any self-awareness. If they have insight into their own perfectionism, this is a good indicator for their ability and willingness to change. If they don't see the perfectionism and defend their tendencies, you're in for a challenge. Improving their insight will be a steep hill to climb, and you'll need to climb it before anything else can change.

If the perfectionist has some insight, it helps to determine if they're exhibiting a *skill deficit* or a *skill impairment* when it comes to prioritizing within the Emphasis Framework. A skill deficit means that the perfectionistic employee doesn't have the skills for prioritizing and selecting an optimal Emphasis level strategy (i.e., they don't know how). A skill impairment means that the employee has the skills to prioritize within the framework, but there are cognitive, behavioral, and emotional factors obstructing the application of those skills. Skill deficits and skill impairments warrant slightly different approaches.

For a skill deficit, you would benefit from instructing and mentoring the perfectionistic employee on the process of prioritization. You can model your own selection of Emphasis levels across tasks, as well as demonstrate how to handle outcomes from those priority choices. Share some insight into your thought processes as you make your decisions and carry out the Emphasis plans. At some point, it helps to provide scaffolded training by observing the employee navigate the Emphasis Framework and offering gentle corrective feedback as needed.[93] Once the employee has learned and understood the skill, be sure to reassess whether they exhibit any skill impairment. Skill deficits and skill impairments are not mutually exclusive. They can present in the same employee.

For skill impairment, the strategy is different. The perfectionist has the necessary skills, but they can't use them effectively. This is usually caused by anxiety, safety behaviors getting in the way of task performance, and perfectionistic thinking patterns (e.g., cognitive biases). Each perfectionist presents with unique patterns of thoughts, feelings, and behaviors, so a uniform plan for addressing a perfectionistic employee doesn't exist. That being said, exposure exercises are one tool in your kit that can help in most circumstances.

---

93 Gentle because of the tendency for perfectionists to be oversensitive.

Exposure Exercises for a Dysfunctional Emphasis Framework. You're (probably) not a qualified psychotherapist, so I wouldn't recommend that you attempt formal exposure therapy. You can, however, use exposure principles to encourage the perfectionistic employee to adopt Emphasis B for a variety of tasks. With a collaborative discussion of the Emphasis Framework and why Emphasis B is important, you can nudge the employee toward completing tasks in an Emphasis B manner. If you can sell this idea to them, your next step involves creating a list of exposure exercises.

A rank order of exposure examples can be listed out to guide progressively more challenging exercises. In my field, we call this an *exposure hierarchy*,[94] which essentially is a metaphorical staircase that starts low and moves the perfectionist higher with each step. In this case, *higher* means more anxiety provoking. We use a subjective scale for measuring anxiety called *Subjective Units of Distress* (SUDs).

See figure 7 for an example of an exposure hierarchy with SUDs ratings that our case, Kabir, could undertake to fight his perfectionism. I've also made a blank copy of the hierarchy available for you to individualize for your own employees. See the end of the book for instructions on how to access it or go to www.gregchasson.com/flawedresources.

94 Abramowitz, Deacon, and Whiteside, *Exposure Therapy for Anxiety.*

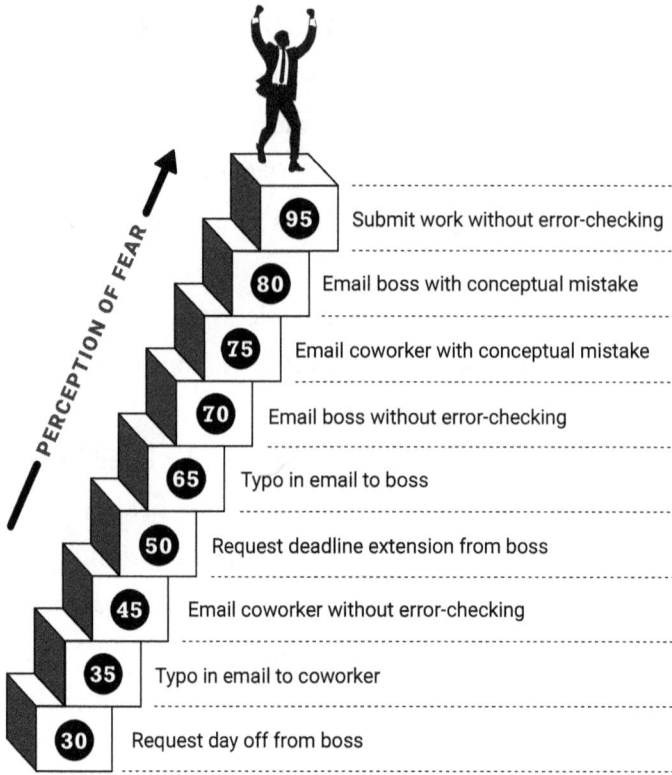

Figure 7: Kabir's Exposure Hierarchy with Subjective Units of Distress (SUDs, 1-100)

When taking an exposure approach, have the employee start with low-level steps on the staircase. For perfectionists, this usually means performing a work task with minor mistakes while curbing any safety behaviors. What constitutes a minor mistake is a matter of individual perspective. In this case, the perfectionistic employee's perspective is the most important, so start with mistakes that the employee finds difficult to make, even if you think the mistake is small. During these exercises, it's important not to invalidate the difficulty of the tasks, sound condescending, or come off as critical. Stay as neutral as possible.

In the introduction to this book, I noted that managing perfectionism can include making mistakes *on purpose*. Exposure exercises are the vehicle for doing so. If you're concerned about permitting or encouraging mistakes in your workplace, however, please note that emerging research suggests that an organization's culture of tolerating mistakes is positively associated with psychological safety.[95] As discussed in the previous chapter, psychological safety is correlated with many employee and organizational benefits.[96] In other words, the more a workplace signals a tolerance for mistakes, the more secure the employees likely feel and the better the individual and company outcomes.

Enabling of a Dysfunctional Emphasis Framework. Maintaining a neutral stance involves reducing your enabling behavior. Remember that perfectionism ropes in people to perform safety behaviors. Examples that you might feel tempted to offer include providing reassurance, rechecking and fixing work on behalf of the perfectionist, and permitting procrastination and other avoidance behaviors.

It's easy to get sucked into these patterns. You probably think you're helping your employee in the moment. After all, as safety behaviors, they are performed with the intention of providing temporary relief, which seems like a positive step you can take. For instance, it seems natural and humane to tell your anxious employee that, "It's alright. No big deal. You did fine."

Unfortunately, this is not positive or helpful in the long-term. It may decrease anxiety momentarily, but safety behaviors carried out on the perfectionist's behalf serve to worsen perfectionism's grip on

95 Wang, Guchait, and Paşamehmetoğlu, "Tolerating Errors in Hospitality Organizations."
96 Edmondson and Bransby, "Psychological Safety Comes of Age."

the workplace over time. It contributes to the sawtooth effect we saw in chapter 2.

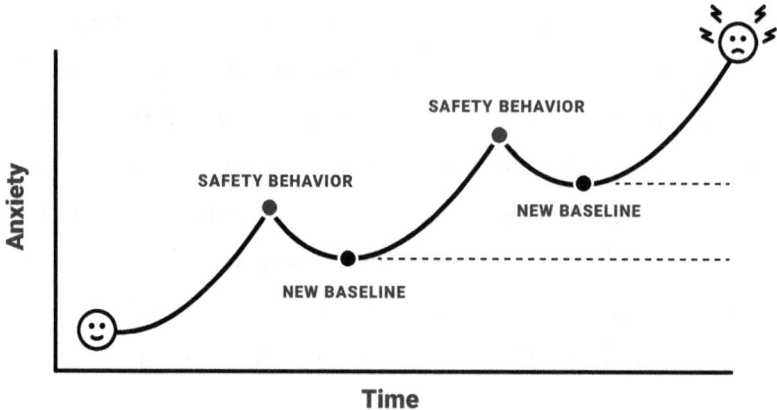

What does this mean for you in the workplace as you navigate working with a perfectionistic employee? If doing antiperfectionism strategies by the textbook, it means that you can help by ceasing all safety behaviors: not providing reassurance, not rechecking and fixing work on behalf of the perfectionist, not accepting unwarranted apologies, and not enabling procrastination and other avoidance behaviors. This might seem harsh, but it's all about the delivery. It doesn't need to be harsh. It can be collaborative and transparent. You also can ease in slowly.

What do I mean by *slowly*? At first, you can help the perfection-istic employee decide which tasks can be tackled with an Emphasis B approach. You can also support them by providing them with reas-surance that it's okay to use Emphasis B. You can reassure them that the risk of bad outcomes is minimal for an Emphasis B approach (e.g., getting fired, messing up). Your goal, however, is to gradually reduce that type of support—reassurance, decision-making, checking, and other safety behaviors in which you partake on the employee's behalf. Ultimately, that type of support falls under the safety behavior umbrella. It may help the employee in the short-term, but it strengthens the perfectionism in the long run.

Some of my messaging may seem contradictory. On one hand, I suggest fostering a work culture that tolerates mistakes to strengthen psychological safety. On the other hand, I also recommend not providing reassurance to perfectionistic employees, as doing so is a safety behavior.

What's a manager to do?

Do you provide reassurance to signal a climate of high tolerance for mistakes (enhancing psychological safety)? Or do you resist providing reassurance and imply that your workplace may not tolerate mistakes (jeopardizing psychological safety)?

It's not as inconsistent as it seems. The contradiction is only a problem at the individual level and not at the group level. A manager would benefit from invariably and publicly fostering a workplace that signals tolerance for mistakes (group level). For perfectionistic employees such as Kabir, however, I would encourage a reduction or elimination of excessive reassurance (individual level).

A discussion with Kabir can be done collaboratively in private and with candid communication: "Kabir, this company expects and grows from blunders. As you know, however, we're working on your perfectionistic tendencies. For this reason, I will purposefully not offer private reassurance when it comes to making errors. Sometimes this may feel to you like a culture of not tolerating making mistakes."

Example of Kabir's Exposure Exercises. When you approach Kabir to discuss exposure exercises, he seems nervous at first but ultimately comes around and understands their importance. It helps that you provided education and described the rationale for the exercises. The education involves two major components. First, it helps to explain to Kabir how safety behaviors provide immediate relief but cause the behaviors to strengthen over time. These safety behaviors don't remedy the anxiety in the long-term. Draw or show the sawtooth effect based on negative reinforcement to illustrate this point (see chapter 2, figure 1). This also is a good time to explain how your enabling responses are a safety behavior that contributes to the sawtooth effect.

Second, explain how completing exposure exercises improves learning. By carrying out these activities repeatedly, systematically, and consistently, Kabir can learn that tolerating anxiety from the risks of Emphasis B is doable, that disastrous outcomes are not likely, and that handling poor outcomes is possible even when they do occur. Overall, he will learn to become more flexible with his thinking, including loosening any inflated sense of responsibility and need for overcontrol.

He agrees to work with you on exposure exercises. You both sit down and develop an exposure hierarchy that seems manageable (see figure 7). Kabir agrees to start with an exercise around the middle of the hierarchy (e.g., SUDs of 50). In our example, this means Kabir asking you—his boss—for a one-day extension for a task. He has agreed to ask you for this extension in person (i.e., no email) and cease any safety behaviors. Some of the safety behaviors Kabir has self-disclosed include scanning and checking the reactions of others to make sure they're not angry at or disappointed with him (e.g., observing microlevel facial expressions, listening for exasperation, overanalyzing ambiguous statements such as "Okay").

You are now savvy with the principles of exposure and understand that you cannot enable these checking behaviors. You remain neutral in your response when Kabir asks for the extension. With a poker face, you simply say, "Okay" to permit the extension but provide no indication of your feelings toward the decision. You both know that this is the plan, but it's nonetheless anxiety-provoking for Kabir. In this sense, you are doing this collaboratively and in an expected manner, so it might help you—as the boss—to feel less inhumane in doing these exercises. You both signed up for this; it's informed consent.

You check back in with Kabir after a few hours and again the next day to see if he's learned anything about his ability to handle the fear of asking for an extension and sitting with the anxiety that you—as the boss—think less of him. You remain neutral throughout the entire process.

Kabir then moves on to the next exercise. This may include asking for another extension (e.g., sticking with the same stair on the exposure hierarchy staircase) or moving on to a higher one. This depends on how he's doing with the previous exercise and whether he is ready to move on to the next one.

Over two-to-three months, Kabir makes tremendous progress. He seems much more flexible in his thinking around making mistakes and asking for help from others. His work efficiency increases, and he shows a marked decrease with involving others in reassurance-seeking, checking and fixing, and procrastination behaviors. Kabir's rockstar aptitude starts to have a positive effect on the workplace; he starts to realize his potential.

➡ Chapter Conclusion and Takeaways

This chapter linked perfectionism to a dysfunctional Emphasis Framework, which is a useful model to communicate about task prioritization and effort allocation. I also provide group- and individual-level strategies to mitigate the negative effects of perfectionism by addressing a dysfunctional Emphasis Framework. Takeaway points include the following:

→ The Emphasis Framework includes three levels of task completion strategies—Emphasis A, B, and C. These strategies differ based on the amount of effort applied.

→ Emphasis A is meant for top priorities that warrant maximum effort. Emphasis B characterizes effort allocation for tasks that need getting done but aren't critical. And Emphasis C is designated for tasks that are not important and can strategically be ignored.

→ A perfectionistic dysfunction of this framework occurs when individuals infeasibly approach too many tasks with Emphasis A, effectively failing to prioritize. When this occurs, Emphasis A turns into a forced Emphasis C.

→ Selecting appropriate Emphasis approaches is based on your core values.

→ Exposure exercises (e.g., making mistakes purposefully and sitting with the anxiety) can nudge perfectionistic employees toward focusing on tasks in an Emphasis B manner. Exposure hierarchies are a method for guiding such exercises.

→ At the group level, exposure exercises via the Emphasis Framework can be encouraged through the workplace culture, such as in new hire orientation and employee handbook materials.

→ For individual-level strategies, assess for skill deficits versus skill impairments. The former indicates the perfectionist lacks the ability to calibrate task effort and prioritization. The latter suggests the perfectionist has this ability but encounters cognitive, emotional, and behavioral barriers to calibration and prioritization.

→ At the individual-level, exposure exercises can be tailored for specific employees in need of assistance with a dysfunctional Emphasis Framework.

As somebody who can influence workplace culture and individual-level performance, you can help your perfectionistic employees understand and communicate from the Emphasis Framework to engage in anti-perfectionistic strategies. You also can guide individual employees through a structured exposure-based perfectionism intervention.

You can start by modeling the antiperfectionistic attitude of Aisha Tyler.

CHAPTER 6

LEAVE IT TO SANTA AND THE ASSASSINS: PROCESS PARALYSIS

"A good plan…executed *now* is better
than a perfect plan next week."[97]

GEORGE S. PATTON
Major General, United States Army

THE LATE AND decorated General Patton springs to mind when you consider well-respected leaders in US history. He must have encountered perfectionism in his leadership duties; likely in others and perhaps even in himself.

His quote summarizes, aptly and concisely, how perfectionism can obstruct a planning process. I can imagine how this obstruction could play out on the battlefield, where lives are at stake and the pressure is unmatched. He is alluding to process paralysis.

You may have heard of paralysis by analysis, or the idea of getting stuck overanalyzing to the point of not reaching a conclusion or finishing a task. This saying exemplifies perfectionism and essentially

97 Patton, Jr., *War As I Knew It.*

characterizes the dysfunctional Emphasis Framework from chapter 5. When you use an Emphasis A strategy to evaluate data and optimize results—for example, overanalyzing marketing data, revenue streams, economic forecasts, stock market patterns, parking trends, employee sick days, etc.—it often leads to Emphasis C. In this case, you'll find yourself getting lost in the data, getting stuck on the details, and becoming so paralyzed that you cannot draw a conclusion or finish the task.

Imagine if analysis paralysis was to occur one step sooner. What if the paralysis occurs when you try to optimize the process for completing the task? What if the goal for optimizing the process is to obtain perfect efficiency? What if you feel compelled to search comprehensively for the perfect strategy? What if you get stuck trying to find the ideal order of operations to complete the task? This is called process paralysis and, much of the time, it's a presentation of perfectionism.

Presentations of Process Paralysis

A perfectionist is liable to get fixated on developing the perfect plan for completing a task. This can show up in multiple ways, two of which will be characterized in this section. Sometimes these presentations occur simultaneously and compound each other. They aren't mutually exclusive.

Choosing an Optimal Strategy or Tactic.[98] With this variant of process paralysis, the perfectionist feels responsible for selecting an ideal approach for working on and completing a task. They may over-analyze the various strategy options, hoping to vet each one compre-

98 For the sake of smooth reading, I will lump strategy and tactic into strategy, even though they are different concepts. Please know that I am referring to both when I use *strategy*.

hensively so that they can make an informed decision. They don't want to be accused of missing an obvious and ideal option for completing the task. Sometimes this coincides with a feeling of not having done enough searching or that they've missed something during their search (e.g., a type of *not just right experiences*).

The Internet can be a black hole and, through process paralysis, the perfectionist can get sucked in by engaging in excessive research. Hours are lost to meandering Internet journeys. The excessive Internet research is another form of safety behavior—the function is to relieve anxiety by researching comprehensively and collecting all relevant information. They attempt to satisfy a need for achieving due diligence with perfection.

We all experience moments in which we get stuck trying to determine the best strategy. It presents in small moments for most of us. For example, when driving, my wife and I have different opinions about which routes are the best to arrive at our destination. Different routes represent different strategies for completing the task—getting from Point A to Point B. Options are varied and may include the long but scenic drive, a quicker but nonscenic approach, or a fast but dangerous path. We might have to select between different routes from the map application, and some of the options have matching estimates of destination time. Spontaneous circumstances (e.g., accidents, construction) often blur what is considered the ideal strategy.[99]

You can probably guess where I'm going with this. It's not feasible to "collect all information" or "vet all options perfectly." For any given task, a countless number of combinations of strategies could be brainstormed and enacted. The ideal combination is dependent on a host of

99 In these situations, the perfectionist may struggle to switch to a new route, even if circumstances suggest it would be optimal. This is an example of cognitive rigidity, discussed in chapter 8.

variables, many of which are dynamic—they change across contexts. What is declared optimal at one point in time isn't necessarily optimal five minutes later.

An appraisal of what is *optimal* is also subjective. Different parties often perceive different ideal strategies.[100] In many instances it's impossible to test different strategies head-to-head because of feasibility. For example, you can't test two work interventions at the same time on the same participant. You can test the interventions serially, or you can compare the interventions in parallel across individuals,[101] but there's no way to know which intervention is better for that specific participant at that moment in their life. You just can't know the counterfactual outcome with certainty.

In addition, perfect vetting would require a crystal ball. You can judge the effort but not the outcome, until the outcome comes to light. Only after the fact can a vetting outcome be appraised as *sufficient* or *successful*. Notice I didn't use the word *perfect* there. Even if a vetting process were excellent, it's not clear what *perfect vetting* would mean.

Ultimately, a perfectionist who exhibits process paralysis around selecting the ideal strategy for completing a task will impact others around them in a workplace. Not only do they slow down processes, but they typically seek reassurance constantly about the universe of possible strategy choices and which one to select. This safety behavior is draining for an organizational culture and diverts energy and time from other employees.

---

100 My wife thinks her route is best, but I think mine is best. We're probably both wrong.

101 You can even match those two different individuals on key characteristics to equate them as much as possible, as if finding a twin. This is a common research design methodology.

Electing an Optimal Order of Operations. In addition to selecting an overall strategy, the perfectionist often gets derailed trying to identify the ideal sequence of steps for finishing a task. They labor over the decision of how to start and what step *should* go first, second, etc. There is a mistaken belief that one perfect approach to the task exists—they just need to find it.

We also experience this type of difficulty in everyday activity. For example, if I have a list of errands to run, the order of operations can become complicated. It seems logical to pick up the dry cleaning first because the dry cleaner opens at dawn. Perhaps you also need to pick up the parcel at the post office, but the place doesn't open until later in the day. The dry cleaner and post office are near each other, but they are both on the other side of town. Combining the post office and dry-cleaning errand during the day is practical because it's a pain to schlep out to that area of town two separate times.

Here's an added problem: Fido needs to be groomed, and the dog groomer is around the corner from your house. The walk-in hours for grooming fall in between the times when the dry cleaner and post office open. This makes it so that you cannot combine the dry cleaner and post office errand if you want to bring Fido to the groomer. None of this inconvenience negates the fact that Fido stinks and has tangled fur.

Optimizing the plan may require sacrificing one or more of the errands. Alternatively, it might require selecting inefficiencies on purpose, such as driving back and forth across town to squeeze in Fido's appointment. Most of us make these decisions intuitively, but the perfectionist often gets paralyzed trying to order the operations.

Much like the discussion of the "perfect strategy," no perfect order of operations exists. It's not static—even the most efficient approaches may change over time and across situations. It also changes across individuals, as each person may bring a different pattern of efforts, strengths, and weaknesses to a task.

When a perfectionist gets stuck trying to optimize the order of steps for completing a task, the impact on others in the workplace is profound. Procrastination and avoidance are common reactions to this type of paralysis. That class of safety behavior slows down productivity and causes resentment in the workplace.

Part of the paralysis typically includes excessive reassurance-seeking, such as asking coworkers about what order of operations makes the most sense. The employee with perfectionism comes across as highly incapable of organizing their efforts and does not instill confidence that everything is handled.

Preoccupation with Efficiency

Obsessing about finding the ideal task strategy and optimal order of operations often boils down to a fear of not being efficient. A perfectionist typically wants to choose the perfect strategy because not doing so would be deemed by them to be *inefficient*. This usually is combined with a should statement—*I should be efficient*—which worsens the tendency.

Similarly, for a perfectionist, getting stuck on finding the optimal order of operations may be a function of wanting to eliminate inefficiencies in the order of steps. They cringe at the thought of doing a task's steps in an inefficient order. Like above, this tends to coincide with should statements such as, *I should do steps in an order that makes sense.*

Irony of Process Paralysis

Perfectionism is highly ironic, specifically via the self-fulfilling prophecy, and process paralysis provides one avenue for seeing this irony clearly. This is particularly true when the process paralysis is driven by a fear of not being efficient enough. Imagine becoming so preoccupied with efficiency that it causes you to engage in behavior that undermines your efficiency dramatically. In these scenarios, in attempting to be more efficient, you are making yourself less efficient.

The examples of this irony extend into the different types of process paralysis. Imagine a taxi driver who is preoccupied with efficiency and therefore becomes paralyzed trying to find the perfect route to pick up a passenger (i.e., optimal strategy). In doing so, the driver gets delayed significantly and loses the opportunity to transport the passenger, who found alternative transportation in the meantime.

Consider a postal carrier who seeks perfect efficiency and therefore gets stuck trying to figure out the order of their job tasks on any given day. They might compulsively analyze different sequences of steps, such as where and when to collect parcels and deliver mail. The postal worker with process paralysis, due to fears of inefficient order of operations, may get so stuck that ultimately no mail is retrieved or delivered.

Process Paralysis and the Emphasis Framework

Sometimes it helps to think about process paralysis within the Emphasis Framework. When a perfectionist freezes trying to optimize the process for completing a task, essentially they are opting to use Emphasis A to plan their approach. When this goes awry, Emphasis

A turns into a forced Emphasis C. The perfectionist gets stuck trying to optimize the process (i.e., Emphasis A) and doesn't end up getting to work on that task (i.e., Emphasis C). It's process paralysis.

Meta-Meetings

One common result of dealing with perfectionists in the workplace is encountering a fundamentally absurd phenomenon in which people have meetings to plan or discuss other meetings. In these moments, I often reflect in awe at how far our species has come in our evolutionary trajectory.[102] I'm sure there's a bumper sticker out there that shows the human evolutionary lineage that concludes with a silhouette of a workplace meeting about meetings.

This type of phenomenon is often referred to as a *meta-meeting*, whereby the meeting process itself becomes the focal point of discussion. This can take various forms, such as a focus on the process of the current meeting in which people find themselves. For example, a leader may pause a meeting and check in with attendees about how the meeting is going and ask them to weigh in on the process. This by itself can lead to its own form of process paralysis, but it's a pretty common process-based approach to holding a meeting and feels a little less absurd than other versions.

Another version of meta-meetings occurs when people hold meetings to discuss other upcoming meetings. This is the worst when it involves meetings that extend at least three degrees. What do I mean? It's not unheard of for a manager to hold a meeting with their team to discuss how to approach a meeting with their client. This represents a two-degree meeting (i.e., a meeting about

102 This is sarcasm.

a meeting). It's also not uncommon for a manager to hold a meeting with their team to discuss how to approach a meeting with their division chief, who in turn called the meeting to discuss strategies for hitting a homerun with an upcoming meeting with a client. This is a three-degree meeting (i.e., a meeting to prepare for a meeting about preparing for a meeting).

Meta-meetings that extend beyond two degrees often cause my consciousness to change. I begin to feel my mind dissociating from my body, as if there has been a rupture in the space-time continuum.[103] This type of torture device—the three-degree meta-meeting—is often a byproduct of problematic human tendencies, such as perfectionism. It may reflect process paralysis, such as a need to optimize meeting strategy and order of operations, often in the name of achieving perfect efficiency. There is a threshold in which meta-meetings reach a point of diminishing returns and become hurtful to efficiency, if not paralyzing.

Compulsive List-Making

Shopping lists, to-do lists, bucket lists, hit lists,[104] any sort of list— they can become the epicenter of process analysis. If Santa Claus was perfectionistic, his naughty list would paralyze him, and there would be no Christmas magic for anyone. A perfectionist becomes immobilized trying to create the most comprehensive and organized list possible. In doing so, they have a difficult time starting the tasks and checking them off their respective list.

The to-do list is the perfectionist's chummiest enabler and closest tormentor. For them, the to-do is the go-to. It can feel like a cozy safety

103 Also sarcasm.
104 Maybe process paralysis could serve a societal benefit when it comes to a hit list.

blanket, but this becomes problematic when the list-making becomes excessive. It creates an illusion of productivity and progress. When checking in with themselves, or if others are checking in with them, the perfectionist experiences a sense of security because it feels like they're making forward movement. They might be thinking, "Yep, I'm feeling good about my progress."[105] It's all an illusion. There isn't much progress, just avoidance. The safety blanket has become the safety behavior.

Not Just Right Experiences (NJREs) and Process Paralysis

The NJREs phenomena often plays a crucial role in process paralysis. Much of the time, the perfectionist adopts a criterion for determining when the process planning is complete and it's time to initiate the task based on the plan. The criterion is often based on how much the perfectionist feels like the planning of the process is done. This gut feeling becomes the threshold for transitioning from planning to doing, but it's subjective and poorly defined. These characteristics turn this gut feeling into a recipe for disaster for perfectionists, who struggle with ambiguous situations (i.e., uncertainty) and interpret context with a host of cognitive biases (i.e., problems with subjectivity). The recipe leads to NJRE-based process paralysis.

Productivity slows to a halt because the perfectionist is waiting for a feeling that the planning is complete.

Case Illustration: Noam

Noam is well-known in his field for being a superb computer programmer. Some have called him the Mozart of program-

---

105 This is a good example of emotional reasoning, by the way.

ming. His code has been used around the globe to train novice programmers on best practices. His products are known to be effective yet efficient and sleek. The code is creative and unconventional. When experts see how it works, sometimes you can see the look of awe on their face.

Noam was noticed at the age of 13 given his natural mastery of programming skills. He was recruited out of high school by a leading software company and set up for a career of software innovation. The employer envisioned that Noam could become a leader in the field. This vision hasn't come to fruition.

Now 24 years old, Noam has become known for being a disappointment. His code is still innovative and serves as a model for training programmers. His genius has never been questioned. His reputation, however, has become clouded by reports of his excruciatingly slow pace. Although his work is considered impeccable and ground-breaking, the rate at which he completes his projects is unsustainable.

The snail pace isn't caused by Noam's inability to code or envision the long-term product. His coding flows naturally and quickly when he engages in the task—like a maestro. His employers were stumped and hired an executive coach to observe and help Noam with a project that he was assigned. It requires coding a new feature of their flagship software.

According to the executive coach, much of Noam's day is spent lurking in the depths of online niche discussion boards to seek evidence of what coding direction makes the most sense for his needs. Sometimes he posts anonymously on these boards to check how others view his ideas. You can often catch him refreshing his Internet browser every few seconds awaiting new discussion board responses. He does this for hours.

The executive coach documented that Noam's excessive planning is characterized by copious list-making. When he considers a coding strategy, he lists the possible pros and cons of the approach, the short-term cost of exploring and fine tuning one strategy, and the long-term costs to implementing this strategy at a larger scale for the company. He creates these lists for each plausible strategy that comes to mind. Items on the lists are supported with links to online sources in case anyone asks for justification. This also requires considerable Internet research.

His employers have essentially written off Noam's work and considered anything he contributes to be a "bonus" to the company's productivity. They have invested considerable resources in Noam's professional development but ultimately determined that it's a sunk cost.

From his employer's perspective, Noam's name alone warrants keeping him on the payroll; however, they humor him when he seeks permission to pursue any of his long-term visions.

Noam's coworkers have noticed his unconventional role at the company. They express a blend of confusion, resentment, and pity. They are confused about why the company retains him but—based on coworker perception—permit him flexibility to do whatever he wants. They resent that he receives a handsome paycheck and has a nice office despite not contributing to overall productivity. But they also see some of Noam's struggles and pity him because of just how far his stardom has dropped since being recruited as a teenager more than a decade ago.

At this point, most of the company—including the C-suite and board of directors—consider Noam to be little more than the company mascot.

Noam's Process Paralysis

The case presentation illustrates process paralysis and what happens to a career when a perfectionist gets drawn into fears about task efficiency and optimization. Noam has become so obsessed with planning that his career has become a mockery. Without his historical reputation, he would have been unemployed long ago.

Noam is consumed by process paralysis in numerous ways, despite having unmatched talent to change the landscape of his field. Noam gets stuck figuring out how to start a programming project and therefore can't get beyond the planning phase. He can visualize the end-goal product but freezes trying to identify the best strategy for accomplishing it and what steps and order of steps make the most sense.

He often starts coding with one approach in mind and then stops, deletes what he has typed, and starts anew. Sometimes he skips around to different steps when he starts to question if a different order of tasks would increase the quality of the product and coding process. His list-making behaviors have become debilitating. The Internet research and discussion board lurking have consumed his workday and mental load. These self-imposed barriers happen persistently and resemble writer's block with a struggling author.

Noam's mindset has been reinforced for years. He has been lauded and rewarded for adopting an optimal coding approach. This is an example of how the cause of perfectionism is unclear in most cases and represents a mix of biology and environment, as noted in chapter 1. Noam likely has genetic vulnerabilities (i.e., biology) that triggered perfectionistic behavior as a child. These behaviors were rewarded over many years (i.e., environment) to worsen the presentation.

At a young age, Noam redefined the very definition of *optimal coding* and, as a result, noticed the high expectations placed on him. He expresses considerable stress from the pressure to live up to his potential. Others have given up long ago on Noam meeting these expectations, and he is aware of how others perceive him. This elicits disappointment in himself, shame, and guilt, and this, in turn, amplifies his feelings of pressure to perform.

Noam's self-perception notwithstanding, the workplace environment also suffers in this scenario. Although Noam's presence seems relatively harmless, coworkers pulling their weight feel resentful that he gets a free ride simply because of his name. They deride him behind his back and often condescend to him.

For a minority of employees, this creates watercooler gossip, which serves as a bonding experience at Noam's expense. For the remainder of coworkers, this type of gossip and disdain creates negativity into the workplace climate and makes them feel "dirty."

Group-Level Solutions for Process Paralysis

Managers have options for curbing process paralysis in their employees. You can emphasize the importance of *product over process*. Specifically, this places the priority on getting the task done, even if the process isn't ideal. Managers and business leaders can promote this messaging by modeling this type of approach in their own work.

Adopt the Emphasis Framework for Messaging. Organizational messaging about planning and processes can use the Emphasis Framework language. This framework can be applied to planning. You can use an Emphasis A approach to create a plan for a task. This would consist of expending tremendous energy and leaning in heavily to the planning process. Emphasis B instead would consist of using far fewer resources to devise a reasonable plan. The goal would be to create a sufficient yet flexible plan to meeting the goal, perhaps with less concern about the end-product. An Emphasis C approach to planning means no planning.

Your messaging can promote Emphasis B approaches to planning in most instances. When planning a task is crucial to the organization or because it's a top priority, Emphasis A planning makes sense. Sometimes, Emphasis C for planning is reasonable. A task may need to get done—and done quickly—regardless of its quality, so Emphasis C planning strategies are indicated. This might look like starting the task and revising the approach as you go.

Stimulus Control. In this book, I've tried to stay away from psychology jargon, but I'd like to introduce a concept to you: stimulus control.[106] It's just a fancy name for adjusting the environment to increase the likelihood of engaging in a behavior or not engaging in a behavior, as desired. It's used intuitively by people all the time. For example, you might place the chocolates out of sight because each time you open the pantry you eat them impulsively. You may place a sticky note on the back door so that you remember to grab the extra set of documents for work, as doing so would be out of routine. If you

106 Sidman, "Reflections on Stimulus Control."

prompt yourself by placing your dog's medications next to her food the night before she needs them, you're leveraging stimulus control.

Let's look at a nonworkplace example to illustrate the use of stimulus control to drive home the concept. Consumer psychologists love to leverage stimulus control to make their clients (i.e., businesses) money. Nothing screams *stimulus control* like creating an airport terminal in which the primary pathway between gates requires potential customers to walk through a retail store to get from Point A to Point B. I don't mean walking around or past a store; I mean walking *through* a store. It's the same as being forced to exit through a souvenir shop when you visit a tourist attraction. In that case, however, it's more expected compared to strolling through an airport.

This type of airport design is intended to increase consumer spending. It forces travelers to enter a shop and observe the goods around them. It has thereby eliminated a critical step for retail success—getting the customer into the store. The design is far from subtle. It seems relatively harmless, except on the pocketbook.

Sometimes this type of stimulus control becomes absurd. Late for an international flight connection, my wife and I sprinted through the airport to arrive at the gate,[107] multiple bags in tow dangling in every direction. My body and belongings at that moment must have been the volume of at least three or four people. The path required navigating a non-linear route through a retail store.

It wasn't just any retail store. It was upscale and displayed some eclectic and expensive goods. For some genius reason, the store lined this meandering path with a series of glass shelves displaying sparkling

---

107 I'm looking at you, Gatwick.

crystal figurines and glass bottles of expensive alcoholic beverages. Needless to say, my pace for catching the connecting flight halted to an amble as I tried not to slam into the expensive products and add thousands of dollars to my vacation bill. I can't even imagine schlepping small children in the same scenario. One of my primary thoughts at that moment was, "whoever designed this should be fired." Yes, it's a should statement. Yes, it's other-oriented moralism. I stand by my statement with (self-) righteous indignation.

As much as I cursed stimulus control in this airport situation,[108] it's not worth it to throw the baby out with the bathwater. Stimulus control can be a powerful strategy for changing behavior in the workplace. No need to abandon it altogether. It can be used to help Noam. Examples of stimulus control strategies in the workplace include the following.

→ Limit access to specific websites (e.g., block social media sites, popular discussion boards).

→ Prohibit administrative privileges on workstations to reduce employee control over the computer (e.g., downloading and installing programs).

→ Institute an advertised, occasional, and random audit of employee Internet behaviors (e.g., search histories).

→ Place workstations out in the open for increased visibility, thereby reducing unwanted employee behavior (e.g., creating excessive lists).

→ Create a system for your employees to declare (privately to you) at the end of a workweek their estimate for the week's ratio of

108 Also, there is the famous stimulus control found in casinos, which are carefully orchestrated to keep you there for spending money. Ever try finding a wall clock or window at a casino? Good luck.

planning to *executing* tasks. Make sure they know the difference between these two. This creates accountability.

You might be doing some of the stimulus control strategies already. Beware that most, if not all, of these suggestions will be despised by your workers. They reek of micromanaging and can create a stressful fishbowl environment. It also doesn't make sense to adopt these strategies to stop just one employee's process paralysis, unless the strategy is needed for other reasons (e.g., blocking social media sites may also facilitate productivity for the nonperfectionist).

You should use these group-based stimulus control suggestions sparingly and consider their use in the context of how they make your workers feel. You might be creating a more toxic environment than if you just do nothing to curb process paralysis. Sometimes the cure is worse than the disease.

Employee-Level Solutions for Process Paralysis

Gather Details about Self-Awareness and Skills. As with the Emphasis Framework discussion, assessment for self-awareness is a helpful place to start. But, unlike the approach to the Emphasis Framework, perfectionists tend to have more self-awareness of process paralysis. They may not appreciate what contributes to the tendencies, but they can identify the planning difficulties and their harmful impact. In some situations, however, the self-insight might be lacking, which means you can help the employee by providing some education.

As with approaches discussed previously, it also helps to determine if the process paralysis is driven by a skill deficit, skill impairment, or both. If a perfectionist presents with a skill deficit with planning, they will require training on how to plan for completing tasks. This includes educating them about the balance between efficiency and effectiveness within the context of available resources.

If a skill impairment in planning is evident in addition to—or instead of—a skill deficit, the next step involves understanding the impairment. For perfectionists, the impairment often stems from a fear of not being efficient or effective when completing a task. I would suggest adopting exposure principles, given what we know about tackling fear and anxiety.

Exposure Exercises for Process Paralysis. For process paralysis, exposure therapy principles would involve a collaborative approach in which the perfectionistic employee carries out work tasks while practicing Emphasis B planning strategies. For example, you could have the perfectionist select a work task and complete it without planning, or by planning with specific boundaries. These boundaries may include a variety of factors, such as time (e.g., plan must be finalized in five minutes) and type of planning (e.g., must plan without consulting others or researching). If the perfectionist is sold on this approach, I'd recommend devising an exposure hierarchy.

Figure 8 outlines an example exposure hierarchy with SUDs ratings that our case, Noam, could undertake to fight his perfectionism. [109]

---

109 As noted in the previous chapter, you can access a blank copy of the hierarchy infographic to individualize for your own employees. See instructions at the end of the book or go to www.gregchasson.com/flawedresources.

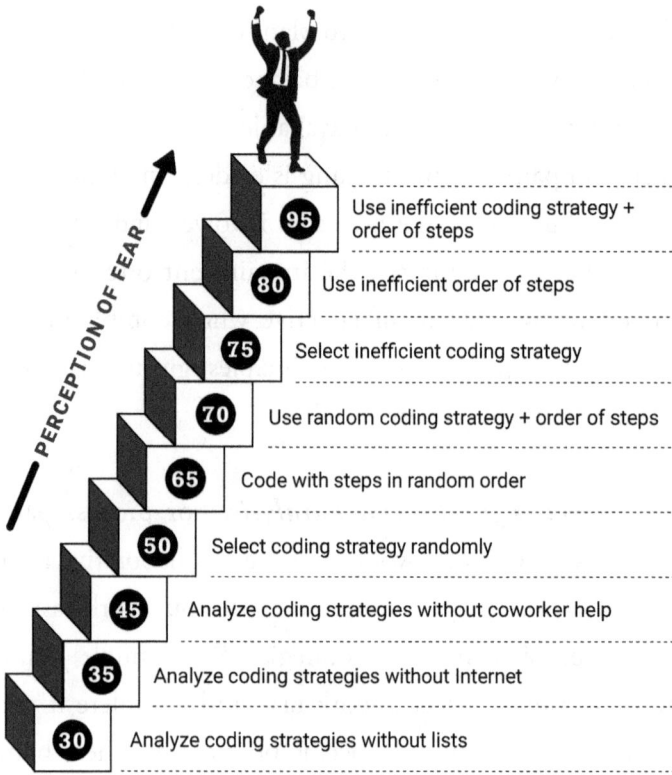

Figure 8: Noam's Exposure Hierarchy with Subjective Units of Distress (SUDs, 1-100)

Enabling of Process Paralysis. The most common way that coworkers and leaders enable an employee's process paralysis is by ignoring the associated safety behaviors. For example, you may allow perfectionistic employees to extend deadlines and seek reassurance about optimal task strategy and order of operations. It helps to set firm boundaries when a perfectionist solicits enabling behavior.

Establishing reasonable boundaries can be done gently and empathically. The perfectionist feels compelled to engage in safety behaviors and, often, the behaviors are carried out automatically and outside of their awareness. Some compassion for their experience can encourage them to address their struggles, as high levels of criticism and hostility tend to worsen this type of compulsive behavior.

Example of Noam's Exposure Exercises. You start by educating Noam about process paralysis and the fear that tends to drive it. You also convey to him a rationale for using exposure exercises to assist. This includes informing Noam about the learning that occurs when he tolerates anxiety and accepts that he may end up using the wrong task strategies and order of task operations. Noam agrees to exposure exercises.

You and Noam develop a feasible exposure hierarchy (see figure 8). You both decide collaboratively to start the exercises in the middle of the difficulty levels (e.g., SUDs of 50). For this example, Noam will use a coin flip to select the order of two steps for programming part of a nonflagship software product. These steps are non-contingent so they can occur in either order to complete the task, but the optimal order is unclear. This exercise requires Noam to abandon his goal of optimizing the order of operations. He is asked to abstain from using the Internet to make an informed decision. Instead, he must rely entirely on chance and accept responsibility for the outcome of his probability-based process.

While he is completing these exposure exercises, you encourage Noam to decrease his safety behaviors more generally during the day. This includes reducing time spent researching on the Internet, seeking reassurance from others in the workplace or online, and making lists. In fact, I would ask Noam to eliminate list-making behavior altogether if he is able and willing to do so. In this age, most of us need to use the Internet to complete our jobs, but you don't need to make lists. Leave it to Santa and the assassins.

Standard Operating Procedures are Complicated

There is no way to avoid the topic of planning and optimizing processes in the workplace. These are universal focuses in the world of work. In some organizations, there is a new or improved standard operating procedure (SOP) being paraded around the office everywhere you turn. The SOP concept exemplifies this focus on processes and probably originated with a perfectionist.

The SOP is a fantastic tool for the perfectionist employee, but it will be pure suffering for them to create it. On one hand, they can use a pre-established SOP to establish certainty; they are handed the "correct" path forward for completing a task. Even if the SOP characterizes a suboptimal strategy or order of operations, it doesn't matter. Why? The perfectionist's perception of control—and therefore their responsibility—is removed. They don't have to decide or plan anything. In that sense, it's equivalent to cooking with a recipe from a cookbook. You can just blame the SOP or recipe for being inefficient.

On the other hand, asking a perfectionist with process paralysis to create an SOP is tricky. They may love the idea of doing so—it leans heavily into the common value of *process optimization*—but it's a loaded request. Perfectionists struggle enough with establishing an ideal process for their own tasks. The struggle amplifies when the stakes are raised by asking them to create a process for universal adoption in the workplace.

Be careful with SOPs in the workplace when dealing with a perfectionist with process paralysis. For them, it can be helpful to use but a nightmare to create.

➤ Chapter Conclusion and Takeaways

This chapter characterized a presentation of perfectionism called *process paralysis*, which refers to getting stuck trying to plan a task perfectly. I provided strategies for mitigating process paralysis. Here are takeaway points:

- → The perfectionist with process paralysis may feel compelled to identify the optimal strategy for completing a task.
- → Process paralysis can also take the form of being preoccupied with identifying the perfect order of task steps.
- → Process paralysis often centers on a fear of not being efficient, which drives concerns about finding the best strategy and order of task steps.
- → It compels the perfectionist to engage in a variety of safety behaviors, such as excessive Internet research, reassurance seeking, and list-making.
- → Group-level strategies for combating process paralysis can include stimulus control, which involves creating a work environment that reduces the likelihood of getting triggered to complete safety behaviors.
- → Individual-level strategies focused on exposure exercises that promote the use of Emphasis B or C strategies to identify a plan and its order of steps.

Process paralysis can disrupt a workplace. When that workplace is a battlefield during war, as was the case for General Patton, lives are at stake. Many of us encounter process paralysis in our colleagues in less serious contexts. Regardless, strategies for mitigating the impact of process paralysis are the same in principle.

As General Patton indicated, don't get stuck on creating the perfect plan. A good plan is often good enough, and waiting for a perfect plan tomorrow may cost you the battle today *and* the war tomorrow.

CHAPTER 7

SMART ALEC: CONFOUNDING RULES AND PRINCIPLES

"Rules are not necessarily
sacred; principles are."[110]

FRANKLIN DELANO ROOSEVELT
32nd President of the United States

FDR SEEMED TO understand subtle distinctions between connected concepts that many people confound: *rules* and *principles*. I will add *values* to the focus of the chapter because they're critical to addressing perfectionism in the workplace, and they often get confused with rules and principles. All these terms are not interchangeable and need to be defined before we explain how they play out in the world of perfectionism.

Defining Our Terms

Rules, principles, and values can best be conceptualized as a pyramid. Figure 9 shows the layered nature of rules, principles, and values.

110 Peters and Woolley, "Franklin D. Roosevelt, Radio Address to the Young Democratic Clubs of America."

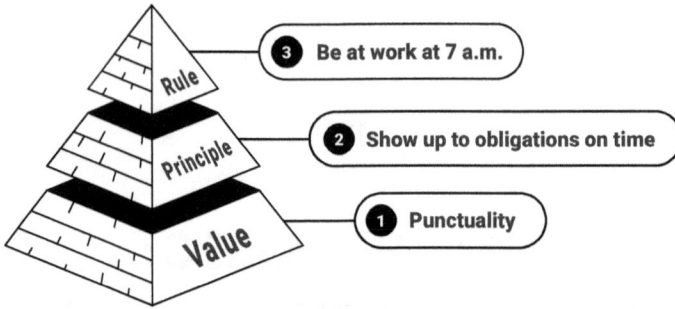

Figure 9: Rules vs. Principles vs. Values Pyramid

Rules are concrete and situation-specific, and they can be measured with certainty. You can determine whether they have been *met* or *not met* at the end state. On the pyramid, rules sit atop the principles upon which they're based.

Principles are abstract frameworks. They are less situation-specific and concrete than rules. You can pursue principles with fidelity, but they have no end state. They cannot be *met* or *not met*, just judged based on degrees of faith and trust. People can pursue a principle with more or less fidelity. Pursuing principles with fidelity provides evidence for your core values. On the pyramid, principles sit atop the values upon which they're based.

Values are even less measurable and tangible than principles. Values are best conceptualized as a broad compass; they provide a global direction of pursuit. They span multiple situations. On the pyramid, they represent the spanning foundation that braces principles and rules.

This is all a bit vague, so let's consider a real-world example.

→ *Arrive to work by 7 a.m.* is the rule;
→ *Being on time to events and obligations* is the principle;

→ *Punctuality* is the value.

With respect to the rule, you can achieve being at work by 7 a.m. It's measurable and concrete. At the end of the day, you can check a box that says "met" or "not met." There is little room for debate. *Being on time to events and obligations* and *punctuality*—as the associated principle and value, respectively—aren't so concrete.

The behavioral framework for being on time to events and obligations establishes broad guidelines, such as showing up at a pre-arranged time, leaving early if it's rush hour, and communicating and apologizing if you're late. All these guidelines reflect a core value of punctuality. You can, over time, behave in a way that aligns with the principle of being on time to events and obligations and the value of punctuality, but no single behavior or moment definitively achieves the principle or value.

Fidelity is demonstrated through long-term averages of behavior. For example, you can say, on average, that you meet the rules that stem from the principle of being on time to events and obligations. You show up to work on time generally, you're rarely late to meetings, and you've seldom been scolded for being tardy and disrespectful. Across the mosaic of evidence, you align with your value of punctuality and its inherent principle of being on time to events and obligations.

This relationship between the pyramid terms has parallels in other areas of life. For organizational leadership, the relationship between values, principles, and rules is somewhat akin to the relationship between the company's values, vision, and policy, respectively. For scientists, values, principles, and rules resemble theory, models, and hypotheses, respectively. For movie buffs and fiction authors, the terms are like the genre, story, and plot, respectively. The relation between morals, ethics, and laws is similar.

Confusion of Terms in Perfectionism

Perfectionism is associated with rigid adherence to excessive and unreasonable expectations, but this problematic presentation is worsened by the perfectionist's confounding of rules and principles.

This causes two primary yet seemingly contradictory issues when working with a perfectionist. First, they often rely heavily on rules and miss the principles or values driving the rules altogether. I refer to this as a *hyperfocus on rules at the expense of principles and values.*

Second, when the perfectionist considers values and principles, they treat them as if they were rules—rigidly and with concrete adherence and unreasonable expectations. More specifically, the rules present typically in the form of goals. For example, a perfectionist salesperson might interpret their job duty as a rule. They might say to themselves, *Your job is to sell, so make this sale.* This self-statement meshes a rule and a goal. If you add, *by rule,* to the beginning of the statement—which is often how a perfectionist interprets their job duties—it becomes more obvious: *By rule, your job is to sell, so make this sale.* The *make this sale* part of the sentence is a self-directive to meet a specific goal. Conversely, the nonperfectionist interprets their job duties more as principles and values, not as rules. I refer to this perfectionistic tendency as *treating principles like rules.*

Let's break down these issues separately. Each amplifies the negative effects of perfectionism in the workplace, specifically when it comes to productivity and workplace culture. Both require slightly different approaches for organizational leadership.

Hyperfocus on Rules at the Expense of Principles. A narrow, rigid, and concrete focus exemplifies perfectionism, and the overreliance on rules is an excellent example of this in action. It's also like the local processing tendency. Zooming in on rules and missing the principles and values is akin to processing at the rule level locally and minimizing the holistic elements (i.e., principles and values).

In an earlier chapter, I provided an example of a cognitive bias and how easy it is to make an incorrect assumption. The scenario included a speeding driver who was rushing their spouse to the hospital. Let's extend this example to illustrate how a perfectionistic overreliance on rules—in a narrow, rigid, and concrete way—may play out in this scenario. Imagine a perfectionistic police officer starts chasing the speeding car and finally catches up when they pull over at the emergency department. The speeding car parks in a disabled parking spot near the emergency room entrance, but it doesn't have a disabled placard. Once the police officer notices the husband rushing his wife into the hospital, the officer infers that the car was rushing because the wife was having a medical emergency.

The police officer could handle this in a rigid rule-bound way, a flexible principle-based way, or somewhere between those two extremes. Let's set aside the idea that the officer's reaction may depend on momentary variables such as whether they had coffee in the morning, or were chastised yesterday by the police chief for being too lenient on traffic violations. At the extreme rule-bound end of the continuum, the officer could get stuck on the notion that the husband violated state law and regulation (i.e., rules), such as speeding. Speeding laws exist for a reason—they are built to ensure public safety (i.e., value) in which reckless driving is unacceptable (i.e., principle). At this point, the rule-focused officer could stop the husband and his ailing wife before entering the hospital, cite them for speeding, tow the car for parking illegally, and possibly arrest the husband for reckless driving.

On the other end of the continuum, the officer could act in a way that shows fidelity to a principle focused on minimizing individual suffering and harm—the wife needed emergency medical attention. In this scenario, the officer would ignore any violated laws and weigh the pros and cons of aligning with this principle (i.e., minimizing individual suffering and harm) at the cost of a value (i.e., public safety). If the officer elects to align with the principle of minimizing individual suffering and harm, they might help the husband transport the wife into the hospital and let the husband go without penalty or warnings. They may even move the husband's car so that it's not towed and ticketed by a different officer.

A perfectionistic police officer in that scenario probably wouldn't react as extremely as arresting the husband for reckless driving, but it wouldn't be outside the scope of believability if they first help the husband transport the wife into the hospital to ensure expeditious medical attention but then, after the situation settles down, meet with the husband and hand him a traffic citation and report that his car has been towed.[111] This would be an example of adhering rigidly to rules, albeit with some flexibility for balancing the value of public safety with the principle of minimizing suffering and harm.

The extreme examples of officer reactions in this scenario might seem ludicrous, but they're meant to illustrate a point about individual differences in rule-based and principle-based responding across contexts. Perfectionism is a dimension. The officer's actual reaction to this scenario would likely fall somewhere between these two extreme

---

111 This example is inspired by a true story. While driving, I was hit by another car and then handed a ticket by a police officer for a traffic violation because my inoperable vehicle was blocking the flow of traffic. Apparently, "it's the law," according to the officer.

versions. Any perfectionistic tendencies likely tip the officer's actions more toward rule-driven behavior.

For further clarification, it helps to consider a slight adjustment to the scenario. Imagine if the husband struck a pedestrian with his car near the hospital entrance and caused major injury. In this scenario, the calculus changes for balancing public safety with individual suffering and harm, so more severe penalties for the husband seem inevitable—and less ridiculous—than in the original scenario. This harsher punishment seems rational, but the main difference between the original and adjusted scenario is that, in the original, the husband was lucky and avoided one of the key negative outcomes (i.e., hurting a pedestrian due to reckless driving) that the laws were designed to prevent (i.e., public harm). It's a bit like saying that if the husband were let off easy in the original scenario, it's because he just didn't get caught—in this case, *getting caught* means hurting a member of the public.

It's not much of a leap from the officer example to see how a hyperfocus on rules can obstruct work productivity and harm workplace culture. Perfectionistic employees who become stuck on rules at the expense of principles often get lost in the details of their work and miss the big picture. Often, they are terrific at ensuring your project is compliant with all formatting requirements and other rules—if they avoid paralysis from perfectionism—but they're less helpful for brainstorming the project's strategy, purpose, process, or structure.

Let's consider the example of a perfectionistic hiring manager. In this case, their primary job duty involves reviewing candidates for job openings. Imagine they're tasked with sifting through dozens of résumés and inviting promising candidates for in-person interviews. A rules-bound hiring manager might tackle their job duty by weeding out candidates based on rule violations rather than principles and values. For instance, they might dismiss a candidate because the résumé had a typographical error. It's easy for the hiring manager to justify this type of rejection: *If the candidate isn't attentive to correcting typos in their application, they'll probably be careless when they're an employee.* It's a fair point, but it places a huge weight on rules and prioritizes the value of *conscientiousness.* There is nothing inherently wrong with respecting rules and valuing conscientiousness,[112] but eliminating candidates for those reasons only makes sense if (a) conscientiousness is a top organizational value, or (b) the applicant doesn't align with more important organizational values. This assumes all other variables are equal (e.g., qualifications).

Treating Principles Like Rules. The perfectionistic employee holds rigid and unreasonable expectations, which is challenging enough, but the problem is intensified by the fact that those expectations often reflect principles, not rules. Expectations work when they are expressed as goals that are defined as rules, not principles and values. Appropriate goals are concrete and measurable. They can be achieved, much like rules can be met. This is not true for principles and values. For these, you can only demonstrate degrees of fidelity to the principle.

How does it look when a perfectionist treats principles like rules? Let's go back to our example of the police officer chasing a speeding car. Imagine the other perspective for a moment. What if the husband is perfectionistic and has been working toward a "goal"[113] of being

---

112 In fact, conscientiousness is a strong predictor of success across contexts.

113 I put the word *goal* in quotes here and in subsequent sentences because it's not really a goal. It's worded as a principle or value.

a more attentive husband? This is problematic because *being a more attentive husband* isn't a rule; it's a principle. You can't achieve being an attentive husband. You can just show degrees of fidelity to the goal.

When goals are based on principles instead of rules, there is no obvious method for determining if they've been achieved. By default, then, perfectionists exhibit a common all-or-none bias to believe that they must abide by the principle at all times, or else they've failed. This creates a situation in which goals become virtually unachievable.

In this example, if the husband is perfectionistic, he might discount his heroic behavior of speeding his wife to the hospital in the context of a medical emergency. Instead, he may focus on the fact that he ignored her distress for 10 minutes and thought she was exaggerating her pain. From an all-or-none perspective, the husband believes he has not always been an attentive husband. His "goal" of being a more attentive husband has not been met. This "goal," however, is based on a principle and not a rule, and therefore it's problematic.

Even then it's not that simple. If all rules for being an attentive husband have been met for the last week, the husband still would likely dismiss the claim that he's met his "goal." This is because a "goal" of being a more attentive husband has no deadline. As principles go, there is no endpoint to achieve this husband-state. There's always more you can do to align with that principle. A principle masquerading as a goal will trigger an endless and futile pursuit. You'll never achieve the concrete outcome of this type of "goal," because it doesn't exist.

You can swap out the husband example to see how this could play out in the workplace. Imagine a perfectionistic employee who seems joyless and believes they're undeserving after receiving the *Employee of the Month* award (perhaps accompanied by a handsome blue ribbon). What is the reason for the discontent and belief of being unworthy? They didn't meet their sales goal during the month. The employee believes their "goal" of success has not been met, but *success* is not a goal in this case. Instead, it's a value. Nobody—including the employee—can meet that "goal" because it has no endpoint or clear criteria for declaring it an achievement. Efforts therefore will seem endless and futile.

Case Illustration: Alec

The following case example of perfectionism in the workplace serves to demonstrate how confounding rules and principles causes issues in an occupational setting.

> Alec is a top performing attorney at a prestigious law firm. He has a reputation for being a perfectionist. He zooms in on the details of law and regulation and, based on industry standards, boasts an excellent record of good outcomes for his cases. His track record for success is mostly due to what his colleagues call "Alec's superpower" for taking advantage of obscure legal details to win via technicalities.
>
> When Alec's colleagues refer to his superpower, it might seem flattering, but it's a back-handed compliment. They recognize his skillset but have tremendous difficulty getting along with him. He comes off as condescending when discussing his rule-driven legal argument, seems to invalidate his peers by undervaluing their principle-based and more holistic arguments, and slows down the team because of his methodical approaches. Alec doesn't intend to come across

this way to his peers, but he becomes fixated on the rules and doesn't notice his impact on others.

The partners of the firm have noted Alec's successful performance, nonetheless. They've assigned him to work on important cases that benefit from a detail-oriented attorney who has a knack for identifying obscure technicalities and procedural errors by the prosecutors or law enforcement. They strategically leverage his skillset.

Though, they rarely assign Alec to serve as lead attorney on cases and have eliminated most of his client-facing duties, despite his junior colleagues receiving ample opportunities for both. Why? First, the partners are confident in his ability to locate detail-oriented evidence to support a case, but they are concerned about his ability to zoom out, see the big picture of the case, and make a compelling legal argument at the holistic level. Clients have noticed this problematic tendency and complained about it to the partners. Second, they have concerns about his efficiency. Alec gets so lost in the details that it requires excessive time for him to complete his work—a luxury that most cases can't afford. Third, Alec has difficulty getting along with his colleagues because he struggles to integrate his work and legal arguments with those of the other firm attorneys on the case.

Despite their concerns, the partners don't want Alec to quit the firm. They see tremendous value in his skillset, believe he can fill a critical niche for them, and therefore strategically extend the offer for him to become a partner of the firm. When they offer the partnership, Alec shows no signs of excitement or pride and instead looks surprised. He declines the offer for becoming a partner on the spot, much to everyone's surprise.

When the partners ask Alec if he's unhappy at the firm and plans to quit, he assures them that he has no intention to leave and plans to stay in this job for the long haul. They ask for clarification—why didn't he accept the offer? Alec asserts that his work performance doesn't warrant a partnership title and its recognition. He rattles off recent examples of his inability to find sufficient evidence to support his cases. He highlights instances in which he merely mitigated his client's penalties instead of finding ways to dismiss the cases altogether.

News of Alec's decision spreads quickly throughout the workplace. His coworkers are confused and start to think he's ungrateful, unambitious, and peculiar.

Although it wasn't his intention, Alec has soured the workplace atmosphere.

Alec's Confounding of Rules and Principles

Earlier in the chapter, I introduced two ways that perfectionists tend to confound rules and principles: (a) hyperfocus on rules, and (b) treating principles like rules. Alec demonstrates evidence for both tendencies, which have detrimental effects on company culture, as well as his work performance and career advancement. It's important to acknowledge, however, that the case also depicts ways in which perfectionism has resulted in some of Alec's successes. Again, nuking the fly works… but it's proven costly to do so.

Alec's Hyperfocus on Rules. The hyperfocus might seem like a "super-power" to his colleagues, but it's also a supervulnerability. Yes, it helps him locate highly obscure details in the law to win his cases, and yes, this is critical for the niche that he fills. The problem, however, is that his approach to cases is so narrow that it results in missed opportunities for big-picture legal arguments and holistic case strategy. Some cases can't be won via a technicality. Alec's superpowers aren't always needed. It's like Aquaman on the moon.

Superpowers notwithstanding, just like when you nuke the fly, Alec's rule-bound tendencies come with considerable collateral damage. Based on the description, Alec is disrupting team dynamics in the workplace via other-oriented perfectionism. His colleagues struggle to work with him because of the way he pushes his rule-bound ideas, invalidates their big-picture approaches, and slows down processes. The disruption in team dynamics disturbs the workplace culture and erodes employee satisfaction.

You might wonder if his tendencies are worth it. After all, his contributions have helped win cases, to the extent that he's been offered a partnership at the firm. Consistent with the themes of this book, however, I believe the partners don't see—or they tend to underappreciate—the negative impact that Alec has on the organizational climate. It's not far-fetched to believe employees have left the firm, in part, because of Alec's interpersonal style and hyperfocus on rules. Based on his restricted client-facing work, Alec's approach has probably repelled potential clients.

Whether Alec's tendencies are worth it to the firm will be dependent on whether the partners can find an alternative means for replacing his level of success with fewer organizational costs, such as loss of human capital.

Alec Treats Principles Like Rules. Much like the previous example of the salesperson not finding success in the *Employee of the Month* award, Alec struggles to accept his successes. In fact, not only does he dismiss the success, but he also punishes himself for his performance by declining the partnership offer. This kind of self-flagellation is common in perfectionism.

Self-punishing behavior disrupts the workplace culture profoundly. It's akin to visualizing the Opus Dei antagonist—Silas— in Dan Brown's *The Da Vinci Code*. Silas whips himself as part of corporal mortification. Alec is the Silas of the office (albeit less violent). It's demoralizing to watch a coworker, who is successful by most industry metrics, whip themselves for not doing enough nor being perfect. Everyone starts to question their worth.

Alec misjudges his value to the firm. It's based on his warped perfectionistic definition of success. He interprets his overall job purpose— to help the firm win cases—as a set of rigid rules, and meeting those rules reflects the primary method of deciding his value. Alec perceives winning cases as the only measure of success. Winning cases is certainly an important metric, but he has an all-or-none bias when interpreting his record. Alec has a goal of winning every case, and he considers himself a failure if he falls short of this outcome in any way.

By most standards in his industry, Alec is demonstrating high fidelity with the value of success. How do I know this? His bosses offered him a promotion for his contributions. He has an uncanny knack for identifying technicalities to win a large proportion of cases.

Everyone other than Alec seems to see his occupational value, but because he treats success like a rule, his pursuit succumbs to all the pitfalls of this tendency. There's no endpoint to his "goal," and winning every case is infeasible. For this reason, his "goal" can never be accomplished. His efforts therefore will be experienced as endless and futile. He can't—and won't—claim success from his work because that conclusion is never 100% certain. Though, he'll whip himself for not meeting the "goal."

Group-Level Solutions for the Perfectionistic Confounding of Rules and Principles

Managers and other business leaders are in an ideal position to influence the climate of an organization. They have opportunities to address a systemic tendency to confound rules and principles. You can identify and recommend changes to any language, behavior, and expectations that fall into this trap.

Similar to group-level solutions for a dysfunctional Emphasis Framework, there are varied top-down solutions for the tendency to confound these concepts, noted below.

→ The employee handbook and new hire orientation can define, and provide examples of, organizational principles and values. These terms can be contrasted with the definition of rules explicitly. Show the pyramid nature of values, principles, and rules using content relevant to your organization.

→ Principles and values can be headlined as part of the organization's identity messaging, such as with the vision, mission, and values statements. This can be done on websites, public relations material, and other public- and employee-facing communication.

→ You can serve as a powerful model. Demonstrate to your employees how to catch and adjust when rules are being confounded with principles. This can be done publicly to the group and privately with specific employees.

→ During annual reviews, provide employees with feedback on their ability to differentiate rules, principles, and values. This feedback can serve as an independent item on the review form. This sends a strong message about the importance of this distinction.

→ Provide training on effective goal setting, discussed later in the chapter.

→ These group-level suggestions aren't tailored for the two different ways in which confounding of terms causes issues in the workplace (i.e., hyperfocus on rules and treating principles like rules). You can differentiate these two issues meaningfully and create top-down approaches for each. For example, when discussing the confounding of rules with principles in a new hire orientation or in the employee handbook, you can describe the two issues independently and provide specific examples for both.

What does a top-down, group-level approach look like for addressing these tendencies? I would recommend being explicit. For example, your employee handbook can include an entire section or subsection devoted to explaining the definitions of values, principles, and rules, as well as their relationships. If it's appropriate for your workplace setting, feel free to adopt some of the language I've provided below.

Employee handbook example of defining terms:

Rules are concrete and situation specific. You can measure them with certainty. You can determine whether they have been met or not met at the end. Example of a rule: Arrive to work on Tuesday by 7 a.m.

Principles are abstract frameworks that serve as the foundation for rules. They are less situation-specific and concrete than rules. You can pursue principles with more or less fidelity, but they have no end state. You cannot meet a principle. Example of a principle: Being on time to events and obligations.

Values are even less measurable and concrete but serve as the foundation for principles. Values are best conceptualized as a broad compass direction. They provide a global direction of pursuit and span multiple situations and areas of the workplace. Example of a value: Punctuality.

You can also provide some language to emphasize the importance of not confounding rules and principles. This also can be provided explicitly. To that end, it makes sense to break down the two different issues that arise with perfectionism.

Employee handbook example for hyperfocusing on rules:

Here at Sham Title LLC,[114] we emphasize values, principles, and rules. All three work together to help us create an inviting, predictable, and fair workplace. Sometimes employees get stuck on rules at the expense of principles and values. For example, please don't get paralyzed writing internal emails. We appreciate timely responses to email communication, even if we spot an occasional typo or grammatical error. Although the rules of grammar are important, we don't want them to undermine our core organizational values of communication and efficiency.

114 This would be a fun, prankish name for a title company.

Employee handbook example for treating principles like rules:

> *Sometimes employees feel stressed or demoralized at work because of poorly designed goals. Goals are most useful when they are concrete. They have a deadline, and you can tell whether they have been met. For example, it's a strong goal to say, "I will be on time to work every day next week." This can be answered with a definitive "yes" or "no." On the other hand, it's problematic when a principle is used as a goal, such as saying, "I will be punctual." This type of goal is unclear and endless. Its outcome of "yes" or "no" can be argued depending on who is defining "punctual." Also, there is no end point to signal when it's time to determine if the goal has been met.*

There are many ways to send your workers a message about the confounding of rules with principles. I recommend finding multiple methods and situations to convey this message. Repetition is key. You don't want employees working toward vague and impossible goals. It's a recipe for frustration and demoralization in your company climate. In some instances, such as with Alec, it can also elicit self-destructive behavior that lowers the mood of the workplace even more. You can reduce negative effects from this perfectionistic tendency from the top down.

Employee-Level Solutions for the Perfectionistic Confounding of Rules with Principles

Gather Details about Self-Awareness and Skills. You can assist specific employees who tend to mix up rules, principles, and values. You would benefit from a careful evaluation of your employee's tendencies.

It helps to determine how often the employee confounds these terms, as well as the impact the confounding causes on the workplace.

I also would recommend evaluating the perfectionist's level of insight into their tendency to confound rules and principles. If you find that your perfectionistic employee lacks self-awareness, you will need to spend extra time providing education, gently challenging misunderstandings, and nudging them toward growth. This is often a slow process and patience is critical.

Individual-Level Strategies for Hyperfocus on Rules. Education is a key component in helping employees at the individual level. If the top-down approaches to influencing the organizational culture have been insufficient for reducing or eliminating an employee's tendency to confound rules and principles, it may be time to teach them individually and directly. In a sense, it's much like correcting a skill deficit, but in this case, it's a knowledge deficit.

For employees who hyperfocus on rules, instruct them on the nature and consequences of doing so and how it creates barriers to seeing the big picture. Drawing from the employee's history of behavior and work output, highlight examples of this hyperfocus and its consequences. Use upcoming tasks as a vehicle for modeling a healthier balance of rules, principles, and values. Offer scaffolding to help the employee plan for a future task and provide gentle feedback if they continue to exhibit an overemphasis on rules and details in lieu of the principles and big picture, respectively.

If the employee struggles to grasp the problem, you can provide a quick overview of a phenomenon called the Simpson's paradox to show why focusing on the details and rules at the expense of the big picture is so problematic. This paradox is a statistical concept in which the relationship between two variables changes drastically (e.g., reverses direction or nullifies) once a third variable is entered into the mix.[115] The Simpson's paradox symbolizes why statistics can be misleading if they're not contextualized properly.

Let's consider a plausible Simpson's paradox in Alec's case to illustrate how it can muddle goals and their interpretation. If you recall, Alec interprets his imperfect win/loss record as evidence of not being successful. Sometimes it's tempting to agree with him in these moments because win/loss records seem so cut and dry when it comes to metrics. It's not that simple.

Please examine figure 10 closely to see a visual depiction of the Simpson's paradox.

The first table shows a direct comparison of wins and losses for Alec versus an average peer, whom we will call Deidre. Let's characterize Deidre as another attorney at the same professional level as Alec. She's good at her job but not a perfectionist. If we had data on case wins and losses for each of them, it could be used for drawing some inferences about their value as employees. But this is not so easy; data can be deceiving.

You can see that Alec looks less successful compared to Deidre in this context. It's easy to see how Alec could interpret himself as not meeting a "goal" of success.

If we add more context to the data, you can see how the pattern—and therefore the interpretation—can shift dramatically. Look at the second table in figure 10, which provides the same data but with one extra variable included in the breakdown: *complexity of the case.*

115 Simpson, "The Interpretation of Interaction in Contingency Tables."

Alec   Deidre

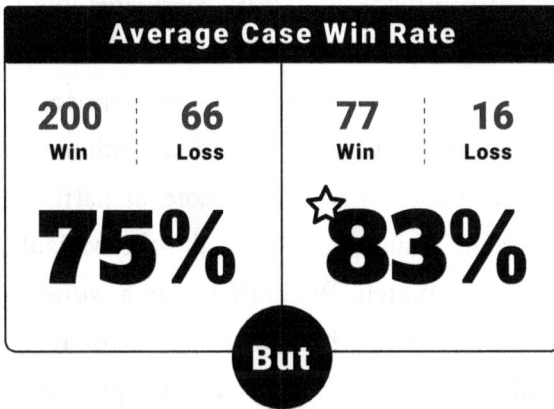

Average Case Win Rate			
200 Win	**66** Loss	**77** Win	**16** Loss
75%		**83%**	

But

Things change when considering case complexity

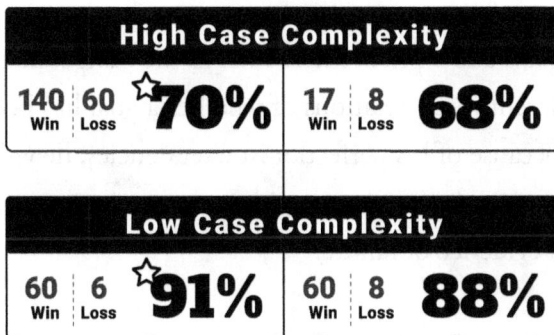

High Case Complexity			
140 Win : **60** Loss	**70%**	**17** Win : **8** Loss	**68%**

Low Case Complexity			
60 Win : **6** Loss	**91%**	**60** Win : **8** Loss	**88%**

Figure 10: Simpson's Paradox Using Alec's Case as an Example

If you analyze the data for Alec and Deidre by complexity level (i.e., high vs. low complexity), you will see how Alec's pattern changes. The new context suggests a much different interpretation—Alec rocks his cases.

So, the context matters for interpreting Alec's win/loss record. His record is far more impressive when you consider the degree of case complexity. On the other hand, his record is less impressive—Alec might even suggest unsuccessful—if it's considered in a context that ignores case complexity. This pattern reversal is an example of the Simpson's paradox. Ultimately, it's problematic to treat an isolated win/loss record as support for a value such as success without more context.

Sure, Alec can use his win/loss record as partial evidence of fidelity to the value of success, holding all other variables constant. That's the problem, though. We don't live in a world in which all other variables are constant. Principles and values are abstract and subjectively defined, and the world is a messy place with countless variables. The world's messiness confuses our ability to draw confident conclusions about vague goals that are defined entirely by principles and values.

Fuzzy goals allow phenomena such as the Simpson's paradox to result in different interpretations of whether a goal has been met. In Alec's case, because of his perfectionistic tendencies, he will interpret the goal's outcome in a narrow, rigid, and negative way. He will see his record as evidence of failure.

Individual-Level Strategies for Treating Principles Like Rules. I would recommend a similar educational approach for employees who treat principles like rules. This will require pointing out how the employee pursues goals defined by principles rather than rules and highlighting why that's a problem. You can draw from the employee's real examples or from your own experience.

This inevitably will lead to discussions of more effective goal setting. For this, I stick to the tried-and-true method characterized by the *SMART* acronym. For those unfamiliar, SMART stands for *Specific, Measurable, Achievable, Relevant*, and *Timed*.[116]

These each represent a key characteristic of effective goals. *Specific* refers to goals that include a precise behavioral target (e.g., *arrive on time to work*). *Measurable* implies that the outcomes are definitive—there is a clear way of stating that the goal has been met or not met (e.g., arrived on time to work at 7 a.m. *each business day*). *Achievable* pertains to whether the goal is reasonable and not excessive (e.g., the goal doesn't require arriving on time to work at precisely 7 a.m. and 36 seconds each business day). *Relevant* connects to values—does the goal make sense for what's important to you and your pursuits? If not, it's a suspect goal. *Timed* sets the deadline (e.g., arrive on time to work each business day *during the business week of December 5th*).

Using a SMART strategy, Alec can revise a vague "goal" that's problematically based on a principle or value instead of rules. This will ensure the goal is more effective. "Being successful" is a great value, but it's a terrible goal. As stated, it's undefined, abstract, endless, and unattainable. A SMART tweak could make a big difference by providing more concrete rules for success. Doing so—and combining it with multiple goals—can provide an array of evidence to support fidelity to a principle and value.

Alec could implement SMART goals. For example, he could create a SMART goal such as, "Read and take notes on the six

116 Sometimes the letter meanings differ across sources; for example, *Attainable* instead of *Achievable* or *Small* instead of *Specific*. The principles are usually similar regardless of labels.

assigned case studies from 1980 to 1990 by the end of the business day on Friday, December 2nd." The wording seems reasonable, but let's examine it more closely.

Does it check off the SMART list of characteristics? Is it specific? Check—the task behavior is well defined as "read and take notes on the six assigned case studies." Is it measurable? Check—you can answer at the end whether Alec has read and taken notes on the assigned case studies. Is it achievable? Check—this seems reasonable, although this criterion is less clear because we don't know about the scope of the case studies, nor whether this is an industry-standard workload. Is it relevant? Check—let's presume this task aligns with Alec's professional values and goals. Is it Timed? Check—the goal states an end date of "by the end of the business day on Friday, December 2nd." All SMART criteria seem to be met.

➡ Chapter Conclusion and Takeaways

This chapter delved into the concepts of rules, principles, and values. These terms are confounded much of the time, especially by those with perfectionistic tendencies. I also provided some tips for how to deal with this confounding of terms. Here are some takeaway points:

- → Rules are built on principles, which are built on values.
- → Rules are concrete and context specific. You can determine with certainty that they have been met.
- → Principles and values are less context specific and concrete. They cannot be met, per se, but you can show degrees of fidelity to them.
- → Perfectionists tend to hyperfocus on rules at the expense of principles and values. This causes them to miss the big picture.
- → They also treat principles like rules, which results in a futile attempt to "meet" principles, which is not possible.
- → Group-level strategies for mitigating the confounding of rules, principles, and values include educating the employees and establishing a workplace culture that applies the terms in an appropriate and consistent way.
- → A primary individual-level strategy for this issue of confounding terms involves adopting SMART goals.

History remembers President Franklin Roosevelt for a host of reasons. His legacy is replete with famous stories and quotes. Perhaps lost in the depths of his legacy, however, was his belief about rules versus principles. His quote at the outset of the chapter noted that principles are "sacred," unlike rules. I somewhat disagree with FDR.[117] Rules aren't a problem, per se; they can be "sacred" in the right context. Instead, I think the problem is that rules and principles are being confounded and, as a result, principles are often overlooked or deemphasized in favor of a rule. This is exactly what happens with perfectionism.

117 Kudos to the readers who had *Author brazenly argues with a dead but celebrated US president* on their bingo card.

CHAPTER 8

SHOULDING ALL OVER THE OFFICE: COGNITIVE RIGIDITY

"Intelligence is traditionally viewed as
the ability to think and learn. Yet in
a turbulent world, there's another set of
cognitive skills that might matter more:
the ability to rethink and unlearn."[118]

ADAM GRANT
Author, Organizational Psychologist

THE QUOTE ABOVE from Dr. Adam Grant sums up the importance of what he refers to as "mental flexibility" and what I've labeled "cognitive flexibility."

Much of Grant's book, *Think Again*,[119] approaches this subject with rich anecdotes, discussion of research, and thought-provoking commentary. This chapter is not meant to rehash the topic but complement it from an angle of perfectionism.

---

118 Grant, *Think Again: The Power of Knowing What You Don't Know.*
119 Grant.

Indeed, perfectionism is the extreme version of what Grant is rallying against in his book: cognitive rigidity.

The opposite of rigidity, cognitive flexibility is a critical ingredient that separates *perfectionism* from *pursuing perfection*. *Pursuing* and *Striving* and *Going* are not static states. They imply a journey, a process. You can embrace the benefits of shooting for perfection even if you miss the mark.

Doing so is what's called an *overcorrection*. This indicates that the agent in the process understands that perfection is unattainable, but they shoot for it anyway because doing so will catapult them well beyond *good*. This is akin to the aphorism: "Shoot for the moon. Even if you miss, you'll land among the stars."

This is all to say that pursuing perfection is not inherently problematic. Workplace culture can integrate messaging about pursuing perfection, but the details of that messaging matter greatly. Talk of perfection in the workplace needs to coincide with messaging that promotes flexible thinking.

Rigidity destroys any nuanced thinking about the world. A perfectionist who achieves the grade of an A instead of an A+ perceives that performance as falling into the category of *Failed*. A more flexible thinker appreciates the proximity of their grade to the highest mark possible. It's not a categorical judgment or binary outcome.

The nonperfectionist would prefer an A+ and they might even be disappointed with the A grade, but the main difference for the flexible thinker is that it's not perceived so categorically as a failure. They can still take pride and contentment in having a strong grade. Both contrasting states can be held in mind simultaneously (i.e., some disappointment plus some pride/contentment). It's not so all-or-none.

Cognitive Rigidity Overview

As a reminder, cognitive rigidity is the tendency to fixate on a mindset, plus difficulty with shifting from that mindset when it's adaptive or reasonable to do so.[120] It's also called *set shifting ability* (i.e., as in, mind*set shifting*). It presents across a variety of contexts in the workplace and ultimately represents a failure to adapt in the moment to an ever-changing environment.

Cognitive rigidity can present throughout the workplace. It's reflected in your employee who can't change their behavior based on feedback; they keep making the same mistakes repeatedly. It explains your team member who can't transition to new agenda items during the meeting until it feels like the previous item has reached closure (i.e., *not just right experiences*). It's the coworker who is being signaled by others to speed up their presentation, but they feel compelled to cover all presentation material anyway, and in the "correct" order. They may put up a fuss about skipping ahead or become extremely anxious about doing so. It's the worker who lags behind when trying to get into a collective mindset of a new top-down strategy for enhancing sales.

Cognitive rigidity is usually to blame for any instance in which your workers struggle to adapt to meet immediate needs. They're on autopilot and can't switch direction. It's the Titanic that can't dodge the iceberg on time.

Much like perfectionism in general,[121] cognitive flexibility is a dimension.[122] Perfectionists are at the extreme end of rigidity. On

---

120 Diamond, "Executive Functions."

121 Broman-Fulks, Hill, and Green, "Is Perfectionism Categorical or Dimensional?"

122 This is an oversimplification. Cognitive flexibility is a multidimensional and complex construct. For the purpose of the point I'm making, however, this will suffice; see Morris and Mansell, "A Systematic Review of the Relationship between Rigidity/Flexibility and Transdiagnostic Cognitive and Behavioral Processes That Maintain Psychopathology."

the other end of the spectrum, you have individuals who are so flexible in their mindset that they may have a difficult time settling on a single strategy or belief and cannot "stay the course" in an adaptive fashion.

As you move toward the middle of the spectrum, where it's most adaptive, you find people who can "go with the flow." They can change strategies as needed to accommodate new information in the environment. All people fall somewhere on this continuum—they are better or worse at stopping the momentum of their mindset and changing trajectory.

Cognitive rigidity worsens all the perfectionism tendencies covered in this book. With respect to the Emphasis Framework, cognitive rigidity prevents the perfectionist from switching adaptively to Emphasis B when they become stuck on overdoing Emphasis A. Cognitive rigidity worsens the tendency to become paralyzed trying to optimize task processes and maximize efficiency; they get stuck on optimizing the process and struggle to shift focus and initiate the task. When a perfectionist hyperfocuses on rules at the expense of values and principles, they struggle to shift this mindset and zoom out to the big picture, even when it's adaptive. Perfectionists who treat principles like rules likewise struggle to pivot to a healthier perspective as needed.

Stubbornly Self-Sustaining

When considering the features of perfectionism, rigidity is the largest barrier to change. With rigidity, people are single-minded and have a difficult time shifting to a new frame of reference. By definition, any attempts to change a perfectionistic worldview will also be relatively stuck. Other ways that perfectionism wrecks the workplace—such as a dysfunctional Emphasis Framework—have solutions for change, such as shifting behavior and expectations. These solutions are undermined considerably by the perfectionistic inflexibility to leverage them for that change.

The primary message is that perfectionism interferes with the ability to change perfectionism. It's a stubbornly self-sustaining feature. In fact, cognitive rigidity may be the most harmful trait of perfectionism in your organization for this reason.

Stop *Should*ing All Over the Office

I should want a partner. I must lose weight. I ought to like this job. The should statement is the most toxic presentation of cognitive rigidity. If there's ever an appropriate use of *should*, it's that people should stop using *should*.[123]

The acknowledgement of harmful should statements is not new. In fact, there have been clever play-on-words to describe this tendency. The luminary psychologist, the late Albert Ellis, coined the risqué term *musterbation*,[124] which has been used to describe the rigid overuse of *must*, to dictate behavior. Similarly, author and psychologist Clayton Barbeau supposedly implored others to "stop *should*ing" themselves.[125]

Play on words notwithstanding, this perfectionistic tendency is quite serious and causes tremendous suffering. These should statements grow like a tumor and contaminate behavior and mood. They become a prison of unattainable dictates. Moreover, they often are built on faulty logic that confounds rules and principles—as discussed in chapter 7.

---

123 It's been a bucket list item of mine to use the same word three times justifiably in a short sentence. Done.

124 Ellis and Harper, *A Guide to Rational Living*.

125 I say "supposedly" only because I can't corroborate the origin of this play on words.

The individual with perfectionism treats all should statements like rules, even if they are principles and values. This is a problem. If you believe that you should be punctual (i.e., combining a should statement with a value), you will inevitably miss the mark. It's impossible to meet this should statement for two major reasons. First, it's not feasible to be on time in every instance. Life happens. Second, when do you make the final determination? At what point does the pursuit of this type of should statement end so that you can determine if it was met? Death? I guess it could be inscribed on your epitaph.[126]

Should statements also play a key role in the Emphasis Framework discussed in chapter 5. For example, an employee may exhibit the rigid belief that anything less than Emphasis A on tasks is unacceptable. Everything *must* receive an Emphasis A effort in their eyes. Should statements abound—for example, "I *should* be good at this job." When they cannot live up to that impossible goal, Emphasis A turns into a forced Emphasis C.

The should statement also plays out with process paralysis discussed in chapter 6. The main motivation for optimizing processes and maximizing efficiency is because the perfectionist believes they should be efficient and adopt the best processes to achieve efficiency. Though, because perfectionists confound rules and principles, this sounds like a goal, but it's not. It's a value (i.e., efficiency). More specifically, it's a value, wrapped up in a should statement, cosplaying as a "goal."

Should Statements and Moralism

As noted in chapter 2, other-oriented perfectionism is associated with a tendency for moralistic condemnation of others' behavior. This

---

126 Here lies Jonah. He achieved punctuality, depending on whom you ask.

moralism is often a symptom of should statements. For example, imagine if an other-oriented perfectionist scoffs self-righteously at a coworker who's running late. They may believe that the late coworker should be on time, should be respectful of others' time, should have managed their time better, and so on.

These moralistic should statements also incorporate elements of treating principles like rules, described in chapter 7. In this scenario, the perfectionist makes a self-righteous judgment about the coworker by treating a principle (i.e., arrive on time to places and events) as a rule. The moralistic judgment of the coworker is based on a single data point. The binary verdict is all-or-none; a common feature of cognitive rigidity. Yes, by running late, the coworker displays a lack of fidelity to the underlying principle, but because the perfectionist is treating the principle as a rule, the all-or-none judgment is overly damning and ignores countless other data points that may show the late coworker is punctual most of the time.

The moralistic behavior of an other-oriented perfectionist will come across to others as self-righteous. This will have an immense negative cascade effect in the workplace. The toxicity of moral judgments from the perfectionist will poison the organizational climate. This necessitates careful action from leadership, because the perfectionist's cognitive rigidity undermines workplace attempts at changing their rigid moral self-righteous mentality. More on other-oriented moralism is provided in the next chapter.

Cognitive Flexibility and Not Just Right Experiences (NJREs)

In chapter 2, I introduced you to the concept of *NJREs*, which refer to a gut feeling and set of beliefs signifying that something is "off."

Your action or product might not feel complete or perfect. This is an example of cognitive rigidity at play.

For perfectionists who get stuck with NJREs, they have a difficult time transitioning to the next activity, place, mindset, etc. They're waiting for a self-defined internal cue that signals it's okay to move forward, but the cue is ambiguous and uncertain to occur. It therefore keeps perfectionists stuck and unable to transition. A flexible employee can move to the next step without satisfying an internal need for it to feel *just right*.

Case Illustration: Libo

Consider the case of Libo, who works as an assistant manager of a large retail department store. The case illustrates cognitive rigidity and its impact on the workplace.

Libo was recently promoted to the assistant manager position after demonstrating dependability and a strong work ethic for the first six months of his employment. During those first six months, he always arrived on time, excelled at tasks required for opening and closing the store, and submitted the most comprehensive inventories of all staff. He was considered shy but friendly, deferential to the general manager, and quiet in team meetings. He interacted professionally with customers.

In his new role as an assistant manager, Libo provides oversight of the other store employees when he's on shift. This requires a much different set of responsibilities than what was required of him before the promotion. Libo seems to struggle with managerial skills.

After Libo's promotion, the general manager observes a new side of Libo that's unexpected. In this role, his interaction style with the staff is not as approachable as it was before the promotion. He seems notably unforgiving of employee mistakes. For example, he hands a written warning to one of his staff for being 20 minutes late to the shift, which might be reasonable in most circumstances, but in this case, the employee is late because of a flat tire. The staff member—who had never been tardy to a shift until this incident—is understandably upset by Libo's lack of accommodation and empathy. They complain to the general manager about Libo's behavior.

The general manager approaches Libo and asks why he was so strict with the staff member. Libo is not surprised and states: "It felt like it was extreme, but it says in the employee manual that being more than 10 minutes late results in a written warning."

The general manager acknowledges the rule but responds that extenuating circumstances—such as a flat tire—warrant some flexibility. Libo seems to understand.

Soon after this incident, Libo finds himself in another difficult situation. Corporate has handed down new policies and procedures to implement in the store. This includes a policy that requires all cashiers to proposition the customer with offers to join the department store's new rewards program. The policy contains instructions outlining what information needs to be conveyed to the customer as part of the cashier's pitch.

A few days after the new policies are launched, the general manager receives a complaint from an irate customer, who accuses Libo of pushing the reward programs too hard on them and not respecting their right to decline the offer. From the general manager's perspective, this seems out of character for Libo, who was characterized as unassuming before his promotion and didn't seem capable of strong-arming anyone.

The general manager approaches Libo and asks for clarification. Libo admits to feeling like his pitch of the rewards program to the customer was too forced. He attributes this forced approach to Corporate's guidelines for pitching effectively to customers, noting that he felt compelled to try all guidelines written in the policy before discontinuing his effort.

The general manager is flummoxed and doesn't understand how Libo failed to learn the lesson about flexibility from the earlier incident involving the tardy employee with the flat tire. The general manager advises Libo to be flexible with implementing Corporate's new policy, especially if the customer is sending strong signals to discontinue the rewards plan pitch. The general manager deeply regrets the decision to promote Libo to assistant manager and begins contemplating solutions that involve removing him.

Libo's Cognitive Rigidity

Libo's case exemplifies cognitive rigidity and how it plays out in a workplace. In this example, tendencies of perfectionism weren't apparent for many months after he was hired and working an entry-level position. Libo's perfectionism may have gone unnoticed during that time. Alternatively, perhaps the perfectionism was appraised by the general manager as an asset and helped impress everyone because the entry-level position was not sufficiently demanding and permitted excessive Emphasis A effort. Maybe Libo's performance didn't suffer because the demands of the position didn't trigger debilitating perfectionism.

It's clear, however, that Libo's perfectionism started to have a harmful impact once he was promoted to a managerial position, which required the use of untested skills for new demands. Examples of untested skills include applying policy flexibly, communicating with employees and customers appropriately, and appreciating principles versus rules. These skills were less critical for his entry-level position, but with his new managerial position, they're vital to workplace health and functioning.

The new demands of the managerial position have pulled back the curtain on Libo's shortcomings, which can be explained in large part by cognitive rigidity. With the employee who was written up for being tardy, Libo was unable to compromise to accommodate the extenuating circumstances—a flat tire. In this case, his thinking processes reflected the all-or-none bias. Libo perceived only two options: adhere to the policy; or do not adhere to the policy.

This all-or-none approach to policy adherence also demonstrates a hyperfocus on rules at the expense of the principles and values—discussed in chapter 7. Libo fixates on the rule of not showing up late to work—spelled out in the employee manual—and cannot appreciate the principle and value on which that rule is based: to prevent employees from showing up for work late without just cause. This reflects the core principle underlying the rule. The tardy employee with the flat tire was not showing a lack of fidelity to this principle; his cause was reasonable.

Libo abided by the policy in the employee manual religiously, even though he recognized that his reaction was extreme. This self-awareness is an important clue that he may not be exhibiting other-oriented perfectionism, specifically moralistic tendencies. His reactions seem more stuck on his own actions and being unable to flex his response to the environment. If instead this response reflected other-oriented perfectionism, there would be an indication that Libo was responding harshly because he believes employees *should* respect the rules, *should* be on time, *should* respect management, and so on. His response would be self-righteous, punitive, and designed to teach a lesson.

The situation with the irate customer also demonstrates Libo's cognitive rigidity. Libo's response to the customer demonstrates a lack of flexibility in two ways. First, as with the situation with the tardy employee, Libo adheres too rigidly to a policy, this time handed down from Corporate. He was unable to generalize the lesson about flexibility, apply it to a similar situation, and alter his response. This is a textbook example of cognitive rigidity—not being able to transfer lessons or skills from one context to another. It signifies that the perfectionist is stuck in a mindset and cannot adapt.

Second, Libo shows an inability to integrate the general manager's feedback. In response to the situation with the tardy employee with a flat tire, the general manager advised Libo to approach store policy with more flexibility. Based on the description of the scenario, Libo understood the advice but failed to implement any discretion. This also characterizes cognitive rigidity. As if driven by momentum, Libo is stuck and unable to change his behavior based on feedback.

Libo Embodies the Peter Principle

The Peter Principle was coined and described by the late Canadian educator Laurence Johnston Peter.[127] The eponymous Peter Principle describes the tendency for people to rise to the level of their incompetence. For example, an adept and valued Chief Technology Officer (CTO) might be offered the recently vacated Chief Executive Officer (CEO) position, perhaps based on an assumption that a CTO is a step down in the organizational chart from the CEO and therefore the obvious successor.

A CTO position doesn't necessarily require the same skillset as a CEO position. If the CTO is promoted and doesn't have the skills necessary for acting competently as the CEO, their shortcomings will become apparent and cause problems. According to the Peter Principle, you can claim that the CTO ascended to the level of their incompetence. They crashed through the ceiling of their ability, with the pieces falling down and damaging everything below.

In this case study, Libo embodies the principle. He was competent at his entry level position. As a result, he was promoted and therefore was given an opportunity to rise to a new level. Unfortunately, as was quickly discovered by the general manager, Libo didn't have the competencies to manage others and implement policy effectively.

127 Peter and Hull, *The Peter Principle.*

Often such incompetency can be corrected with training and support, but in Libo's case, it doesn't bode well. He struggled to integrate the general manager's feedback and generalize the lesson to a new but similar situation. His cognitive rigidity obstructed his performance, caused dissatisfaction in the workplace with his employees, angered a customer, and may have cost him his job.

Group-Level Solutions for Cognitive Rigidity

Cognitive rigidity is difficult to address at the group-level because its presentation is so unique to the individual experiencing it. Nonetheless, there are ways for managers to promote a flexible cognitive style in the workplace. Doing so will reduce the top-down signals that reinforce cognitive rigidity in your organizational climate to limit its effects.

Business leaders and managers have the chance to target systemic cognitive rigidity patterns in the workplace culture by communicating the value of cognitive flexibility via language, behavior, expectation, and reward; and there are many vehicles for meeting this goal. The employee handbook offers real estate for communicating the definition of cognitive flexibility, some examples, and its inherent value. As a complement to changes to your employee handbook, adding an item measuring cognitive flexibility in the annual employee reviews is an excellent way to convey its importance and strengthen its sustainability.

The same is true for the new hire orientation materials. The orientation could integrate some exercises for new hires to practice. This could leverage common workplace examples as vignettes or anecdotes to train new employees in identifying and altering cognitive rigidity.

Feel free to borrow some of the cognitive rigidity examples from Libo's case when building your example vignettes.

You can act as an authoritative model for demonstrating how to identify cognitive rigidity and use strategies for shifting mindsets more flexibly. This type of modeling can be done one-to-one in private with a rigid employee, or it can be carried out at the group-level in public. If you have strong rapport with, and have garnered respect from, your employees, this type of modeling can be a powerful tool for maximizing cognitive flexibility in your workplace.

One extreme approach could be adopted in your workplace, but it's a bit radical and needs some careful planning. If your workplace has a finite number of daily tasks as part of its routine, and if their completion is mostly non-contingent on order of operations (e.g., Task A doesn't need to be completed before Task B), you can have the tasks completed in a random order that has been determined at the outset of the workday. Let's call this the *random daily structure* technique.

Here's an example of adopting a random daily structure. Let's say part of your team's daily workplace routine involves (A) calculating product sales figures from the previous day, (B) reviewing and answering customer feedback, (C) conducting inventory, (D) depositing checks and cash at the bank, and (E) appraising advertising efforts. A random daily structure strategy would involve randomizing the daily order of Tasks A-E for the team. The randomization would occur at the beginning of the workday. Whatever order is determined via randomization is the order your team knocks out tasks for the day. See figure 11 for an example workweek.

Weekly Tasks

A Calculating product sales figures from the previous day

B Reviewing and answering customer feedback

C Conducting inventory

D Depositing checks and cash at the bank

E Appraising advertising efforts

No task contigencies

MON	TUE	WED	THU	FRI
C	D	B	C	E
A	C	E	E	A
B	A	D	D	B
E	B	C	A	D

Task A must occur before task D

MON	TUE	WED	THU	FRI
C	A	B	A	E
A	C	E	E	A
D	D	A	D	B
E	B	D	C	D

Task A must lead into task D

MON	TUE	WED	THU	FRI
A	B	B	A	E
D	C	E	D	C
B	A	A	E	A
E	D	D	C	D

Task A must occur first each day

MON	TUE	WED	THU	FRI
A	A	A	A	A
D	C	E	B	C
B	E	B	C	E
E	D	D	D	C

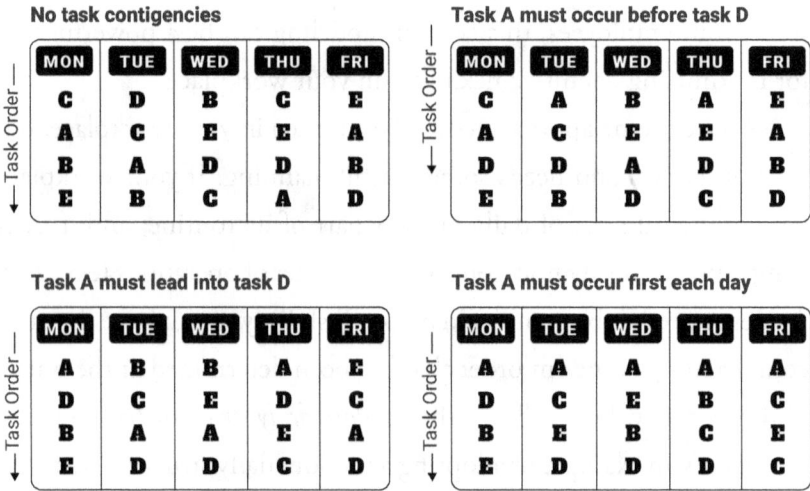

Figure 11: Example Workweek Schedules Using the Random Daily Structure Technique

For one of the examples, you may notice that Task A and Task D are always in the same order—Task A universally occurs before Task D. This was purposeful because you've determined that Task A is a necessary step before starting on Task D. You can randomize with this contingency in mind. Tasks can be sequentially paired (i.e., Task D immediately follows Task A in the order—no task in between). Alternatively, tasks can be paired but you can permit spacing (i.e., Task D always follows Task A, but there can be other tasks between them).

You can also randomize blocks of tasks. For example, perhaps you'd create a block of tasks for public-facing company needs (e.g., Tasks B and E) and another block for tasks to address the company's financial needs (e.g., Tasks A, C, and D). You can randomize the order of blocks in each day (e.g., On Monday the public-facing block goes before lunch and the financial block goes after lunch, but on Tuesday the order of blocks switches.)

This system has some flexibility, which is apropos of its function to reduce cognitive rigidity. You can randomize the order of blocks and tasks within blocks. You can add as many tasks and blocks as you need, and you can link tasks based on order contingencies (e.g., Task D must come before Task A). You could even create temporal blocks. For example, for an April fiscal year closing date, there could be an April month block that specifies order of April-specific tasks and blocks (e.g., budget and spending reconciliation tasks, tax filing tasks). The options seem endless.

Why does this work? Depending on the implementation strategy, it forces team members to adjust their daily routines to fit the randomization scheme. For some implementation approaches, the employee may not have a concrete answer to their daily tasks until it's handed to them after they fill their coffee mug in the morning. This requires flexible thinking and inevitable adaptation. It encourages your team members to sit with and accept unpredictability. It's difficult to stay rigid about daily structure when the daily structure is constantly in flux—on purpose.

Why did I describe the random daily structure as *radical*?

Other than it being unconventional, the strategy is a naturalistic exposure exercise at the group-level. It would require all members of your team to sit with the unpredictability of a randomly structured day. Unpredictability is highly anxiety-provoking for many people.[128] Humans crave routine; predictability is a potent anxiolytic. Fortunately, the *random daily structure* technique is not wholly unpredictable. It has predictable tasks and parameters. There's a finite universe of combinations for most days. Once the team members get used to the fluctuations in routine, the anxiety will largely dissipate but preserve the cognitive flexibility it evokes. It becomes predictable unpredictability.

Why did I specify that the strategy *needs some careful planning*?

Without careful planning, your daily routine will be confusing, frustrating, and ineffective. A leader needs to ensure that randomized task orders are appropriate (e.g., task contingencies addressed) and communicated clearly at predictable times. Here is where predictability is crucial. If it is not planned with care, the *random daily structure* approach turns into chaos—a nightmare for all involved. If done properly, however, it keeps employees on their toes, flexible and adaptive, and engaged.

Employee-Level Solutions for Cognitive Rigidity

Gather Details about Self-Awareness and Skills. As I've noted previously, you would benefit from a careful evaluation of your employee's perfectionistic tendencies. In this case, that means characterizing the perfectionist's cognitive rigidity, when it's most likely to express itself, and the damage it causes to the workplace. I would also recommend evaluating whether NJREs are playing a role in the cognitive rigidity.

---

128 I bet many readers—especially those who succeed and fail by routine—are freaking out even thinking about this idea. It's deeply unsettling at first. I get it. Start small, try a feasible trial, and see how it goes.

It's also critical to assess the perfectionist's degree of self-awareness. With a limited level of insight into their own cognitive rigidity, the perfectionist will be more resistant to change. This makes sense. If they don't think they have a problem with cognitive rigidity, why would they attempt to correct it?

Exposure Exercises for Cognitive Rigidity. The strategies for managers to work with rigid employees resemble those described in the group-level section, but on a micro scale. The most effective approach involves using exposure exercises to loosen fixed mindsets. For example, the random daily structure technique outlined above can be tailored to an individual employee rather than used as a group-wide framework. A cognitively rigid team member could be provided a randomized task or block list of tasks each day, with the same guidelines specified above. You can provide guidance and monitoring to assist the employee with tolerating the unpredictability and focusing on flexibility. As an added benefit of implementing this technique at the individual rather than group level, you will avoid causing distress among employees who are not rigid and don't need this exercise.

Exposure exercises at the individual employee level can be expanded even more. The spirit of these exercises is best conceptualized as *adaptation*. If you see a rigid employee carry out the same procedures for completing a task each time, challenge them to create a new procedure. For example, if an employee is required to take inventory, and you find that their strategy involves clustering the approach by department (e.g., shoes, electronics), have the employee test a new strategy of clustering by manufacturer instead. Then, have them use a strategy of clustering by price. The trick is to keep the employee fluid in their approaches and not allow them to solidify a seemingly mandatory procedure. This might cost the organization some efficiency, but this cost will be defrayed by the gains from having a more flexible employee.

A similar approach can be used for the list of assigned duties in general. If the employees in your company have cross-training to help them work in different roles or to do tasks that lie outside their normal responsibilities, you can vary up which employees complete specific functions. You can request that a rigid employee rotates at random through a finite universe of tasks for which they trained. For example, a perfectionistic employee could be assigned to wait tables one day, serve as host the next, act as food runner on the weekend, and take inventory and order supplies every third week. The order and type of task can be randomized and mixed to keep the to-do list fresh and unpredictable.

When it comes to rigid adherence to policies and expectations, such as is the case with Libo, you can set aside time to work with this type of perfectionistic employee. Discuss with them the policies and their underlying principles and values. Examine some likely scenarios in which the policies might be violated and how to handle these violations. This can include a careful assessment of whether the violation of the rule also violated the principle and whether extenuating circumstances warrant accommodation and leniency.

Overall, if you're working individually with a specific employee who exhibits cognitive rigidity, I'd recommend discussing this tendency gently and outlining your concerns about how it can interfere with the employee's duties. You then can provide reassurance that you're an ally and will help them tackle these tendencies. Doing so will help loosen a rigid employee for your organization's needs, and you may help the employee transfer their new flexibility to other areas of their life and future jobs. Win-win.

➤ Chapter Conclusion and Takeaways

This chapter provided an overview of cognitive rigidity, including a discussion of an especially harmful presentation—the should statement. Group- and individual-level strategies were introduced for reducing the negative impact of this perfectionistic tendencies. Here are some takeaway points:

- → Cognitive rigidity is particularly challenging because of its self-protective nature; the rigidity itself prevents perfectionists from reducing that rigidity.
- → Should statements are problematic in part because they are tied to other perfectionism problems, such as treating principles as rules, becoming mired in process paralysis, and undermining a healthy Emphasis Framework.
- → Should statements are associated with other features of perfectionism, such as moralism and NJREs.
- → The random daily structure approach could be useful as a group- and individual-level strategy. It integrates uncertainty and flexibility into the workplace culture and task routine.
- → Cognitive flexibility can also be combatted with exposure exercises that promote adaptability, such as requesting that your perfectionistic employee switch up their task strategy.
- → Cross-training to implement employee versatility is a natural exposure-based method for improving cognitive flexibility.

Perfectionism, by its nature, implies cognitive rigidity. It does not, however, imply that a pursuit of perfection is wrong. The pursuit of perfection is not synonymous with perfectionism, and so long as the pursuit is combined with cognitive flexibility, it can be adaptive.

Indeed, as Grant put it at the beginning of the chapter, with cognitive flexibility you can "rethink and unlearn" to adapt to a "turbulent" world.

CHAPTER 9

SOCIAL CAPITAL PUNISHMENT: OTHER-ORIENTED MORALISM

"He was a solemn, unsmiling, sanctimonious
old iceberg who looked like he was waiting
for a vacancy in the [Holy] Trinity."[129]

MARK TWAIN
Author

MARK TWAIN KNOWS how to paint a vivid picture with words, and this quote is no exception. The character that he describes here embodies the negative energy that so often accompanies the self-righteous person with whom you're talking. This energy is palpable and unpleasant. It can be toxic to the workplace culture.

This chapter covers a social dynamic that often occurs in the workplace and makes for a difficult organizational culture: other-oriented moralism. If you recall from chapter 2, this involves the perfectionist projecting unreasonable and rigid standards onto other

129 Twain, *Travels with Mr. Brown.*

people. Most of the time, this type of projection is not communicated kindly to the recipient, nor is it received well.

This brand of perfectionism can vary in its presentation. It might look like the coworker who polices your comings and goings to keep track of your time on the clock. They can become preoccupied with your work assignments and become preachy about an "unfair" balance of work. They might perceive special treatment for some coworkers and vocalize this at the watercooler.

This drama can create pockets of dissent—cliques—that ultimately lead to fractured workplace cohesion. These individuals enforce company policy rigidly as if it were moral law that, if broken, should be punishable by guillotine. Sometimes their enforcement seems so draconian they might as well physically throw the employee manual at you.

I'm not saying that it's acceptable to act against company policy, such as rebelling against the time clock; I'm not suggesting that unfair balance of workload or special treatment for certain employees is okay. Following company policies is a standard expectation. My positioning on this doesn't suggest the Wild West mentality in the office.

My position is that there is a civil and healthy way for employees to address concerns in the workplace. The moralistic examples provided above are not healthy, and they disrupt the workplace culture substantially. In many situations, the other-oriented moralistic behavior has a worse impact on the workplace culture than their coworker's original problem behavior (e.g., chronic lateness) being judged by the perfectionist. There is a certain irony to this form of perfectionism.

This presentation of perfectionism looks and feels separate from what we've covered so far in this book. For this reason, this chapter will seem different. With previous topics, the perfectionism problems were due to expectations applied inward. The perfectionist exhibits a dysfunctional Emphasis Framework and experiences process paralysis. They demonstrate their own tendency to confound rules and principles and to think rigidly. These tendencies negatively impact others in the workplace, but they don't involve targeting others. The target has been themselves—the perfectionist. This chapter, however, focuses on perfectionism applied outward—when the perfectionist targets others. This results in a different workplace dynamic.

Other-oriented moralism can devastate a positive workplace spirit. Working around moralistic perfectionists in the office can feel like walking on eggshells. You're always worried about doing or saying something the perfectionist perceives is "wrong." It requires a hypervigilance that exhausts everyone. They may show visible disapproval via nonverbal cues (e.g., eye roll) or react passive-aggressively (e.g., purposefully leave a poor customer review of your service out on the counter for the boss to see). These are the types of coworkers for whom you're willing to lose 20 minutes of sleep to arrive at the office extra early, just to avoid running into them. Their behavior results in a large percentage of employee turnover, plain and simple.

When it comes to psychological safety specifically, it's possible there's a double whammy effect from other-oriented moralism. The first whammy is direct. Workplace bullying is associated with reduced psychological safety,[130] and other-oriented moralism resembles bullying.

The second whammy is indirect. When an employee exhibits other-oriented moralism in the workplace, their coworkers may have a tendency to stay silent and hesitate to share knowledge out of fear of

130 Edmondson and Bransby, "Psychological Safety Comes of Age."

triggering the perfectionist (i.e., walking on eggshells). Staying silent and hesitating to share knowledge have been associated with lower perceptions of psychological safety.[131]

Unfortunately, management may miss much of the toxic moralistic behavior, as the other-oriented perfectionist is likely to offer their unsolicited judgments to peers and supervisees, but not to the boss. Why? The very reason they express moral outrage to their peers and supervisees is the same reason they wouldn't dare question an authority figure—rigid and all-or-none perception of *right* and *wrong*.

For many with perfectionistic moralism, it feels like a righteous duty to call out others for their "improprieties." At the same time, it's righteous to remain deferential to your boss and not question them directly. This pattern results in a lopsided display of self-righteousness loaded heavily toward peers and supervisees.

In addition, employees who quit often don't provide honest feedback to the company about an obnoxious coworker. The field is small, and retaliation is a very real concern. As a result, leadership may not see these uncomfortable interactions, even though it's shattering in terms of job satisfaction for your other employees.

I've placed the chapter on other-oriented moralism near the end of the book for two reasons. First, as noted above, this chapter feels different than the others because of its focus on a form of perfectionism that targets others. Second, other-oriented moralism is a complicated form of perfectionism that encompasses many of the elements already discussed in this book. In that sense, the other chapters are foundational to the discussion of other-oriented moralism.

---

131 Edmondson and Bransby.

Moralism and Other Perfectionism Tendencies

Dysfunctional Emphasis Framework. Moralistic judgments of others imply that the target of the criticism has done something "wrong." If you carry out a task using an Emphasis B approach because you deemed it unworthy of more attention, the other-oriented perfectionist may scoff and suggest that you're not giving the job your full energy. They might perceive you as loafing, which is "wrong" from their perspective. The same pattern is true if you opt to use Emphasis C for a task—they might be shocked at your "irresponsibility" for ignoring a job task.

Process Paralysis. Sometimes the other-oriented moralist gets so focused on policing others that ironically it obstructs their own productivity. They get stuck on local processing and become hyper-vigilant to the details of what others are doing wrong. They miss the big picture. This doesn't cause overwhelming paralysis, but it does slow them down.

Confounding Rules and Principles. Moralistic perfectionists judge others for not meeting rules. This is a major problem—as discussed in Chapter 7—because they often confound rules and principles, and principles can't be met. You can only show degrees of fidelity. Moreover, they tend to get stuck on moral principles (e.g., good employee, bad person). For this reason, moralistic perfectionists express criticism toward coworkers for not "meeting" abstract moral constructs, as if they were rules that could be met concretely.

Cognitive Rigidity. This is the most obvious perfectionism tendency implicated in other-oriented moralism. Moralistic reasoning is full of cognitive biases, such as all-or-none thinking and should statements. The moralistic perfectionistic misinterprets and overemphasizes abstract moral principles and sees them as rigid rules, often expressed as should statements. They show little ability to flex their thinking around these rules and morals. There are no shades of grey. They see you only falling into categories with judgmental labels (e.g., good person, bad employee, awful parent).

This is Not Canceling Cancel Culture

Some may see similarities between my description of other-oriented moralism and the recent trend of *cancel culture*. This trend refers to eliminating support for and disengaging from a public figure because their behavior has been judged as socially and culturally unacceptable. For example, after making insensitive racial remarks, a celebrity might lose a substantial social media following because of being "canceled" by the public. Their reputation takes a hit, and often their industry loses interest in working with them (e.g., the celebrity can no longer get acting jobs) because it's a public relations nightmare.

Other-oriented moralism and cancel culture are not interchangeable. They have important differences, but they are not mutually exclusive. You can cancel somebody in a way that is not perfectionistic. In other words, the approach is sensitive to context, appreciates shades of grey, and balances all sides of the situation. This includes demonstrating patience for awaiting the full landscape of evidence. The potential cancel-worthy behavior can be evaluated in a way that isn't rigid and all-or-none and considers the underlying fidelity to principles rather than a breaking of rules. There is an openness to the celebrity carrying out amends to right their wrongs.

You can also cancel someone from a framework of other-oriented moralistic perfectionism. Such an approach would consist of jumping quickly to place the celebrity in the bin of "bad," seeing no shades of grey or extenuating circumstances, treating the celebrity's behavior as a rigid violation of an abstract moral construct, and offering no flexibility for a celebrity carrying out appropriate restitution. In general, the perfectionist demonstrates little openness to changing their mind.

Ultimately, there are important differences between other-oriented perfectionistic moralism and cancel culture. They seem related and it's easy to confuse them. It's helpful to think of perfectionism as the reason for a subset of cancellations that are extreme, rigid, and sometimes unreasonable.

As an analogy, you can approach a job task with varying degrees of perfectionism, from little to a lot. Similarly, you can cancel a public figure with varying degrees of perfectionism, from little to a lot.

Case Illustration: Anya

Here is the case of Anya, who works for a large cancer non-profit as a development associate. Her role focuses on strengthening donor relations, facilitating fundraising prospects, and cultivating new development opportunities. Let's use Anya's case to highlight individual- and group-level approaches to addressing other-oriented moralism.

Anya is mostly quiet and agreeable in meetings and when interacting with her superiors at the non-profit. She seems deferential and compliant and performs her development duties well. Her products are exemplary, her efficiency laudable. She maintains strong donor relations and boasts some of the highest fundraising totals on the team.

From a leadership perspective, managers hear very little about Anya's engagement in the workplace. They assume she mostly keeps to herself, given her interaction style in meetings and in their one-to-one encounters with her. They see her as a valuable, loyal, and agreeable member of the team.

When it comes time to consider her candidacy for promotion to development manager, they become frustrated at the lack of detail they can obtain from her peers about her performance. When they probe her coworkers, everyone agrees that Anya is stellar when it comes to her work quality and pace. Objective productivity metrics corroborate these statements about Anya's job performance.

They do notice, however, a strange pattern by her coworkers when they start asking around about her. Most of her peers become quiet and look guarded when they first hear about the purpose of the questioning (i.e., to evaluate Anya). It's as if they are worried about saying something wrong, and therefore they start to shut down. Many of them question whether their comments will be on record and made available to Anya.

Seeing only that Anya has met or surpassed all her job goals and done so with little evidence of workplace difficulty, leadership promotes her to development manager. Everyone in the office congratulates her. It all looks like a genuine and universal celebration of her advancement.

It's not.

Her peers' celebration is performative and self-preserving. They despise Anya and are concerned about her new role. The leadership has been oblivious to the ways that Anya has poisoned the work environment.

What are the peers experiencing? Anya is holier than thou. Despite her unassuming interaction style in meetings and with her managers, Anya makes everyone in the office uncomfortable. She has a few close colleagues with whom she gossips, but even those colleagues are wary of her and keep her close as a strategy and out of fear. They also don't like her and don't want to be the target of her judgment.

As if it were part of her job description, Anya often holds everyone around her accountable to the company policies. She does so in a rigid and rule-driven way, offering little wiggle room for extenuating circumstances. She complains about imbalanced workload and unfair special treatments. This often leads her to campaign against others in shrewd yet quiet ways to "correct" such workplace "wrongs."

Her communication style isn't visibly aggressive. In fact, some of her colleagues miss some of her subtle passive-aggressive comments and body language. She presents as friendly, but her approach is so powerful that it has everyone anxious about encountering her. They see Anya as a crusader and a narcissist. They avoid her at all costs.

In the months following Anya's promotion, a trend emerges in the company's workforce. The rate of employees quitting in the development division increases to a much higher rate than usual. Exit interviews don't reveal anything consistent about the reasons for the turnover.

One company manager stumbles on some reviews on a website that provides a safe platform for employees to discuss their experience working for an organization. The manager is dismayed to read a dozen recent anonymous reviews that blast the organization, particularly the development division, for bullying behavior. When the manager investigates further using more direct questioning, the employees in the development division start opening up about their experience with Anya.

It's too late; the damage has been done. Workplace engagement has been decimated, and excellent staff have departed for greener pastures. It's time to rebuild... and Anya will *not* be a part of that process.

Anya's Other-Oriented Moralism

Anya's case is a classic example of other-oriented perfectionistic moralism. Though, admittedly, the example is a bit extreme. It resembles toxic high school drama. The dynamic and behavior are reminiscent of the movie *Mean Girls*.[132]

This type of drama and behavior is not always—nor even commonly—attributable to other-oriented perfectionism. Many variables can result in ugly workplace dynamic such as this, most of which have nothing to do with perfectionism. Other-oriented moralism, however, can explain some egregious examples of animosity in the office between coworkers. This is what's occurring in Anya's case.

Anya is careful not to show disrespect to her managers. This approach may be driven by her perfectionistic interpretation of the

---

132 Apologies if this triggers traumatic memories.

principle of *respect authority figures*. Additionally, or alternatively, Anya's approach may be a sly attempt to manipulate her environment. Either way, it's causing rifts in the workplace dynamic, and leadership doesn't see it.

Anya feels a duty to act as the sheriff in her workplace, keeping everyone in line. This includes preoccupations with having a "fair" and "good" workplace and compulsions to correct any disturbances to those qualities. It also includes rigid and binary beliefs about what is *fair* and *unfair,* as well as *right* and *wrong*—but Anya's appraisal of fairness and goodness in her workplace is subjective. Others may not, and often *do* not, agree with her assessment. This doesn't stop Anya from thrusting her version onto others.

The biggest issue for this workplace, however, is not Anya's subjective beliefs about fairness and goodness. Rather, it's *how* she preaches, abides by this rigid system, and demands others follow suit. If Anya internalized these expectations, kept them to herself, and didn't demand anything of others, the workplace would be far less negatively impacted by her perfectionism. It would probably look more like a case study from previous chapters— self-oriented perfectionism.

In Anya's case, however, her behavior externalizes outwardly and throttles her peers metaphorically so that they cannot breathe. Her conduct is so poisonous that her colleagues feel unsafe voicing their concerns to leadership—often due to a fear of Anya's retaliation. They only feel protected by posting anonymously on websites. Even then, the posts are kept vague purposefully, to stop a reader from deducing the identity of the poster.

Coworkers steer clear of Anya at all costs, sometimes with the ultimate avoidance strategy: quitting. Not only does her interpersonal approach splinter the workplace culture, but it also results in turnover. The company's bottom line therefore takes a hit.

In short, Anya is a dangerous liability to the company. Any positive results from her strong productivity are negated—if not overwhelmed entirely—by the detrimental baggage she brings to the organization. The leadership starts to strategize about terminating her employment, but there might be other solutions.

Group-Level Solutions for Other-Oriented Moralism

Social Capital Framework. I would suggest adopting a social capital framework as a top-down strategy for safeguarding against other-oriented perfectionistic moralism and its disruptions to workplace morale. The concept of social capital works much like the concept of financial capital, except it has nothing to do with liquidity. Instead, it involves a framework—a metaphor—for understanding social gains and losses within the context of our complex social world. Let me explain how the concept of financial capital translates to social dynamics.

Each social relationship automatically includes a social bank account. Our behaviors can deposit or withdrawal social capital from that account at any given moment. The more capital you have in a social bank account, the stronger the social relationship.

The social bank accounts are based on partnerships and go in one direction only. I have an account with my wife, and she has a separate account with me. My account with my supervisor is independent from the one with my mechanic. My account with my therapist is distinct from the one with my brother. This is the case for all social relationships.

How much capital you have in that social bank account is dependent on a variety of factors. Some accounts are created with a robust deposit from the outset, such as a child's relationship with their parent. Some accounts have a minimum balance and require substantial deposits to reach a healthy level. Unfortunately, some balances dip below zero and are in the red, requiring a bit of digging to get out of a social capital hole.

Some of your behaviors spend from the social bank account. For example, if I walk into the house with muddy shoes, I've just burned through some of my social capital with my wife. The size of the expenditure is relative. My cost is tiny compared to the scenario in which I walk into the house with muddy shoes *plus* a mistress. This would lead to a sizable and instant negative balance. It's a social capital punishment.

Just as you can spend from the social bank account, you can also replenish capital. If I send a spontaneous text message to a friend and check in with them, this builds some capital. I earn capital if I notice that my wife's favorite rock band is coming to town and thoughtfully buy us tickets. Each time I rub that one spot behind my dog's ears, I've earned some social capital with him.[133]

What's the point of this metaphor? It helps people understand that their actions have an impact on their relationships and that often these impacts are not considered properly when analyzing the pros and cons of carrying out actions. Your behaviors deposit or withdrawal social capital in the context of your relevant relationships. Social capital is not infinite, and it's wise to monitor the balance of important social bank accounts and consider making some deposits

---

133 We all could learn a thing or two from dogs and their social capital dynamics.

when necessary. The message is straightforward: don't bounce social capital checks;[134] instead, spend wisely and replenish as necessary.

Social Capital in the Workplace. When you go to the doctor for a check-up, it's customary for them to evaluate all your vital signs including blood pressure and heart rate. For a workplace, social health is a vital sign. Social health in this context is a broad characterization of how well the interpersonal dynamics of a workplace yield positive well-being among the team, effective communication, strong worker vitality, high job satisfaction and low dissatisfaction, and soaring workplace pride and loyalty.

Social health needs monitoring and—when needed—intervention. Social capital is a framework for contextualizing one key social health indicator of a workplace.

For the concept of social capital, each relationship in the workplace has a designated social bank account. Generally, as a new employee is on-boarded, they're afforded a reasonable, positive balance in their accounts with each coworker. This isn't true in all cases. Sometimes entrenched employees can be salty about a new hire and treat them poorly from the outset. Every so often, a jealous employee refuses to grant social capital to a new hire. Nonetheless, as a new hire builds a reputation and establishes relationships in the workplace, they're depositing and withdrawing from respective social bank accounts.

It's important for employees to realize that their behaviors and decisions have an impact on their social capital. Nothing they do exists in a vacuum in our complex social ecosystem. For example, if you choose to seek a promotion, but your peers think the move

134 Or "cheques" for the British readers.

is premature and entitled, you've spent social capital with them and may not have realized it. Even hinting at seeking promotion can cost capital, but the act of pursuing it costs more.

Let me illustrate with a real-world example.[135] My friend is an oncology nurse at a major hospital. He loves his job, especially when he gets to work with patients directly. He's also a big fan of his colleagues, which makes going to work a joy. After several years with this satisfying job arrangement, my friend received a notice sent to all oncology nurses. It asked if anyone would be willing to transfer over to the hospital administration offices to assist with important non-clinical tasks. My friend was hesitant to do so initially given how much he enjoyed his colleagues and working with patients.

As the hospital's need continued to remain unmet, however, he decided that it was worth the social capital he would earn by taking the plunge. He agreed to the transition. It was a wise move—hospital leadership publicly praised him for his selfless decision. He started making critical connections with key personnel who could facilitate his professional development. My friend understood the power of social capital and opted to make a sacrifice to grow his account.

You may note similarities between political and social capital. They overlap as concepts and operate similarly but are distinct. Political capital involves figurative bank accounts that provide capital for carrying out successful political[136] moves, such as adding pork barrel to legislation by influencing opponents. This process can be successful even if the opponents despise each other—they have zero

---

135 Identifying details have been changed to ensure anonymity.

136 This means *politics* broadly construed—governmental, organizational, familial.

or even negative social capital bank accounts with each other. Often social and political capital positively correlate but not always.

The two types of capital are linked in many political circumstances. It helps for political action if the parties maintain high social capital with each other. This is why politicians make an effort to schmooze. Doing so earns political capital indirectly through enhancing social capital. This also means that controversial political actions by one party can deplete social and political bank accounts at the same time.

Social Capital Messaging. How do you integrate this framework into the workplace in a top-down manner? It's very similar to approaches you might take with introducing and adopting the Emphasis Framework. Organizational leaders can integrate antiperfectionism messaging into the workplace, and this can include language that describes the social capital framework. Below are some examples of how it can be integrated at the office from the top down.

- → Add language about the social capital framework to the employee handbook.
- → Orientation for new hires can introduce and focus on this framework.
- → The social capital framework can become an important and explicit element of workplace decision-making processes. For example, when employees are tasked with deciding on Strategy A versus Strategy B, an explicit workplace guide for making that decision can include weighing the pros and cons of each strategy for relevant social bank accounts.

→ As a leader, serve as a faithful model to demonstrate how to adopt this framework when navigating the social dynamics of the workplace.

→ Integrate social capital framework language into yearly employee evaluations, particularly with items that measure a worker's social behavior.

Let's consider an example of how the social capital framework can become embedded in the culture of the workplace.

Imagine if a leader is required to decide which two coworkers will be assigned to spearhead an important project. The twist, however, is that the two coworkers best suited to take the assignment hate each other. Perhaps the two coworkers have complementary skillsets that would make for an excellent product. Is it worth it for the leader to take the risk and assign the two coworkers to the project?

A leader who emphasizes social capital considers the impact of their decision on the social bank accounts of all those involved, as well as the social climate of the workplace. The two coworkers may deliver a great product together, but at what social capital expense? If they leave a wake of workplace destruction in their path when finishing the product, it may not have been worth it.

Often leaders consider the financial and logistical effects of choosing one option over another. For example, in the scenario above, the leader might focus narrowly on the financial benefits of a quality project—it increases company revenue. Similarly, they may emphasize the logistical benefits, such as choosing two coworkers for the project that have resource availability to do so. In many cases, however, social capital consequences get overlooked, and potential negative effects on the workplace culture are neglected.

Social bank accounts represent an abstract concept, but it is helpful for visualizing the delicate social relationships we maintain in our lives, including those in the workplace. When we make decisions and act in a workplace, the results extend beyond the financial. It also impacts relationships with coworkers.

Anonymous Feedback Mechanism. One other group-level strategy for the office might be useful for addressing the dysfunctional social dynamic caused by Anya's behavior. You can develop a mechanism for coworkers to submit anonymous feedback, reducing fears of retaliation and excessive social capital expenditure. You then can hope that a peeved employee provides details about Anya's behavior.

This feedback technique is not perfect.[137] An anonymous feedback mechanism can be used for evil, such as a group of bullies in the workplace ganging up on a coworker. In our case study, Anya might even use the anonymous feedback mechanism to complain about her coworkers and their perceived trespasses. The feedback you might receive is best interpreted with a grain[138] of salt.

Employee-Level Solutions for Other-Oriented Moralism

Gather Details about Self-Awareness and Skills. A thorough assessment of the social health of a workplace is critical, but how do you handle the situation when you discover a complicated social dynamic associated with tension and drama? As with previous chapters, the first step is to carry out a careful evaluation of the forces at play that contribute to the tension and drama. Most of the time, there are

137 As nothing is perfect. Have I belabored this enough?
138 Or "heap" or "pinch."

multiple factors and players implicated but, even in those situations, the investigation leads to one or two key individuals who instigate and maintain the tense social dynamic. When uncovering the details, you may find that some of the problem is attributable to other-oriented perfectionism.

If this is the case, it helps to identify the specific moral "code" and the associated rules that seem to be driving the perfectionist's behavior. I'd also recommend creating a comprehensive inventory of the perfectionist's social behavior and estimates of social capital costs. Knowing these details will help craft an individualized remediation plan for the perfectionist who is disrupting the social dynamics of the workplace.

Anya seems oblivious to the concept of social capital. This speaks to a lack of self-awareness, another key characteristic that needs careful assessment. How you approach Anya will depend on her level of insight into her own behavior. If Anya exhibits poor self-awareness, your task becomes much harder for teaching her and motivating change. It also predicts a much more confrontational path forward as you deal with Anya. She'll probably put up a fight with change efforts.

Individualized Strategies. As noted, other-oriented perfectionistic moralism often represents a blend of all perfectionism problems discussed in this book—dysfunctional Emphasis Framework, process paralysis, confounding rules and principles, and cognitive rigidity. Once you've evaluated the nature of a perfectionist's other-oriented moralistic behavior and its social capital impact, part of the solution will likely involve implementing techniques described for each of these perfectionism problems.

Let me illustrate. Other-oriented moralistic behavior often includes cognitive rigidity. As a result, it would benefit the astute reader to apply strategies discussed for addressing cognitive rigidity (see chapter 8). For example, imagine a perfectionist who is harassing others for taking too long for lunch breaks, which violates the employee manual. It may be time to meet with the perfectionist, discuss their cognitive rigidity, and create some exposure exercises to help them navigate scenarios in which their coworkers disobey organizational guidelines. Part of this would include having the perfectionist abstain from commenting to others or exhibiting nonverbal cues of disapproval—a strategy for ceasing safety behaviors (i.e., compulsions to fix their coworkers' "transgressions" and teach them a lesson). It also might help to send the perfectionist a message that it's not their job to police the lunch policy.

Assertiveness Training. Evidence supports the use of assertiveness training to help those with ineffective communication styles.[139] Entire books have been written on assertiveness training, so it's not feasible to give it full justice here. I nonetheless highlight some key concepts and strategies to help get you started. If you're intrigued, you may want to consult resources that provide more extensive coverage of the topic. At the end of the book, I've provided some instructions for accessing a list of resources.

Assertiveness training starts with education. Figure 12 (see following pages) shows a breakdown of four communication styles, including a workplace example, common characteristics, pros, and cons. The communication approaches are *Aggressive, Passive, Passive-Aggressive,* and *Assertive.*

139 Speed, Goldstein, and Goldfried, "Assertiveness Training."

Aggressive Communication Style. This is exactly how it sounds—forceful; hostile; combative. When you're using an aggressive style, you impinge on other people's rights in the service of meeting your needs and at the expense of their needs. It shows little respect for the person with whom you're communicating. It destroys relationships because it feels abusive to people receiving the aggression. In other words, it obliterates social capital.

I like to use a parking lot scenario to illustrate differences in communication styles. Imagine you're trying to park at a busy shopping center during a cold and icy holiday season. Parking spots are rare, especially ones that are near the front of the center entrance. As luck would have it, you see a patron enter their car and about to leave. You drive to the spot, stop conscientiously with enough room for the car to back out, and turn on your signal to indicate proudly that you've "claimed" the enviable spot.

Now imagine if another driver pulls up at the last minute—nowhere near the spot moments ago—and steals your prime spot. This thief pulls in as the departing driver backs out, leaving you in disbelief. In this scenario, you could engage an aggressive communication style. This might look like honking in a fit of road rage, screaming, getting out of the car, yelling at the driver, and perhaps smashing their windshield or car.[140] You might think the parking spot thief deserves it—and maybe you're right—but what is the cost? They could hurt you or involve the police (i.e., in this situation, you're probably the one getting arrested, not the thief).

---

140 "Towanda!" If you know, you know.

Figure 12: The Four Communications Styles as Part of Assertiveness Training: Coworker Example

Passive

Nonconfrontational, submissive, timid, ingratiating

> Sure, no problem. Happy to help.

PRO
Avoid confrontation; Please others; Stay under the radar

CON
Don't meet your immediate needs; Lose self-respect; Build resentment of others

Passive Aggressive

Sneaky, sarcastic, cowardly, indirect

> Sure, it's not like my work is that important.

PRO
Feel a temporary sense of retribution

CON
Destroy relationships; Lose self-respect and respect from others; Attract possible behavioral consequences (e.g., job termination)

Aggressive

Combative, theatening, loud, obnoxious, oppositional

> No, your perfectionism makes you so self-serving. You don't care about other people's time.

PRO
Often get your immediate needs met

CON
Destroy relationships; Lose respect from others; Attract behavioral consequences (e.g., job termination)

Assertive

Respectful, nonjudgmental, authoritative, nonthreatening, nonblaming

> I can't help because I'm too busy at the moment. I'm also concerned that reviewing it again would promote perfectionism in the workplace.

PRO
Protect relationships; Often have your needs met; Preserve self-respect and respect from others

CON
People may not be used to your assertiveness and treat you differently

Let's see if the aggressive parking lot response meets all the criteria. Did you impinge on the thief's rights? Yes—you threatened their safety or property. Was it at the service of meeting your needs? Yes—it satisfied the impulse to give the thief a piece of your mind for stealing from you. Does it show little respect to the thief? Yes—though this one might be warranted, as it's not clear they have earned or deserve your respect. Does it destroy your relationship with the thief? Yes— the two of you probably won't be squash buddies, but imagine if you later learn that your daughter is dating this thief. In this case, the relationship damage might be especially problematic.

Passive Communication Style. Now, let's turn to passive communication, which is the opposite of aggressive. You can envision them as two extremes on a dimension. When you adopt a passive communication style, you meet other people's needs at the expense of your own. It shows little respect for yourself. It's self-abuse; you are neglecting yourself, and neglect is a form of abuse. It does preserve your social capital in the short-term, as you are placing no demands on others and, in fact, are assisting others with their needs.

Short-term benefits to social capital notwithstanding, relationships are damaged by passive communication in the long-term. Over time, passive interpersonal styles corrode the well-being of the person being passive. Others start to take advantage and resentment grows. At some point, the passive communicator may explode and turn aggressive in a difficult moment, but it's often not directed appropriately. It's displaced anger, and it's often a result of the "straw that broke the camel's back." Whoever is nearest the passive communicator is the unfortunate target, and this is terrible for relationships. So, passivity costs social capital in the long run.

For the parking lot incident, a passive response to the thief would look very different than the aggressive version. If you're being passive here, you might be angered by the thief and even curse at them in the privacy of your own car, but you decide it's not worth the imposition to express your anger to, or attempt a resolution with, the thief. You ultimately park way out in the boonies and mumble to yourself in anger as you trek for 10 minutes in the bitter cold to the shopping center through ice and snow.

This scenario checks off all the features of passive communication. Your needs have not been met, unlike the thief's needs. Your actions demonstrate little respect for yourself. My guess is that you'll feel terrible about yourself after this incident, probably as you're taking the treacherous walk to the shopping center entrance. The relationship between you and the thief is non-existent and unaffected by the scenario, but you might explode at innocent others as soon as the straw breaks the camel's back.

Passive-Aggressive Communication Style. No doubt, aggressive and passive communication styles are problematic, but passive aggression is the king of disastrous communication approaches. It involves indirect aggressive communication—it's aggressive behavior masquerading as passivity. With this approach, everyone loses. If you're being passive-aggressive, your original need isn't being met, but you might gain some temporary satisfaction from hurting the person you're targeting. For the targeted person, their original need may have been met, but as a result, they will receive disproportionate punishment in an unrelated context.

This style is a blend of the worst parts of aggression and passivity. The passive-aggressive style is associated with little respect. There's no inherent respect for yourself, nor is there any respect for the victim of the passive-aggressive behavior. In many respects, it's self-abuse plus abuse of the targeted person.

I can say without hesitation that passive-aggressive communication styles are relationship killers. Few people stick around for relationships in which the other person acts passive-aggressively. The relationship feels—and probably is—abusive and disingenuous. I'd venture a guess that most people would prefer a slightly aggressive coworker over a slightly passive-aggressive coworker. Though, I suppose it would depend on your stomach for conflict. Ultimately, passive aggression obliterates social capital.

Circling back to the parking lot incident, a passive-aggressive response to the thief could take on various forms. As an example, you might park a long distance away but then place sharp nails upright and underneath the thief's two back tires. When they back out, it causes a flat in both.[141] It's aggressive with a passive twist—the thief knows it was an intentional attack, but there is no direct communication. The culprit remains in the shadows in a passive way.

The passive-aggressive response also checks off all the boxes. Your original needs were not met—you didn't get the parking spot and still parked a distance away. The thief's original needs were met—they secured the parking spot—but the punishment severity far exceeded the "crime." Their well-being therefore was violated. This incident and response show little respect for any of the parties involved, yourself included. You might feel satisfied for "getting them back," but many people feel dirty after engaging in passive-aggressive behavior. It also adds to a perception by others that you are passive-aggressive, which repels others. The relationship between you and the thief is minimal

---

141 I realize this is suspiciously and oddly specific. I assure you that I've never done this before.

but, if they discover it was you, their response might be worse than what would have occurred if you were aggressive with them instead.

Assertive Communication Style. This style of communication is the appropriate approach for respectful discourse in most instances. Using this style, you articulate your needs and feelings in a way that acknowledges and respects all parties involved in the communication. You maximize the chance your needs get met while still preserving your relationships with others. None of the other communication styles offer this balance.

Assertive approaches and passive-aggressive approaches both represent hybrids between the passive and aggressive extremes, but that's where the similarities end. In many respects, assertive and passive-aggressive styles are opposites. Passive-aggressive approaches come with all the downsides of passive and aggressive approaches but none of the upsides. Inversely, assertive approaches come with all the upsides and none of the downsides.

Let's look at how assertiveness works. Assertive responses are non-judgmental, focus on you and not the recipients, and communicate your feelings and needs while respecting those of the recipients. For example, let's say you make the following statement to a coworker: "You're so manipulative—you always take the credit for our work."

This is an aggressive statement. Why? You're blaming the recipient and being judgmental. It instantly sparks a defensive reaction from the recipient. This approach is very likely going to cost you social capital with this coworker and probably doesn't help you change their behavior. It might even cause them to dig in their heels.

Instead, an assertive approach with this coworker would minimize the possibility of these consequences. An assertive version of this message might look like the following: "I'm frustrated because I'm not getting the recognition I deserve for the work we submit—I would like more credit, please."

Notice the absence of accusatory language, judgment, and harsh labels (e.g., manipulative). The assertive statement is about the communicator, not the recipient; the use of *I* instead of *you* often helps with this focus. It articulates a need and feeling. This approach preserves social capital by reducing the likelihood of a defensive response.

As a note, much of the time, when I provide assertiveness training, the client practices changing the *you* statements to *I* statements in a way that makes them retain the aggressive messaging. They might give an example such as, "*I feel* like you're so manipulative."

Nope, but clever try.

These attempts are not assertive. You can't just add *I feel* or some equivalent in front of a *you* statement to make it assertive. The subtext matters greatly. For it to be assertive, the message needs to be centered on you (i.e., the communicator), non-judgmental, and respectful.

Assertiveness extends beyond verbal communication and includes nonverbal cues. Eye gaze, eye rolls, closed-off posture, crossed arms, negative facial expressions, etc.—these all matter greatly when it comes to demonstrating assertive communication. If you express an assertive statement but it's joined by your silent sneer or eye roll, then your nonverbal cues have invalidated any attempt at being assertive and therefore any benefits.

Note that I haven't offered any promises. Assertive communication does not guarantee that you'll get what you want or that others will validate your feelings. It does, however, protect your relationships while also allowing you to stick up for yourself, set boundaries, and exercise self-respect.

Others may react differently if you switch your communication styles. If people are accustomed to your passivity, they may balk at your assertive communications and resist any boundary-setting attempts. This is particularly true if they're accustomed to walking all over you and getting what they want.

Similarly, if people are used to your aggression, they may react surprised at any assertiveness. In some instances, if you're aggressive and surround yourself with other aggressive people, you may find that people around you perceive you as *getting soft* once you switch to assertive communication. You may need to prepare for this reaction.

Please also note that assertiveness is not ideal in all situations. Assertive approaches are the most appropriate for most contexts, but there is a time and place for each type of communication style. Imagine being held up at gunpoint. Being assertive in this situation is dangerous: "Mr. Gunman, I do not want to give you my money and feel upset right now."

Perhaps a passive approach makes the most sense for survival.

As another example, imagine your toddler keeps running into the street and into oncoming traffic. They seem to enjoy the resultant attention from their behavior and don't seem nervous about upsetting you. This might be a time to increase the aggressive communication—just slightly—to make it clear to your toddler that this behavior is not acceptable and is dangerous. I'm not suggesting any form of child abuse, but the situation might call for more aggressive tone and volume of voice, forceful body language, and punishment threats. In this situation, catastrophic injury and death are probable consequences if the child doesn't learn to stop their problem behavior. This scary outcome seems to outweigh concerns about the aggressive communication style.

I can't think of many commonplace situations in which passive-aggressive communication styles are adaptive. Though, I'm sure that such circumstances exist. Perhaps there are rare scenarios in which violently oppressed individuals need to meet their needs indirectly and, to do so, they feign allyship but lash out at the oppressive party anonymously and in a way that won't cause violent reprisal by those in power. It's a *Game of Thrones* strategy. I would nonetheless urge you not to adopt a passive-aggressive style; it's destructive and unnecessary most of the time.

Anya's Communication Style and Social Capital. Anya has depleted her social bank account. In fact, given the degree to which she has infuriated her coworkers, she's probably in considerable social capital debt. The details of her communication style are unclear, but it would be consistent with the case description if she were engaging in considerable aggressive or passive-aggressive behavior. This behavior is wreaking havoc on her social bank account.

You can check in with Anya about her understanding of the social capital framework. If it's a knowledge deficit, I'd advise you to fill in the lacking information with education and examples. If Anya exhibits a skill deficit related to her communication style (i.e., she doesn't know how to express herself assertively), I suggest assertiveness training. You can show her figure 12 as a starting point for teaching her assertiveness skills.

I've also created a worksheet for you to use when carrying out assertiveness training (see figure 13). For instructions on how to access a full-size and blank copy of the worksheet, please see the end of the book or go to www.gregchasson.com/flawedresources. The worksheet walks you through a guided process for analyzing a social interaction to determine the communication style. It also provides a decision process and some prompts for crafting assertive responses.

Social Capital & Assertiveness Worksheet

Page 1 of 3

Situation

Describe:

Anya and Mason got into a verbal altercation at work. This caused an escalation which resulted in the two raising their voices at each other and disrupting the workplace. Coworkers were very uncomfortable.

Analysis

Behavior:

Anya made a loud, sarcastic comment to Mason when he was 10 minutes late

Thoughts

Mason shouldn't be late to work. It's rude and against organizational rules. He shouldn't be able to get away with this.

Feelings:

Annoyance

Response by other parties:

Mason snapped back at the sarcastic comment and said, "Who made you the police? Mind your own business!"

Any social capital spent during the situation?

☑ Yes   ☐ No   *If yes, please check off any of the aggressive or passive-aggressive behaviors you exhibited:

Physical behaviors exhibited:

☐ Physically harm others

☐ Physically touch others without harming them

☐ Physically break property (yours or not yours)

☐ Physically threaten others

☐ Physically mock or taunt

☐ Steal from others

☐ Violated others' personal bubbles

☑ Roll your eyes

☐ Cross your arms

Other

Figure 13: Example of Worksheet for Anya's Assertiveness Training

Social Capital & Assertiveness Worksheet

Verbal behaviors exhibited:

☐ Verbally threaten others

☑ Raise your voice

☐ Use sarcasm

☐ Verbally mock or taunt

☐ Insult, name call, or make unkind comment

☐ Use profanity

Other

Relational behaviors exhibited

☐ Blame others

☑ Judge others

☐ Manipulate others

☐ Sabotage others

☑ Step out of your role to police others

☐ Spread rumors, gossip, or lies

☐ Spread others' information (e.g., photos, secrets) without consent

☐ Excluding others socially to hurt them

Other

Your needs and well-being

Please rate the degree to which you undermined your own well-being or blocked your own needs in the situation

Circle: None   (A little)   Some   A lot   All

Needs and well-being of others

Please rate the degree to which you violated the well-being or blocked the needs of other parties in the situation

Circle: None   (A little)   Some   A lot   All

Self-respect

Please rate the degree to which you showed self-respect in this situation

Circle: None   A little   (Some)   A lot   All

Respect for other parties

Please rate the degree to which you showed respect to other parties in this situation

Circle: (None)   A little   Some   A lot   All

Relationship preservation

Please rate the degree to which you preserved your relationship with other parties in this situation.

Circle: (None)   A little   Some   A lot   All

Social Capital & Assertiveness Worksheet

Assertiveness

What messages did you wish to communicate in this situation:

I am annoyed by Mason and the fact that he is late and will get away with it. I am most annoyed, however, with the organization for not enforcing their own rules. We all are expected to be on time. It's not fair when others don't follow these rules. I want him to be respectful of the rules. This isn't okay.

Were the other parties the most appropriate for receiving this message?

☐ Yes ☑ No   *If no, please describe the most appropriate parties for receiving this message:

Supervisor

Please provide examples of communicating these messages in an assertive way.
Do not use any of the aggressive or passive-aggressive behaviors from the lists above:

It's confusing to know which rules, like punctuality, are a priority for the organization. The organization needs to clarify.

I prioritize being to work on time, but others don't share that priority.
It's demoralizing.

It sets a problematic example when employees don't show up to work on time.

I'm frustrated by the organization not enforcing punctuality rules.

This worksheet could serve as a rich tool for Anya's assertiveness training. Figure 13 provides an example of a completed worksheet for a hypothetical altercation. The first section ("Situation") provides a thumbnail sketch of the circumstances surrounding the conflict.

The second section ("Analysis") provides an in-depth breakdown of the scenario. This includes jotting down the presentation of Anya's CBT triangle (e.g., thoughts, feelings, and behaviors), as well as the other party's behavioral response to Anya (e.g., sarcastic comment). The section drills down into more specificity by cataloguing Anya's aggressive verbal, physical, and relational behaviors (e.g., raised voice, eye roll, and being overcritical, respectively). As part of the overall analysis, the section includes assessments of respect, needs, well-being, social capital, and relational harm.

The third section ("Assertiveness") creates space for developing assertive alternatives to aggressive behaviors. It includes a request to distill down the core message of what Anya wishes to convey (e.g., the organization is letting her coworker get away with breaking rules). Then, the worksheet asks whether the target of the altercation was the appropriate party in the first place, and if not, who might be a better fit for receiving the message. The worksheet concludes with a prompt to create assertive statements conveying the core message.

Once Anya has a sense of the differences between the communications styles, you can practice assertive delivery by role playing examples. During the role play, you can model assertiveness and then switch roles and have her perform. When you notice her interacting with her colleagues and you notice a problematic communication style,[142] you can use this observation as an example when you meet with her privately. Discuss how her approach could have been more effective with assertiveness and demonstrate it for her.

142 Granted, you may never see her engage in aggressive or passive-aggressive behavior directly, because she doesn't act that way toward authority figures and her coworkers are reluctant to disclose this information. It could be a good opportunity to use an anonymous feedback mechanism.

➤ Chapter Conclusion and Takeaways

This chapter is different from the previous ones because individuals with other-oriented moralism in the workplace tend to project perfectionistic standards on coworkers instead of themselves. Others become the target of the perfectionist's rigid and unreasonable standards. I've provided an overview of this type of presentation and offered group- and individual-level strategies to reduce its negative impact.

Here are some chapter takeaways:

→ Other-oriented perfectionistic moralism often takes the form of self-righteous behavior, which can poison a work environment.

→ It often worsens the various types of perfectionistic problems outlined in this book, such as focusing exclusively on Emphasis A approaches, contributing to process paralysis, falling into the trap of confounding rules and principles, and resisting change due to cognitive rigidity.

→ Group-level strategies for addressing other-oriented moralism focused on the social capital framework, which is a metaphor for characterizing the costs and benefits of your behavior within the context of social relationships.

→ Employee-level strategies for other-oriented moralism emphasized assertiveness training, which enhances communication approaches to preserve and grow social capital among your team members.

All these strategies promote a healthy social environment in the workplace. You have an opportunity to create an office environment that protects against social capital debt. Ultimately, you can help your other-oriented moralistic employee strengthen their social skills and mitigate their reputation as "a solemn, unsmiling, sanctimonious old iceberg."

CHAPTER 10

LIKE A BOSS: HOW TO HANDLE A PERFECTIONISTIC LEADER

"I had several different bosses during the early years of *Dilbert*. They were all pretty sure I was mocking someone else."[143]

SCOTT ADAMS
Cartoonist and Author of Dilbert

MOST PEOPLE HAVE dealt with a difficult supervisor. The ubiquity of this challenge has inspired countless movie tropes, fodder for primetime television shows, and rich material for fiction and non-fiction books alike. Apparently, it inspired Scott Adams to serve up a generation of laughs.

There are so many reasons to detest a boss that analyzing them comprehensively could serve as the primary focus of a different book— even a series of them. Perfectionism is one reason for a ruptured supervisor-supervisee relationship. Though, unlike other chapters of

---

143 Zachary Kanin, "An Interview with the 'Dilbert' Cartoonist Scott Adams," *The New Yorker*, October 27, 2008. https://www.newyorker.com/cartoons/cartoon-lounge/an-interview-with-the-dilbert-cartoonist-scott-adams (accessed January 10, 2024).

this book, this chapter is focused on the boss's characteristics, instead of being concentrated on those of the employee.

A perfectionistic boss can drive poor management. This type of leadership often gets in the way of productivity and, when severe, devastates it. What are employees to do? Do they have any power in these situations? How do they deal with a supervisor who manages from a perfectionistic worldview?

Employees have options for reducing the damage caused by a perfectionistic manager. Many of the strategies outlined in this book will help, but suggesting and implementing them can get thorny. The primary reason is the power differential between the supervisor and supervisees, which makes communication tricky and increases the potential for unwanted consequences.

This chapter provides some tips. First, I highlight ways that employees can infer that perfectionism explains some of their boss's difficult behavior. Second, I outline ways in which working with a perfectionistic boss can challenge well-being and productivity. To conclude, I provide some techniques for approaching a perfectionistic boss to mitigate its impact.

Spoiler alert: the techniques do not involve anonymously and passive-aggressively slipping a neatly wrapped copy of this book under their office door as a hint.[144]

Characterizing a Perfectionistic Boss... Like a Boss[145]

Instead of rehashing all the indicators of perfectionism from earlier chapters, I'll focus on the ones that are particularly relevant for

144 Instead, ship them an entire crate. 😜

145 For those unfamiliar, *Like a Boss* is an idiom that indicates doing something with confidence, style, and effectively. For example, somebody might say, "They tweeted that response like a boss."

spotting perfectionism in management. Some of these indicators

spotting perfectionism in management. Some of these indicators weren't emphasized previously—largely because they are predominant when they present at the management level (e.g., stinginess). Some indicators are unique to bosses (e.g., role-reversal reassurance-seeking, which is introduced below). Ultimately, however, all indicators of perfectionism covered in prior chapters are relevant for identifying these characteristics in your supervisor or line manager.

Cognitive Rigidity. This feature of perfectionism often affects a manager's expectations. Perfectionistic bosses hold themselves (i.e., self-oriented) and others (i.e., other-oriented) to standards that are impossible to meet or are excessive relative to industry standards. Their mindset might seem so fixed that it feels like it would take an act of war to move it. Their expectations are resistant to changing circumstances (e.g., short-staffed for a day) and new contexts (e.g., selling a new product). They may have low self-awareness and not appreciate the unreasonableness of the expectations. Alternatively, they may have insight into the unreasonableness but feel unable to waver.

As part of cognitive rigidity, the perfectionistic supervisor may get stuck with distorted thinking patterns, such as the cognitive biases outlined in figure 3 from chapter 2. This includes the common tendency for all-or-none thinking and the should statement.

If should statements characterize a boss's worldview and managerial behavior, it can come across as moralistic, especially if it's driven by other-orientated perfectionism, as described in chapter 9.

Safety Behaviors. Bosses with perfectionism will invariably carry out safety behaviors to deal with mounting anxiety around their performance and the performance of their team. This is true even in the case of the supervisor ultimately delivering high-quality projects. Safety behaviors often consist of reviewing and rehashing the details of work products and returning products compulsively to employees for fixing or improving. While these behaviors are standard job duties of a supervisor, they present in an extreme manner. They go well beyond what's reasonable for the purpose of the project and its stakes.

These tendencies typically rope in the entire team. It can become a group-wide affair to handle a supervisor's full inventory of safety behaviors. The entire culture of the organization or division might be built on a supervisor's avoidance, escape, and ritualizing behavior. Think of the movie tropes of the personal assistant having a coffee and dry cleaning ready to go for their boss at the same time each morning. Now imagine that type of employee responsiveness but with safety behaviors. Here's an example:

Lucia runs a tight ship as the supervisor of the distribution division for her organization, which produces coffee filters for vendors around the globe. Every morning is like clockwork. She arrives at 8:30 a.m. precisely, checks in with her assistant about messages and mail, waits for the assistant to praise the chicness of her outfit, and sits down to review her email.

When Lucia checks her email, her process is formulaic. Her first step is to make sure each employee in her division emailed her that morning when they sat down at their computer—much like asking them to punch a time card. She then scans for emails from her boss to make sure she answers any of his inquiries by 8:45am. Lucia then sends her team an email praising them for their efforts the previous day, providing some key data about their distribution of coffee filters, and closing by asking them if they felt supported by her at work. She then awaits responses to her question, which all her employees provide in the affirmative within five minutes. She's not aware that several of the affirmative responses are disingenuous.

At the daily division meeting at 9 a.m., Lucia asks each member of her team to comment on how their morning has been going. If anyone appraises their morning as anything other than positive, she immediately asks whether something at work has soured their day. They never suggest that work is a cause and therefore attribute negative experiences to non-work experiences (e.g., rush hour traffic). Much of the time, these are white lies.

The remainder of Lucia's day is similarly regimented. From an outsider's perspective, her day would look highly choreographed, much like watching Snow White tidy up her home with anthropomorphic help from adorable forest animals.

Though, because this isn't a cartoon, the workplace scene is high on the Kookometer.

This example illustrates a series of safety behaviors—prompted by Lucia—that have deeply integrated into her team's workday. Her team functions according to Lucia's regimented activity, such as her assistant being at work and ready for her arrival to hand her messages and comment religiously on the boss's outfit. Her coworkers have similarly arrived on time to "punch in" to the time clock before she arrives.

Lucia has conditioned her team to give her specific responses. They've been prompted to reassure her that she's a good supervisor, and they do so by responding to the group email request quickly. The team has similarly learned not to disclose anything negative about their morning. In the event they can't hide a bad morning, they've learned to attribute it to non-work-related causes. Lucia needs considerable reassurance via positive responsivity and predictability from her team.

Let me introduce one subtle variant of checking behavior: *role-reversal reassurance-seeking*—a red flag for a boss's perfectionism. For a supervisor, role-reversal reassurance-seeking consists of asking for feedback excessively from supervisees about one's supervisory performance. Lucia exhibits this tendency.

This is the wrong direction of reassurance-seeking. Employees are naturally expected to solicit reassurance from their bosses, not the other way around. This reversal is akin to a parent seeking feedback from their child about whether they've made the right parenting decision or have been acting appropriately as a parent. It's high on the Kookometer.

In addition to reassurance-seeking, avoidance of a boss's perfectionism and often takes the form of procrastination. Another presentation of avoidance occurs when a perfectionistic supervisor refuses to delegate tasks to a capable team. This tendency is often driven by fear that others will not complete the task properly. Even when a supervisor does manage to delegate tasks, it often coincides with a hefty dose of micromanaging.

Avoidance can also present at the managerial level in the form of process paralysis. This might take the form of a supervisor calling unnecessary meetings to develop plans for completing projects, waffling when it comes to deciding on the order of task steps, and feeling compelled to carry out extreme due diligence when vetting options. The latter may manifest as debilitating levels of Internet research.

Stinginess. As noted in chapter 2, individuals with perfectionism often exhibit a tendency toward being stingy with their spending. When dealing with a perfectionistic boss, this can take many forms, but it often feels like penny-pinching. Office resources may feel thin because a perfectionistic supervisor micromanages the budget and refuses to spend the necessary amount of money to ensure a comfortable work environment.

Sometimes it's necessary for an organization or division to tighten the belt. This is not the circumstance that I'm describing. I'm referring to the perfectionistic boss who maintains a constant worldview and behavior shaped by stinginess.

If the supervisor has control over salary and benefits, the perfectionism can be particularly problematic. As a result of stinginess, employees may be underpaid and have a difficult time fighting for equitable pay raises consonant with industry standards. Perfectionistic managers may resist grassroots efforts to address salary compression.

The perfectionistic stinginess often mixes with other-oriented moralism. In this case, the boss digs in their heels when it comes to employee pay and might do so with self-righteous indignation. In their mind, they may see working as part of the team as a privilege worthy of its own value that offsets a need for a reasonable salary.[146]

Oversensitivity. Perfectionistic managers often exhibit oversensitivity when they receive feedback. They tend to overvalue criticism and discount positive comments. Neutral comments are often viewed through a negative lens. Often, perfectionistic managers misread evidence and interpret it negatively.

The oversensitivity might dovetail with excessive reassurance-seeking. When a perfectionistic boss is oversensitive to an employee's perceived criticism, they may react by seeking confirmation that

146 I've seen organizations so haughty that they didn't even try to hide the fact they paid employees 30% less than industry standard. They believed the privilege of working for them made up for the monetary difference. It was practically a point of pride.

they haven't caused too much harm, that they aren't a bad boss, and that the employee is "okay." Often the manager's behaviors look as if they're being thoughtful about the welfare of the employee, but the response functions chiefly to calm the boss's anxiety.

Advocating for Employees. Another problematic tendency associated with perfectionistic managers has to do with advocacy. On one hand, a perfectionistic supervisor may have tremendous difficulty advocating for their employee when the situation requires it. It's common for a perfectionist to remain deferential to their superiors and to authority. On the other hand, they may feel a duty to speak up for their employee, when necessary, on account of other-oriented moralism.

In some instances, the perfectionistic supervisor may feel particularly distressed and paralyzed as they waffle between advocating for an employee and comporting themselves respectfully with their superiors. It's a tug-of-war between two characteristics of perfectionism.

Workplace Effects from a Perfectionistic Boss

The impact of a perfectionistic boss can be intense and pervasive. For employees asked to meet unreasonable and rigid expectations, it can feel like a never-ending marathon with little to no reward along the way. The goals seem insurmountable. It's demoralizing to work at an extreme level without having the satisfaction of meeting goals and reaping the benefits of doing so. These perfectionistic expectations spread through a workplace and sour the team dynamic.

A manager's safety behaviors are similarly problematic for the team. Returning to Lucia's case, it would be unsurprising to learn that her employees are miserable fulfilling their boss's every perfectionistic demand like robots.

The subtext of the Lucia example suggests that many of the employees have learned to abide by the manager's safety behavior regimen. This type of compliance often results from fear. It's unclear how Lucia handles non-compliance but, based on the degree to which her team falls in line, the employees are probably terrified of her response.[147]

Excessive reassurance-seeking as a ritualistic behavior has a particularly harmful effect on the workplace. Many of the consequences of this type of safety behavior were outlined in previous chapters and won't be rehashed here. Focusing specifically on perfectionistic supervisors, however, this safety behavior can have a robust negative effect, especially when it's role-reversal reassurance-seeking. When managers engage in role-reversal reassurance-seeking, it reeks of low self-confidence and therefore undermines a supervisor's credibility and leverage.

I'm not recommending that organizations stop seeking feedback from employees. Managers benefit greatly from obtaining feedback and evolving themselves and the workplace culture. As with many of the behaviors discussed in this book, the problem is more about the degree and intensity. Role-reversal reassurance-seeking is reasonable in small doses and when done systematically, but perfectionistic supervisors tend to blow past this dose level and seek out reassurance haphazardly.

Micromanaging can feel smothering and sends a toxic message: the supervisees can't be trusted to complete tasks competently. Refusing to delegate tasks sends a similar message. Both shatter employee confidence and morale.

Stinginess can disrupt a work culture. Yes, it may preserve financial capital, but the impact is profound. Penny-pinching damages

147 The Lucia case may conjure up memories of *The Devil Wears Prada*, Lauren Weisberger's 2003 novel and the 2006 film adaptation. The boss in that story—played by the inimitable Meryl Streep in the movie—seems like an illustrative case study of perfectionism and its impact on the workplace. This includes the adverse impact of perfectionism, as well as some of the positive results it can yield.

a positive workplace atmosphere. It's like maintaining a strict family budget when times are tough—it requires extra mental energy and careful planning. Employees often dread having to devote their mental energy to processing seemingly asinine budget issues.

Beyond being disruptive, stinginess can also devastate a work culture when a perfectionistic manager has decisional control over employee salary and benefits. As noted, perfectionism can result in rigid beliefs and behavior around budgeting for personnel. Salary figures often don't stay private in a work setting. It's likely that employees will realize that they're being underpaid. Inequitable pay kills workplace morale and builds tremendous resentment toward coworkers, management, and the organization. This is further worsened by high rates of turnover that occur from a systemic undervaluing of human capital.

With respect to cooperating with a perfectionistic manager, employees will experience a boss's oversensitivity as a tremendous obstacle to healthy communication. It can feel like walking on eggshells. This oversensitivity makes it very difficult to practice many of the assertiveness skills recommended in chapter 9.

The negative impact of a supervisor's oversensitivity on the workplace cannot be understated. Employees will stop communicating important details, even neutral ones, out of concern that their supervisor will receive the message poorly. When this occurs, the organization will be unresponsive to an ever-changing set of needs and circumstances because of the limited communication. Psychological safety in the workplace crumbles when employees feel uncomfortable communicating.

I'd like to highlight one final adverse impact from a perfectionistic boss. A work culture can be affected negatively when employees sense passivity from their supervisor in circumstances in which assertive advocacy on the employees' behalf is necessary. It can feel devastatingly unsupportive. This is leadership 101. Few behaviors will undermine a manager's ability to lead a team more than not sticking up for employees when necessary.

Handling a Perfectionistic Boss... Like a Boss

You may think it's futile to challenge a perfectionistic boss given what was described above. Yes, such managers are oversensitive to feedback. Yes, they think rigidly and hold employees to unreasonable standards. Yes, they may stick their heads in the sand when confronted with anxiety-provoking situations. Yes, they often lack awareness and don't see the effect they have on the workplace. This amounts to a recipe for a poor outcome when trying to communicate your concerns.

That being said—no—it's not futile. Most, but not all, perfectionists exhibit some self-awareness and wish to present in a more flexible and adaptive manner. They don't want to manage poorly and impact the organizational culture, productivity, and bottom line negatively.

There are strategies for mitigating the effects of a perfectionistic manager, and two entwined and overarching approaches include setting boundaries and being assertive.

Setting Boundaries with a Perfectionistic Boss. It's critical to set reasonable boundaries when dealing with perfectionistic supervisors. Get a sense of the organizational culture and industry standards. Reasonable expectations change across contexts—there is no uniform definition. Some organizations expect 60-hour workweeks. A subset of industries necessitates going into the office on weekends or working overnights. Certain professions require seasonal shifts in workload and expectations.

It might help to discuss expectations within and outside of your organization. Social media (especially platforms catered toward professional networking) and web postings (e.g., discussion boards and blogs) make it easier than ever to glean information about what is considered *reasonable* for a given professional circumstance. Don't be shy in your investigation.

Once you have a good sense of how to characterize reasonable expectations, be sure to define your boundaries. They can vary depending on your schedule or the context in which you're working. For example, if you're an accountant, you might have a different set of boundaries for workweek hours during tax season. Sometimes it's wise to shift your boundaries to complete a critical project. Selected contexts change based on career stage. For example, you might need to work overnight shifts as a new employee to pay your dues.

How do you know when to make a shift in your boundaries? It's all about your values, just like when deciding what task deserves an Emphasis A approach (see chapter 5). Set boundaries when and where it's important to you. Use your values as a guide.

An employer may expect one set of boundaries from you, but you may disagree. If opposing those employer-backed boundaries would undermine your job and career (e.g., you get fired), it might not be worth picking that battle. In other words, you may value the specific job—or its benefits to your career—more than you might value the benefits of adhering to your optimal boundaries (e.g., valuing work-life balance).

Assertiveness with a Perfectionistic Boss. Chapter 9 provides a framework—and its rationale—for adopting an assertive communication approach. I won't rehash the details, but I'll provide some tips and examples for implementing assertiveness when communicating with a perfectionistic boss. It's the best strategy for communicating in general, and that includes the scenario in which a perfectionistic boss needs confronting.

Above all, keep in mind that assertiveness is about respect. This includes self-respect, as well as respect for the other party. This means speaking in a firm and direct tone, which minimizes passivity. At the same time, the message would benefit from not being judgmental, accusatory, or too personal, all of which are aggressive. Keep the volume and tone civil.

See figure 14 on the following pages for some differences between communication styles covered in chapter 9 (i.e., assertive, aggressive, passive, and passive aggressive).

One helpful approach is to use "I" statements that communicate feelings instead of "You" statements, which tend to put the recipient on the defensive almost immediately. For example, with a boss that gets stuck asking you to fix a project repeatedly, a "You" statement might sound like: "You keep sending this back to us. Why are you being so indecisive? What do you want from us? Your perfectionism is making us miserable."

An "I" statement in this situation would establish a more respectful and effective dynamic. For example: "I'm confused by the number of edits we seem to be making to this project. The changes seem excessive, and I'm not sure how we're making the project better. It would be helpful if you could explain."

Notice this message centers on the communicator and not the recipient. This style reduces the likelihood that your supervisor becomes defensive—although it's not guaranteed. The communicator is offering a statement about how they're feeling about the situation. It's difficult for a recipient to argue with the message.

Figure 14: The Four Communications Styles as Part of Assertiveness Training: Boss Example

Passive

Nonconfrontational, submissive, timid, ingratiating

> Sure, no problem. Happy to help.

PRO
Avoid confrontation; Please others; Stay under the radar

CON
Don't meet your immediate needs; Lose self-respect; Build resentment of others

Passive Aggressive

Sneaky, sarcastic, cowardly, indirect

> Sure, I will help. God may have needed to rest on Sunday, but God never worked in corporate America.

PRO
Feel a temporary sense of retribution

CON
Destroy relationships; Lose self-respect and respect from others; Attract possible behavioral consequences (e.g., job termination)

Aggressive

Combative, theatening, loud, obnoxious, oppositional

> No, you always do this and don't seem to care about your team's work-life balance.

PRO
Often get your immediate needs met

CON
Destroy relationships; Lose respect from others; Attract behavioral consequences (e.g., job termination)

Assertive

Respectful, nonjudgmental, authoritative, nonthreatening nonblaming

> Unfortunately, this is not enough notice. I cannot help this weekend, as I already have important plans, but I can work extra next week to assist.

PRO
Protect relationships; Often have your needs met; Preserve self-respect and respect from others

CON
People may not be used to your assertiveness and treat you differently

Figure 14 mirrors figure 12 from chapter 9 but demonstrates a scenario involving a perfectionistic boss instead of a colleague. It provides an example of how to handle a situation in which the manager asks for the employee to sacrifice their weekend for work. The different types of responses—passive, aggressive, passive-aggressive, and assertive—illustrate appropriate and inappropriate ways for an employee to respond.

Caveat Emptor—Boundaries and Assertiveness with a Perfectionistic Boss. Not all supervisors and situations are appropriate for assertiveness or boundary setting. Some managers and work settings don't encourage these approaches or even seem hostile to them. Assertive communication can help you approach an oversensitive manager, but you can't control how they will interpret your message and respond.

Each situation is unique and warrants careful consideration of the pros and cons of broaching issues with management. Don't gaslight yourself or let others tell you that retaliation isn't a concern. It is. When attacked, humans have an instinct to retaliate,[148] whether it's conscious or otherwise. If you decide to pursue action, do so with this potential cost in mind.

In organizations where workers have sufficient rights, employees have self-determination. They get to decide their actions. They can and often do quit when a workplace or job becomes unbearable. If your values are too compromised when attempting to set reasonable boundaries—or if your manager responds harshly to assertiveness or refuses to address their perfectionism—you have the power to walk away from the job. That's your decision; that's your prerogative. Leaving a role isn't always feasible, but it's a choice.

148 Jackson, Choi, and Gelfand, "Revenge."

➤ Chapter Conclusion and Takeaways

Written for managers, this book has focused exclusively on how to deal with perfectionistic employees. This chapter, however, has flipped the script. Here, I provide some strategies to identify and deal with perfectionistic bosses, which can negatively impact the workplace. Here are some key takeaways:

→ Bad bosses are everywhere. In some circumstances, perfectionism may explain why they're so challenging.

→ Perfectionistic managers often exhibit many of the tendencies covered in previous chapters, although some features are more prominent when part of a boss's profile. Examples include role-reversal reassurance-seeking, stinginess, and oversensitivity.

→ Managers with perfectionism often display characteristics that disrupt the workplace culture, productivity, and employee well-being.

→ Boundary setting is crucial for working with a perfectionistic supervisor, but doing so requires investigating what is considered reasonable in your industry. It also warrants careful assessment of your values.

→ Assertiveness is the optimal communication strategy for engaging with a perfectionistic boss, as well as with setting reasonable boundaries.

Hopefully some of the strategies offered herein help mitigate the damage caused by a manager's perfectionism and provide avenues for sustaining a healthy team dynamic. Ultimately, however, dealing with a perfectionistic boss is challenging and often outside of your control.

Sometimes acceptance is the only option other than finding new employment. Well, that's not entirely true; I guess you can imitate Scott Adams by creating funny cartoons about it and etching your name into history.

CONCLUSION

CRAIG IS UBIQUITOUS

WHILE YOU CAN find ample self-help and family-based resources for targeting perfectionism, there are no dedicated books for helping business leaders approach employees on their team who exhibit these tricky characteristics. This is an unfortunate void, and it's particularly curious given that perfectionism is no stranger to the organizational setting. To that end, by writing this book, I hope that I've filled a void with this useful guide.

I've used case studies as an important vehicle for illustrating my points throughout this book. No need to stop in the final section. Let's end the book with one final example. It's one that conveniently brings together many of the perfectionistic problems highlighted in this book.

Craig, who is nearly finished authoring a book, was asked by his editor to write a concluding chapter. Craig is a self-described perfectionist and freezes up when asked to tackle this task. Craig believes an author should write the conclusion using a formulaic and nongimmicky style that ties the book content together in a neat package. From his perspective, a conclusion section is the closing argument and therefore makes or breaks the message of the book. It should be conventional and to the point.

Craig fears that his perfectionism will overwhelm him—and he is correct. This belief creates a self-fulfilling prophecy, as his feelings of being overwhelmed cause him to freeze even more. This results in considerable procrastination and checking behavior. For example, he gets stuck researching the best strategies for writing a book conclusion but ends up with a series of different and equally compelling options. He finds himself staring at a blinking cursor on the word processor, praying to the writing gods that he finds inspiration for a creative conclusion angle, and wondering how he managed to write the rest of the book in the first place.

As Craig's thoughts of failure and imposter syndrome crush him, his publishing company becomes increasingly aggressive. The book isn't finished, and—sunk costs be damned—the publisher resentfully invests extra resources into pushing back the book's launch date.

Then the publisher starts to threaten litigation.

Craig's editor, who also exhibits some perfectionism, is equally furious because she has defended him to the publisher. In one heated call, she tells Craig that he's irresponsible and selfish. This worsens Craig's mood and heightens his anxiety, which in turn aggravates his procrastination.

Other collaborators are less hostile and instead express concern about Craig's anxiety and lack of productivity. For example, when the book illustrator reaches out to Craig, he reminds Craig of antiperfectionism strategies. The illustrator saves the day, as Craig's gentle reminder prompts progress.

Craig reviews all the strategies he learned. This includes maintaining a healthy Emphasis Framework. He struggles much of the time to allocate his effort adaptively to tasks according to his values. Instead, he tries to give his best effort on every task, failing to discriminate levels of importance. Craig realizes that he's been adopting an Emphasis A mentality for the book conclusion, but his efforts have turned into a forced Emphasis C, a common perfectionism pattern that blocks success. He reviews solutions to break this pattern. He was drawn to the idea of doing his own exposure exercises by sitting down and typing a conclusion with an Emphasis B approach.

Craig also recalls lessons he learned about avoiding process paralysis, which occurs when he tries to identify the perfect strategy or order of steps to complete the task. He has an epiphany—he's stuck in process paralysis with writing the book conclusion. He checks in with himself and realizes he's trying to find the perfect strategy for ending the book. He opts to practice exposure exercises by completing the conclusion by using Emphasis B to select the writing strategy from several options. This helps him get started.

In a moment of insight, Craig realizes that he's been confounding rules and principles. He remembers some of his lessons—principles are abstract and cannot be met concretely. You can only show degrees of fidelity. Craig appreciates that he's been treating his values—such as *being an effective author*—as a rule. In other words, he's been preoccupied with being an effective author, as if that could ever be attained concretely.

As he examines his tendency to confound rules and principles, Craig notices that his thinking is hampered by should statements. There is no universal law that authors should use "a formula" to write a conclusion and that it should be "conventional and to the point." Craig recognizes these should statements as unhealthy signs of cognitive rigidity, a common—if not hallmark—feature of perfectionism.

With his new insights, Craig realizes that he can violate some rules about writing a book and still demonstrate fidelity to the value of *being an effective author.* This also helps him to increase his flexible thinking and undermine his should statements. He decides to deviate slightly from the common formula for writing a conventional conclusion, thereby breaking some rules.

As Craig overcomes his anxiety, he strategizes how to approach his perfectionistic editor, with whom he's upset for some of her offensive language (i.e., "irresponsible" and "selfish"). He recalls some of the assertiveness training that he practiced and begins devising some assertive messages conveying to his editor how he feels and why her language was hurtful. Craig's journey through this process of challenging his perfectionism has empowered him to speak candidly with his editor while preserving social capital.

Overall, Craig finishes his book conclusion using antiperfectionistic strategies. The publisher and editor are pleased with the finished product. Craig becomes a *New*

York Times bestselling author and sells 100 million copies of the book.

I've used Craig's case to review the most challenging presentations of perfectionism in the workplace. This includes a dysfunctional Emphasis Framework, process paralysis, confounding rules and principles, cognitive rigidity, and other-oriented moralism. In each instance, I've detailed some of the problems it causes to Craig and the organization. The case also provides an overview of some of the strategies that I recommend for dealing with perfectionism in the workplace.

Craig is ubiquitous. There are Craigs in every organization. You probably have a Craig on your team or in your division. If not, you will likely have encountered them in past jobs. Maybe *you* are the Craig, or perhaps you work for a Craig. Regardless, this book can help leaders who deal with Craigs every day and need solutions to sustain a healthy and productive workplace.

In the end, Craig is flawed. You can tell him to join our club; billions of members strong. It's not the flaws that cause the workplace problems, but rather, Craig's insistence that he's not *allowed* to be flawed. It's this belief, and the associated dysfunctional behavior, that disrupts productivity and disturbs the organizational climate. Perfectionism offers nothing positive to the equation that can't be provided by having flexible and reasonable *high standards*.

As you lead your organization and inspire your team, focus on high standards and relinquish messages that reinforce perfectionism. Foster psychological safety. Cultivate an environment built on anti-perfectionistic messaging. Engage in values-based task prioritization. Promote adaptable processes and planning. Embrace principles and not rules. Practice flexible thinking patterns and check biases. Preserve social capital and exercise assertive communication. Don't forget to model being flawed with grace.

As your team members learn to navigate their perfectionism and mitigate problems that it might cause, you can foster and emphasize its positive features simultaneously. These include desirable qualities such as conscientiousness, honesty, industriousness, and loyalty. By minimizing the harm and amplifying the positive effects through thoughtful leadership, you can create a team with rockstar employees.

Ultimately, if you've heard my book message, then you'll think differently when a job candidate replies, "I'm a perfectionist," after you've asked them to describe their greatest weakness or area for growth.

Use this as an opportunity to learn more about why the interviewee answered this way and what they meant by it. Are they replying this way strategically—as a way to spin the question to relay a strength—or is this a bona fide weakness for them that warrants your attention?

"I'm a perfectionist," replied Gary, the job interviewee. He looked confident and safe in his response.

"Thanks, Gary. Let's explore that answer some more."

PLEASE REVIEW MY BOOK

If you found yourself enjoying this book—even though it isn't *perfect*—please leave a review online. I'd love to hear from you. Writing and publishing a book is exhausting, but I find it enormously helpful to receive reader encouragement and feedback.

Leave an Amazon review by going to
www.gregchasson.com/amazon or by scanning

Leave a Goodreads review by going to
www.gregchasson.com/amazon or by scanning

RESOURCES

Visit the link or scan the QR code below to access a host of extra resources. They're designed to help you translate the antiperfectionism tips and insights from my book to improve your organization's productivity, workplace culture, and profitability.

Accessible resources include the following:

1. Full-sized figures from throughout the book to use in your workplace to educate workers and leaders, as well as develop and implement antiperfectionism solutions.

2. A blank copy of the fear hierarchy (figures 7 and 8) that can be used in your workplace to design exposure exercises for addressing perfectionism-based fear.

3. A blank copy of the Social Capital and Assertiveness Worksheet (chapters 9 and 10) to use in the workplace to improve team dynamics, interpersonal relationships, and overall communication.

4. Example of antiperfectionism language to borrow for your organization's employee handbook and annual evaluations.

5. A list of up-to-date resources for individuals with perfectionism and their families looking for education, support, and treatment.

6. A video from me on how to address a self-righteous coworker or boss who presents with other-oriented perfectionistic moralism.

Obtain the valuable resources by visiting my website at www.gregchasson.com/flawedresources or by scanning

BIBLIOGRAPHY

Abramowitz, Jonathan S., Brett J. Deacon, and Stephen P. H. Whiteside. *Exposure Therapy for Anxiety: Principles and Practice, 2nd Ed.* New York, NY: The Guilford Press, 2019.

Antony, Martin M, and Richard P Swinson. *When Perfect Isn't Good Enough: Strategies for Coping with Perfectionism.* 2nd ed. Oakland, CA: New Harbinger Publications, 2009.

Baer, Lee. *The Imp of the Mind: Exploring the Silent Epidemic of Obsessive Bad Thoughts.* Penguin Publishing Group, 2001.

Broman-Fulks, Joshua J., Robert W. Hill, and Bradley A. Green. "Is Perfectionism Categorical or Dimensional? A Taxometric Analysis." *Journal of Personality Assessment* 90, no. 5 (September 2008): 481–90. https://doi.org/10.1080/00223890802248802.

Coles, Meredith E., Richard G. Heimberg, Randy O. Frost, and Gail Steketee. "Not Just Right Experiences and Obsessive–Compulsive Features:: Experimental and Self-Monitoring Perspectives." *Behaviour Research and Therapy* 43, no. 2 (February 1, 2005): 153–67. https://doi.org/10.1016/j.brat.2004.01.002.

Covey, Stephen R. *The 7 Habits of Highly Effective People: Powerful Lessons in Personal Change.* New York, NY: Simon and Schuster, 1989.

Curran, Thomas, and Andrew P. Hill. "Perfectionism Is Increasing over Time: A Meta-Analysis of Birth Cohort Differences from 1989 to 2016." *Psychological Bulletin* 145, no. 4 (April 2019): 410–29. https://doi.org/10.1037/bul0000138.

Curran, *The Perfection Trap: Embracing the Power of Good Enough*. New York, NY: Scribner, 2023.

Deng, Hong, Kwok Leung, Catherine K. Lam, and Xu Huang. "Slacking off in Comfort: A Dual-Pathway Model for Psychological Safety Climate." *Journal of Management* 45, no. 3 (2019): 1114–44. https://doi.org/10.1177/0149206317693083.

Derenne, Jennifer, and Eugene Beresin. "Body Image, Media, and Eating Disorders—A 10-Year Update." *Academic Psychiatry* 42, no. 1 (February 2018): 129–34. https://doi.org/10.1007/s40596-017-0832-z.

Diamond, Adele. "Executive Functions." *Annual Review of Psychology* 64 (2013): 135–68. https://doi.org/10.1146/annurev-psych-113011-143750.

Dunkley, David M., David C. Zuroff, and Kirk R. Blankstein. "Specific Perfectionism Components versus Self-Criticism in Predicting Maladjustment." *Personality and Individual Differences*, 40, no. 4 (March 2006): 665–76. https://doi.org/10.1016/j.paid.2005.08.008.

Edmondson, Amy C. *Right Kind of Wrong: The Science of Failing Well*. New York, NY: Atria Books, 2023.

Edmondson, Amy C. *The Fearless Organization: Creating Psychological Safety in the Workplace for Learning, Innovation, and Growth*. Hoboken, NJ: Wiley, 2018.

Edmondson, Amy C., and Derrick P. Bransby. "Psychological Safety Comes of Age: Observed Themes in an Established Literature." *Annual Review of Organizational Psychology and Organizational Behavior* 10, no. 1 (2023): 55–78. https://doi.org/10.1146/annurev-orgpsych-120920-055217.

Egan, Sarah J., Tracey D. Wade, Roz Shafran, and Martin M. Antony. *Cognitive-Behavioral Treatment of Perfectionism*. New York, NY: The Guilford Press, 2014.

Ellis, Albert, and Robert A. Harper. *A Guide to Rational Living.* Englewood Cliffs, NJ: Prentice-Hall, 1961.

Flett, Gordon L., Paul L. Hewitt, Joan M. Oliver, and Silvana Macdonald. "Perfectionism in Children and Their Parents: A Developmental Analysis." In *Perfectionism: Theory, Research, and Treatment.*, edited by Gordon L. Flett and Paul L. Hewitt, 89–132. Washington, DC: American Psychological Association, 2002. https://doi. org/10.1037/10458-004.

Fox, Michael J. *Lucky Man: A Memoir.* New York, NY: Hachette Books, 2003.

Frost, Randy O., and Patricia Marten DiBartolo. "Perfectionism, Anxiety, and Obsessive-Compulsive Disorder." In *Perfectionism: Theory, Research, and Treatment.*, edited by Gordon L. Flett and Paul L. Hewitt, 341–71. Washington, DC: American Psychological Association, 2002. https://doi.org/10.1037/10458-014.

Frost, Randy O., and Rachel C. Gross. "The Hoarding of Possessions." *Behaviour Research and Therapy* 31, no. 4 (May 1993): 367–81. https://doi.org/10.1016/0005-7967(93)90094-B.

Frost, Randy O., Patricia Marten, Cathleen Lahart, and Robin Rosenblate. "The Dimensions of Perfectionism." *Cognitive Therapy and Research* 14, no. 5 (October 1990): 449–68. https://doi. org/10.1007/BF01172967.

Goulet-Pelletier, Jean-Christophe, Patrick Gaudreau, and Denis Cousineau. "Is Perfectionism a Killer of Creative Thinking? A Test of the Model of Excellencism and Perfectionism." *British Journal of Psychology* 113, no. 1 (February 2022): 176–207. https://doi.org/10.1111/bjop.12530.

Grant, Adam. *Think Again: The Power of Knowing What You Don't Know.* New York, NY: Penguin Books, 2023.

Greenaway, Rebecca, and Patricia Howlin. "Dysfunctional Attitudes and Perfectionism and Their Relationship to Anxious and Depressive Symptoms in Boys with Autism Spectrum Disorders." *Journal of Autism and Developmental Disorders* 40, no. 10 (October 2010): 1179–87. https://doi.org/10.1007/s10803-010-0977-z.

Habke, A. Marie, and Carol A. Flynn. "Interpersonal Aspects of Trait Perfectionism." In *Perfectionism: Theory, Research, and Treatment.*, edited by Gordon L. Flett and Paul L. Hewitt, 151–80. Washington, DC: American Psychological Association, 2002. https://doi.org/10.1037/10458-006.

Happé, Francesca, and Uta Frith. "The Weak Coherence Account: Detail-Focused Cognitive Style in Autism Spectrum Disorders." *Journal of Autism and Developmental Disorders* 36, no. 1 (January 1, 2006): 5–25. https://doi.org/10.1007/s10803-005-0039-0.

Hewitt, Paul L., and Gordon L. Flett. "Perfectionism in the Self and Social Contexts: Conceptualization, Assessment, and Association with Psychopathology." *Journal of Personality and Social Psychology* 60, no. 3 (March 1991): 456–70. https://doi.org/10.1037/0022-3514.60.3.456.

Huo, Meng-Long, and Zhou Jiang. "Trait Conscientiousness, Thriving at Work, Career Satisfaction and Job Satisfaction: Can Supervisor Support Make a Difference?" *Personality and Individual Differences* 183 (December 1, 2021): 111116. https://doi.org/10.1016/j.paid.2021.111116.

Jackson, Joshua Conrad, Virginia K. Choi, and Michele J. Gelfand. "Revenge: A Multilevel Review and Synthesis." *Annual Review of Psychology* 70, no. 1 (2019): 319–45. https://doi.org/10.1146/annurev-psych-010418-103305.

King, Michelle Penelope. "How To Ditch The 'Good Girl' Routine." *Forbes*, March 8, 2018. https://www.forbes.com/sites/michelleking/2018/03/08/how-to-ditch-the-good-girl-routine/?sh=6f9a3cfe4a02.

Lafontaine, Marie-France, Stéphanie Azzi, Breanna Bell-Lee, Titania Dixon-Luinenburg, Camille Guérin-Marion, and Jean-François Bureau. "Romantic Perfectionism and Perceived Conflict Mediate the Link between Insecure Romantic Attachment and Intimate Partner Violence in Undergraduate Students." *Journal of Family Violence* 36, no. 2 (February 2021): 195–208. https://doi.org/10.1007/s10896-020-00130-y.

Mackinnon, Sean P., Simon B. Sherry, Martin M. Antony, Sherry H. Stewart, Dayna L. Sherry, and Nikola Hartling. "Caught in a Bad Romance: Perfectionism, Conflict, and Depression in Romantic Relationships." *Journal of Family Psychology* 26, no. 2 (April 2012): 215–25. https://doi.org/10.1037/a0027402.

Martinelli, Mary, Gregory S. Chasson, Chad T. Wetterneck, John M. Hart, and Thröstur Björgvinsson. "Perfectionism Dimensions as Predictors of Symptom Dimensions of Obsessive-Compulsive Disorder." *Bulletin of the Menninger Clinic* 78, no. 2 (Spr 2014): 140–59. https://doi.org/10.1521/bumc.2014.78.2.140.

Montesquieu. *Essays on Montesquieu and on the Enlightenment.* Edited by David Gilson and Martin Smith. Oxford, England: Voltaire Foundation for Enlightenment Studies, University of Oxford, 1988. https://www.voltaire.ox.ac.uk/publication/essays-montesquieu-and-enlightenment/.

Morris, Lydia, and Warren Mansell. "A Systematic Review of the Relationship between Rigidity/Flexibility and Transdiagnostic Cognitive and Behavioral Processes That Maintain Psychopathology." *Journal of Experimental Psychopathology* 9, no. 3 (July 1, 2018): 2043808718779431. https://doi.org/10.1177/2043808718779431.

Mowrer, O. Hobart. "On the Dual Nature of Learning—a Re-Interpretation of 'Conditioning' and 'Problem-Solving.'" *Harvard Educational Review* 17 (1947): 102–48.

Nelson, Elizabeth A., Jonathan S. Abramowitz, Stephen P. Whiteside, and Brett J. Deacon. "Scrupulosity in Patients with

Obsessive-Compulsive Disorder: Relationship to Clinical and Cognitive Phenomena." *Journal of Anxiety Disorders* 20, no. 8 (2006): 1071–86. https://doi.org/10.1016/j.janxdis.2006.02.001.

O'Connor, Sarah. "The Term 'Quiet Quitting' Is Worse than Nonsense." *The Financial Times, Opinion Corporate Culture* (blog), September 12, 2022. https://www.ft.com/content/a09a2ade-4d14-47c2-9cca-599b3c25a33f.

Ojserkis, Rachel, and Dean McKay. "Scrupulosity and Slowness in OCD: Perfectionism as a Central Mechanism." In *Obsessive-Compulsive Disorder: Phenomenology, Pathophysiology, and Treatment.*, edited by Christopher Pittenger, 119–28. New York, NY: Oxford University Press, 2017.

Ong, Clarissa W., and Michael P. Twohig. *The Anxious Perfectionist: How to Manage Perfectionism-Driven Anxiety Using Acceptance & Commitment Therapy.* Oakland, CA: New Harbinger Publications, 2022.

Patton, Jr., George S. *War As I Knew It.* Boston, MA, US: Houghton Mifflin Company, 1947.

Peter, Laurence J., and Raymond Hull. *The Peter Principle.* New York, NY: William Morrow & Company, Inc., 1969.

Peters, Gerhard, and John T. Woolley. "Franklin D. Roosevelt, Radio Address to the Young Democratic Clubs of America." The American Presidency Project, August 24, 1935. https://www.presidency.ucsb.edu/node/209054.

Phillips, Allison, and Brian Fisak. "An Examination of the Factor Structure of the Penn Inventory of Scrupulosity-Revised (PIOS-R) in Atheist and Christian Samples." *Psychology of Religion and Spirituality* 14, no. 2 (May 2022): 222–28. https://doi.org/10.1037/rel0000322.

Platon, Adelle. "Last Laugh: Aisha Tyler On Being A Woman In Comedy." *Vibe*, March 10, 2015. https://www.vibe.com/features/editorial/vibe-league-aisha-tyler-interview-333689/.

Robinson, Anthony, and Amitai Abramovitch. "A Neuropsychological Investigation of Perfectionism." *Behavior Therapy* 51, no. 3 (May 2020): 488–502. https://doi.org/10.1016/j.beth.2019.09.002.

Rotter, Julian B. "Generalized Expectancies for Internal versus External Control of Reinforcement." *Psychological Monographs: General and Applied* 80, no. 1 (1966): 1–28. https://doi.org/10.1037/h0092976.

Shafran, Roz, Sarah Egan, and Tracey Wade. *Overcoming Perfectionism: A Self-Help Guide Using Scientifically Supported Cognitive Behavioural Techniques.* Little, Brown Book Group, 2010.

Sherry, Simon B., Paul L. Hewitt, Dayna L. Sherry, Gordon L. Flett, and Aislin R. Graham. "Perfectionism Dimensions and Research Productivity in Psychology Professors: Implications for Understanding the (Mal)Adaptiveness of Perfectionism." *Canadian Journal of Behavioural Science / Revue Canadienne Des Sciences Du Comportement* 42, no. 4 (October 2010): 273–83. https://doi.org/10.1037/a0020466.

Sidman, Murray. "Reflections on Stimulus Control." *The Behavior Analyst* 31, no. 2 (2008): 127–35.

Simpson, E. H. "The Interpretation of Interaction in Contingency Tables." *Journal of the Royal Statistical Society. Series B (Methodological)* 13, no. 2 (1951): 238–41.

Speed, Brittany C., Brandon L. Goldstein, and Marvin R. Goldfried. "Assertiveness Training: A Forgotten Evidence-based Treatment." *Clinical Psychology: Science and Practice* 25, no. 1 (March 2018). https://doi.org/10.1111/cpsp.12216.

Stoeber, Joachim. "Dyadic Perfectionism in Romantic Relationships: Predicting Relationship Satisfaction and Longterm Commitment." *Personality and Individual Differences* 53, no. 3 (August 2012): 300–305. https://doi.org/10.1016/j.paid.2012.04.002.

Stoeber, Joachim, Kathleen Otto, and Claudia Dalbert. "Perfectionism and the Big Five: Conscientiousness Predicts Longitudinal Increases in Self-Oriented Perfectionism." *Personality and Individual Differences* 47, no. 4 (September 1, 2009): 363–68. https://doi.org/10.1016/j. paid.2009.04.004.

Szymanski, Jeff. *The Perfectionist's Handbook: Take Risks, Invite Criticism, and Make the Most of Your Mistakes.* Hoboken, NJ: John Wiley & Sons Inc, 2011.

Twain, Mark. *Travels with Mr. Brown.* New York, NY, US: Alfred A. Knopf, 1940.

Wang, Xingyu, Priyanko Guchait, and Aysin Paşamehmetoğlu. "Tolerating Errors in Hospitality Organizations: Relationships with Learning Behavior, Error Reporting and Service Recovery Performance." *International Journal of Contemporary Hospitality Management* 32, no. 8 (June 13, 2020): 2635–55. https://doi.org/10.1108/IJCHM-01-2020-0001.

Wetterneck, Chad T., Tannah E. Little, Gregory S. Chasson, Angela H. Smith, John M. Hart, Melinda A. Stanley, and Thröstur Björgvinsson. "Obsessive–Compulsive Personality Traits: How Are They Related to OCD Severity?" *Journal of Anxiety Disorders* 25, no. 8 (December 2011): 1024–31. https://doi.org/10.1016/j. janxdis.2011.06.011.

Woods, Carol M., David F. Tolin, and Jonathan S. Abramowitz. "Dimensionality of the Obsessive Beliefs Questionnaire (OBQ)." *Journal of Psychopathology and Behavioral Assessment* 26, no. 2 (June 2004): 113–25. https://doi.org/10.1023/B:JOBA.0000013659.13416.30.

STOP PROMOTING PERFECTION AND GET UNSTUCK!

Perfectionism quietly sabotages an organization's productivity, profitability, and culture. Understanding how to spot and overcome perfectionism is mission-critical for improving the well-being and functioning of your organization's workplace. Let me help!

My antiperfectionism services include, but are not limited to, the following:

1. Delivering an engaging and powerful keynote address, which provides insights and actionable tools for guiding your organization to overcome perfectionism by turning the concept of 'control' on its head.

2. Offering workshops and group consultations, all aimed at helping your organization overcome specific group- and individual-level perfectionism pitfalls, such as a dysfunctional Emphasis Framework, process paralysis, confounding of rules and principles, cognitive rigidity, and other-oriented moralism.

3. Receive individual consultations from Dr. Chasson for your organization. Services are individualized to each organization and may include (a) a comprehensive evaluation of perfection-

ism in your workplace, (b) the development of antiperfectionism solutions for your organization, (c) guidance on the implementation of these strategies, and (d) organizational support
for the long-term maintenance of antiperfectionism gains.

4. Offering wholesale discounts on bulk quantities of this book if
   you wish to provide your company employees or other groups
   with their own copies.

Learn more—visit www.gregchasson.com/speaking or scan the QR code
below. You can also email me directly at gchasson@gregchasson.com

ACKNOWLEDGMENTS

Pro tip: don't ever attempt to write and publish a book without support. I couldn't imagine this journey without the encouragement, faith, expertise, and brilliance of the people who helped me along the way.

Before launching into talking about the specific people whom I'd like to spotlight, let me offer a pre-emptive apology. As we've established, nothing is perfect, including acknowledgments sections. It's possible that I've omitted people who have been helpful during the making of this book. I promise it wasn't on purpose.

If I missed you, I'm truly sorry.

Indie publishing is no different than bobbing on a raft by yourself in the middle of an ocean. It's challenging to ascertain which direction leads to land. The isolation, hypnotic view of the horizon, and self-doubt can be distressing. A shiver of swindling cyber-sharks always circles the raft and waits patiently to dine on naïve indie authors, who are simple targets. It's very easy to make a mistake by taking a dip in the seemingly calm waters, exposing yourself to the hungry cyber-sharks, and losing a part of yourself in the process.

Fortunately, I was guided to land relatively unscathed with the help of the stars in the sky as my compass. The stars included Internet resources like Reedsy, Tucker Max and his crew, David Chesson at Kindlepreneur (who spells his last name incorrectly), Wesley Atkins at Publishing Altitude, Jason McDonald, David Gaughran, and Tammi Labrecque.

Just like the stars in the sky, these resources are distant and passive guides. They have no idea how helpful they've been on my journey, but they have my sincerest thanks.

It's through Reedsy that I assembled my marvelous team, which I consider my Avengers of indie publishing.

The first Avenger is David Woods-Hale, editor extraordinaire. One of his superpowers includes an impressive balance between the big picture and the details. He has figured out the formula for juggling efficiency and quality. Somehow his constructive feedback isn't deflating but instead pumps you up. David's editing preserves the author's voice and ideas. His involvement also included a tremendous amount of advising, not all of which was related to his editorial role. In that way, he felt integral to my project as a coach. My book is qualitatively better because of David.

The second Avenger is George B. Stevens, who brings many superpowers to the team. His conceptualizations of the book cover and interior layout were remarkable. I admire his knowledge of the industry, especially how designs catch the eye and appeal to prospective readers. Also going beyond the job description by acting as a coach, he taught me a ton in this process. My book is qualitatively better because of George.

The final Avenger is Rodney Hatfield, who wears a utility belt chock full of marketing gadgets and tools, all of which complement years of wisdom. He assisted with book marketing, which is the step of book publishing that was the most mysterious to me and left me maximally terrified. Rodney's work is powerful and next-level sophisticated. My publishing experience has been qualitatively better because of Rodney.

Other than Avengers, my journey included superhero team-ups with other people who enriched this publishing experience and provided tremendous support. With her HR superpowers, Crystal Matthews provided vital feedback as an early beta reader—thank you. With eagle-eye powers, Lucy Morton provided much-needed proofreading. Thank you to Paul Duda for his example and audio recording prowess.

Many thanks to my generous Advanced Review Copy team for their help: Jason Baum, Nick Beem, Lionel Bejean, Becca Belofsky, Robyn Caruso, Kathleen Crombie, Alyce Dailey, Jelani Daniel, Shmuel Fischler, Josh Goodman, Kevin Grodnitzky, Andrew Leventhal, Kaycee Lindeman, Lee Maliniak, Josh Margulies, Glen Mee, Marrietta Merito, Chris Moreno, Loren Nelson, Kirsten Pagacz, Daniel Passov, Heather Patrick, Liz Raigoza, Pam Rogers, Shannon Shy, Tim Tumilty, Rondalyn Whitney, Liz Williams-Clark, Rob Winston, and Domino Wirth.

Jason Nazar is quite the inspiration, and I am so grateful that he agreed to write such a powerful foreword. He was a rockstar from the moment we met as undergraduates and through AEπ at the University of California, Santa Barbara more than 20 years ago. I appreciated his guidance even then.

My professional foray into the world of obsessive-compulsive and related conditions—including severe perfectionism—has been shaped by many mentors and advisors over the years. I'd like to highlight some people who made this book possible through their training and support early in my career: Drs. Thröstur Björgvinsson, John Hart (who, incidentally, inspired chapter 7 and probably doesn't realize it), Michael Jenike, and Sabine Wilhelm. This small list skims the surface of colleagues and friends who have contributed to my professional identity and success. Listing everyone would take too much real estate, but you know who you are, and I thank you.

Although the case examples in *Flawed* were composites and don't represent specific people or circumstances, much of the book content was crafted from my interactions with my students, trainees, and patients. They've inspired me to write this book about perfectionism and disseminate my experience and knowledge to help others. They have my sincerest thanks.

Dr. Adam Leventhal needs to be acknowledged [for] just-in-case (JIC). Adam is my brother from another mother (and father). His support and friendship have helped me thrive.

Please give a round of applause to Joe Tumilty, who illustrated the engaging figures in this book. It's not easy to convey complex information in a visual medium. Joe has his own superpowers that enable him to distill down the essence of knowledge and convey it in a simple way via infographics. He also happens to be my future brother-in-law. Be good to my sister and please have her home by 9:30 p.m.

Dr. Brenda K. Findley—a successful indie author in her own right, among many other intimidating accomplishments—provided tips and connections along the way. She also happens to be my mother-in-law, who was the butt of a joke in chapter 1. Sorry about that.

I owe much of my success and happiness to my late parents. I miss them both considerably but am so grateful that they never, for one second, had me guessing whether they were proud.

This book wouldn't exist without my wife and children. Tasha, my endearing wife, has also been the butt of a few jokes in this book. She's a great sport and has had my back with this project since day one—no hesitation. I'm very grateful that she picked up my slack as part of this book process.

If I'm the idiot bobbing around the ocean as an indie author, Tasha represents the raft. She keeps me afloat and steady, prevents me from falling into the water, and makes it so that I don't drown. Also, as a bonus, even if I were to fall in the water, I could dry myself with some symmetrically folded towels because of her.

My two boys, Zachary and Carter, are why I do this. All of it. They inspire me every day with their curiosities, mistakes, triumphs, laughter, and love. It has been my greatest privilege in life thus far to watch them develop into good humans.

Given all the wonderful people who've helped me along the way, I guess you don't really need *perfection* when you have what I have.

COME HANG OUT WITH ME ON SOCIAL MEDIA

Connect with me on social media and post your thoughts about my book—I want to hear from you. And please don't forget to tag me!

- → Facebook: www.facebook.com/DrChasson
- → Twitter: @GregChasson
- → LinkedIn: www.linkedin.com/in/gregchasson
- → Goodreads: www.goodreads.com/gregchasson
- → Threads: @gregorychasson
- → Instagram: www.instagram.com/gregorychasson

You can also find links on my website:
www.gregchasson.com/socialmedia or scan:

JOIN MY AUTHOR AND SPEAKER MAILING LIST

Click the link or scan the QR code below to join my author and speaker email list. Email content

1. Is original and separate from material found in my blog, this book, etc.

2. Remains exclusive to mailing list recipients.

3. Delves into topics that help your teams overcome perfectionism, which in turn improves your organization's efficiency, workplace culture, and profitability.

   Example topics: Quiet quitting; burnout and perfectionism; perfectionism and the Herzberg Two-factor Theory; and perfectionism and the Peter Principle.

4. Covers topics on mental health more generally, specifically those pertinent to the workplace.

   Example topics: Overcontrol and responsibility; fear versus anxiety; hopelessness versus helplessness; and the Yips (for the sports enthusiasts).

5. Provides alerts and early access to new freebies (e.g., videos, tip sheets, articles), author and speaker updates, and sneak peeks (e.g., chapters from new book releases)

Join the mailing list by visiting here: www.gregchasson.com/mailing or by scanning: